T0330281

Paying the Carbon Price

NEW HORIZONS IN ENVIRONMENTAL AND ENERGY LAW

Series Editors: Kurt Deketelaere, *Professor of Law, University of Leuven, Belgium and University of Dundee, Scotland* and Zen Makuch, *Reader in Law, Barrister, Imperial College, London, UK*

Environmental law – including the pressing considerations of energy law and climate change – is an increasingly important area of legal research and practice. Given the growing interdependence of global society and the significant steps being made towards environmental protection and energy efficiency, there are few people untouched by environmental and energy lawmaking processes.

At the same time, environmental and energy law is at a crossroads. The command and control methodology that evolved in the 1960s and 1970s for air, land and water protection may have reached the limit of its environmental protection achievements. New life needs to be injected into our environmental protection regimes – perhaps through the concept of sustainability in its environmental, economic and social forms. The same goes for energy policy and law, where liberalization, environmental protection and security of supply are at the centre of attention. This important series seeks to press forward the boundaries of environmental and energy law through innovative research into environmental and energy law, doctrine and case law. Adopting a wide interpretation of environmental and energy law, it includes contributions from both leading and emerging international scholars.

Titles in the series include:

Paying the Carbon Price

The Subsidisation of Heavy Polluters under Emissions Trading Schemes

Dr. Elena de Lemos Pinto Aydos

Lecturer, University of Newcastle, Australia

NEW HORIZONS IN ENVIRONMENTAL AND ENERGY LAW

 Edward Elgar
PUBLISHING

Cheltenham, UK • Northampton, MA, USA

Published by
Edward Elgar Publishing Limited
The Lypiatts
15 Lansdown Road
Cheltenham
Glos GL50 2JA
UK

Edward Elgar Publishing, Inc.
William Pratt House
9 Dewey Court
Northampton
Massachusetts 01060
USA

A catalogue record for this book
is available from the British Library

Library of Congress Control Number: 2017947256

This book is available electronically in the **Elgar**online
Law subject collection
DOI 10.4337/9781786439413

ISBN 978 1 78643 940 6 (cased)
ISBN 978 1 78643 941 3 (eBook)

Typeset by Columns Design XML Ltd, Reading
Printed and bound in Great Britain by TJ International Ltd, Padstow

I dedicate this book to my parents Eduardo and Regina

Contents

Acknowledgements

This manuscript would not have been written without the advice and support from many scholars, but I would particularly like to thank my PhD supervisors Celeste Black, Rosemary Lyster and Panagiotis Delimatsis. I would also like to express my appreciation for the three anonymous reviewers for their reading of my manuscript and their feedback. Finally, I would like to thank my parents, Regina and Eduardo, for their unconditional support and wisdom and my siblings, Manoela and Guilherme for their friendship always.

Abbreviations

AAU	Assigned amount unit
ACCU	Australian Carbon Credit Unit
ACU	Australian Carbon Unit
ADP	Ad Hoc Working Group on the Durban Platform for Enhanced Action
ALP	Australian Labor Party
AR5	Fifth Assessment Report
AU$	Australian Dollar
AUS	Australia
AUS CPM	Australian Carbon Pricing Mechanism
AWG-KP	Ad Hoc Working Group on Further Commitments for Annex I Parties under the Kyoto Protocol
AWG-LCA	Ad Hoc Working Group on Long-term Cooperative Action
BAU	Business-as-usual
BCA	Border Carbon Adjustment
CDM	Clean Development Mechanism
CFI	Carbon Farming Initiative
CH_4	Methane
CMP	Meeting of the Parties
CO_2	Carbon Dioxide
CO_2-e	Carbon Dioxide Equivalent
COP	Conference of the Parties
CPRS	Carbon Pollution Reduction Scheme
EC	European Commission
ECJ	European Court of Justice
EITE	Emissions-Intensive Trade-Exposed
ERU	Emission Reduction Units

ETS	Emissions Trading Scheme
EU	European Union
EU ETS	European Union Emissions Trading System
EUA	European Union Allowance
FAR	First Assessment Report
FVA	Framework for Various Approaches
GATT	General Agreement on Tariffs and Trade
GDP	Gross Domestic Product
GHG	Greenhouse Gas
HFC	Hydrofluorocarbon
ICAO	International Civil Aviation Organization
IPCC	Intergovernmental Panel on Climate Change
JI	Joint Implementation
LNG	Liquefied Natural Gas
LULUCF	Activities Related to Land Use, Land-use Change and Forestry
N_2O	Nitrous Oxide
NAMAs	Nationally Appropriate Mitigation Actions
NAP	National Allocation Plan
NAP2	National Allocation Plans for the Second Trading Period
NER	New Entrants' Reserve
NF_3	Nitrogen Trifluoride
NGER	National Greenhouse and Energy Reporting
npr-PPM	Non-product-related Process and Production Methods
NZ	New Zealand
NZ ETS	New Zealand Emissions Trading Scheme
NZU	New Zealand Unit
PFC	Perfluorocarbon
ppm	Parts Per Million
PPM	Process and Production Methods
QELROs	Quantified Emission Limitation or Reduction Objectives

REDD+	Reducing Emissions from Deforestation and Forest Degradation
RMU	Removal Units
RTAs	Regional Trade Agreements
SCM Agreement	Agreement on Subsidies and Countervailing Measures
SF$_6$	Sulphur Hexafluoride
SOT	Senior Official Talks on Climate Change
UNFCCC	United Nations Convention on Climate Change
US	United States
WTO	World Trade Organization

1. Contextualising the issue

> There is no Plan B, because we do not have a Planet B
>
> *Ban Ki-moon, UN Secretary General, September 2014*

1. INTRODUCTION

This book analyses the methodology of the free allocation of permits in Emissions Trading Schemes or Emissions Trading Systems (ETSs). What motivated the research in the first place was an insight from an earlier work[1] on the implementation of carbon taxes in Brazil. The author came into contact with literature suggesting that carbon taxes and ETSs, by unilaterally adding a carbon cost to domestic industries, could lead to carbon leakage and competitiveness distortions.

The aim of carbon pricing is to mitigate greenhouse gas (GHG) emissions. It is intuitive, therefore, that impacts on the profits and, occasionally, on the actual viability of certain businesses are a necessary consequence of an effective environmental policy. However, even now, many heavy polluters participating in ETSs are not paying the full price of carbon.

Concerns with the loss of competitiveness, vis-à-vis international competitors who are not liable under a carbon pricing mechanism, have been at the centre of the political discussions on climate policy in several countries.[2] Carbon leakage, that is, the risk that the environmental goals of ETSs might not be achieved if energy-intensive industries move offshore and global GHG emissions, therefore, remain unchanged or increase, has also been a key concern. Nevertheless, the extent to which

---

[1] Elena Aydos, 'Tributação Ambiental no Brasil: Fundamentos e Perspectivas' (2010) <http://www.egov.ufsc.br/portal/sites/default/files/anexos/33953-447 34-1-PB.pdf>.

[2] See also Harro Van Asselt and Thomas Brewer, 'Addressing competitiveness and leakage concerns in climate policy: An analysis of border adjustment measures in the US and the EU' (2010) 38 (15/09/09) *Energy Policy* 42.

pricing carbon could affect specific sectors remains unclear in most jurisdictions.[3]

Paying the Carbon Price discusses the theory and practice of carbon leakage in the context of three independent ETSs. It demonstrates that risk of carbon leakage is not as high as initially predicted by policymakers. Furthermore, the significant discrepancies in the policy framework for free allocation in independent ETSs is problematic as it discriminates between liable entities within and across the different ETSs. If the combined effects of the carbon price and free allocation are not the same for two firms operating in different jurisdictions, which are in competition in relation to the product they produce, then these firms will still face different price constraints. Different allocation rules could affect their profit margins, thereby distorting trade.

Economic data that assesses the sectors liable under ETSs is often discussed within the economics sphere, with little attention from legal scholars.[4] As a result, the legal implications of the World Trade Organisation's (WTO) laws applicable to the free allocation method have been largely disregarded. The final chapters of this book analyse the issue of free allocation of permits in light of the definition of a subsidy in the Agreement on Subsidies and Countervailing Measures (SCM Agreement). As a result, a number of recommendations are made for future scheme design rules that will be both legally robust and will support the effectiveness of the ETSs while limiting any negative impacts on international trade.

2. THE GREAT EXTERNALITY OF ALL TIMES

The Fifth Assessment Report (AR5) of the United Nations Intergovernmental Panel on Climate Change (IPCC)[5] on the physical scientific basis of climate change concluded, with unprecedented levels of

---

[3] European Environment Agency, 'Market-based instruments for environmental policy in Europe' (European Environment Agency, 2005) 9. According to the European Environment Agency 'there is no evidence that existing economic instruments have a major adverse effect on competitiveness at the macro and sector level'.

[4] Sanja Bogojevic, 'Ending the Honeymoon: Deconstructing Emissions Trading Discourses' (2009) 21(3) *Journal of Environmental Law* 443.

[5] Intergovernmental Panel on Climate Change <http://www.ipcc.ch/>. The IPCC is a scientific body established in 1988 under the auspices of the United Nations (UN) with the aim of providing 'a clear scientific view on the current state of knowledge in climate change and its potential environmental and

certainty, that the atmosphere and oceans are warming at increasing rates.[6] Each of the past three decades has been warmer than all the previous decades in the instrumental records, and the first decade of the twenty-first century has been the warmest yet.[7]

Based on meteorological data independently collected by different centres around the globe, the IPCC concluded that it is *virtually certain* that maximum and minimum temperatures over land have increased on a global scale since 1950.[8] It is also *virtually certain* that the upper ocean (0–700m) warmed from 1971 to 2010.[9]

A growing body of scientific evidence demonstrates that the cumulative concentrations of human-induced GHG[10] emissions are the primary cause of climate change.[11] In 2011, the atmospheric concentrations of carbon dioxide (CO_2), methane (CH_4) and nitrous oxide (N_2O) exceeded

---

socio-economic impacts.' While the IPCC reviews and assesses scientific, technical and socio-economic information produced worldwide, it does not conduct any direct research and/or monitor climate related data or parameters. The IPCC work is conducted by three Working Groups (WGI, WGII and WGIII), coordinated and administrated by a Technical Support Unit (TSU). The WGI assesses the physical scientific aspects of the climate system and climate change. The WGII assesses the vulnerability of socio-economic and natural systems to climate change, consequences of climate change and adaptation options. The WG III assesses mitigation options, including emissions reductions and removals, adopting a solution-oriented approach. Between 1988 and 2015 the IPCC released five Assessment Reports (AR) of the state of knowledge on climate change.

[6] Intergovernmental Panel on Climate Change, 'Climate Change 2013: The Physical Science Basis – Technical Summary' (2013) <www.ipcc.ch>.

[7] Ibid.

[8] Ibid. Also see Intergovernmental Panel on Climate Change, 'Climate Change 2013: The Physical Science Basis – Summary for Policymakers' (2013) <http://www.ipcc.ch/>. Note that '*virtually certain*' indicates a 99–100 per cent assessed likelihood of the outcome or result.

[9] Intergovernmental Panel on Climate Change, above n 8.

[10] There are seven main Greenhouse gases (GHGs) in the atmosphere: Carbon dioxide (CO_2), Methane (CH_4), Nitrous oxide (N_2O), Hydrofluorocarbons (HFCs), Perfluorocarbons (PFCs), Sulphur hexafluoride (SF_6) and Nitrogen trifluoride (NF_3). The first three GHGs occur naturally in the atmosphere, while the others are synthetic. Natural (non-anthropogenic) GHGs are essential to life in this planet. They absorb solar radiation and keep the earth warm enough to support life. However, human activities such as energy production, land clearing and agriculture have increased the volume and variety of GHGs present in the atmosphere, with severe impacts to the climate system.

[11] Intergovernmental Panel on Climate Change, above n 8, 2.

the pre-industrial levels by approximately 40 per cent, 150 per cent, and 20 per cent, respectively.

The present concentrations of CO_2, CH_4 and N_2O are the highest ever recorded in ice cores in the last 800,000 years.[12] More than half of anthropogenic GHG emissions are generated by energy use and production, with land-use changes, such as deforestation and industrial activities, also playing an important role.[13]

Concentrations of GHG in the atmosphere are cumulative and the effects to the climatic system are only experienced decades and centuries after the emissions were created. Even in the event of a complete cessation of emissions in the near future, global warming would still remain constant for centuries, representing a 'substantial multi-century climate change commitment created by past, present and future emissions of CO_2'.[14]

Therefore, a large percentage of climate change is already irreversible and will continue throughout the late twenty-first century and beyond, including the increase in surface temperatures and the heat transfer from the ocean surface to lower depths.[15]

2.1 Global Emissions Trends

Historically, the developed countries have been responsible for the vast majority of the GHG emissions increases that the world has experienced since the years prior to the industrial revolution. In the 1970s, developed countries were emitting approximately two-thirds of global emissions.[16] This trend only started to shift in the twenty-first century, with the reduction in the energy-intensity of big economies, such as the United States (US).

In 2013, the developed countries accounted for approximately 40 per cent of global emissions, while the developing countries (including

---

[12] Ibid., 7. CO_2 concentrations have increased from 280 parts per million (ppm) in pre-industrial times to over 400 ppm in 2013.

[13] Intergovernmental Panel on Climate Change, above n 6; International Energy Agency, 'Key Trends in CO2 Emissions' (2015); Rosemary Lyster and Adrian Bradbrook, *Energy Law and the Environment* (Cambridge University Press, 2006) 51.

[14] Intergovernmental Panel on Climate Change, above n 8; Intergovernmental Panel on Climate Change, above n 6, 61.

[15] Intergovernmental Panel on Climate Change, above n 8, 20.

[16] Ross Garnaut, *The Garnaut Climate Change Review: Final Report* (Cambridge University Press, 2008) 55.

transitional economies) emitted 60 per cent of the global GHGs.[17] At the forefront of this increase are China and India, followed by Indonesia and Brazil, countries which are 'at stages of development in which growth is highly energy-intensive'.[18] In 2013, China, alone, was responsible for 60 per cent of the global coal consumed in industry.[19]

Emissions in developing countries have increased about eight times faster than those in the developed countries,[20] with projections for developing countries to contribute approximately 70 per cent of the global 'business as usual' emissions by 2030.[21]

China's emissions growth levels since 2000 are larger than the total level of emissions in 2012 of the other BRICS (Brazil, Russia, India, China, South Africa) countries combined. Olivier, Janssens-Maenhout and Peters reported that 'the increases in China and India caused by far the largest increase in global emissions of 1.0 billion tonnes in 2011'.[22] In contrast, the majority of other developing countries contributed very little to global GHG emissions.[23]

However, China is undergoing a major structural transformation, with focus on sustainability, and GHG emissions from energy are expected to peak before 2025, at least five years before its international commitment to peak emissions around 2030.[24]

A recent slowdown in global CO_2 emissions from energy suggests that peaking GHG emissions in the next decade is still possible.[25] Still, there

---

[17] International Energy Agency, 'Redrawing the Energy-Climate Map: World Energy Outlook Special Report' (IEA, OECD, 2013) 22, 13.

[18] Ross Garnaut, 'Garnaut Climate Change Review Update: Global Emissions Trend' (Commonwealth of Australia, 2011) 15. Despite the issues with the increasing emissions levels, the current stages of development of the large non-OECD countries are promoting a much needed 'improvement in living standards in the regions that had been home to the most desperate and deeply entrenched development problems, including in most of Africa' and the 'augmentation of opportunity for better lives for most of the world's people': at 7.

[19] International Energy Agency, above n 17, 33.

[20] Garnaut, above n 16, 56.

[21] Garnaut, above n 18, 24–8.

[22] International Energy Agency, above n 17.

[23] Jos Olivier, Greet Janssens-Maenhout and Jeroen Peters, 'Trends in global co2 emissions: 2012 Report' (The Hague: PBL Netherlands Environmental Assessment Agency; Ispra: Joint Research Centre, 2012) <http://www.pbl.nl/en/publications/2012/trends-in-gobal-co2-emmissions-2012-report> 10.

[24] Fergus Green and Nicholas Stern, 'China's changing economy: implications for its carbon dioxide emissions' (2016) *Climate Policy* 1.

[25] International Energy Agency, *IEA Finds CO2 Emissions Flat for Third Straight Year Even as Global Economy Grew in 2016* (17 March 2017)

is much yet to be done and any serious attempt to stabilise the global temperature increase at 2°C above pre-industrial levels will necessarily involve large contributions from the highest emitters, including the developed countries and transitional developing countries such as China and India, combined with substantial contributions from other countries.

3. THE PARIS AGREEMENT

In 1994, a near-universal assembly of countries under the auspices of the United Nations Framework Convention on Climate Change (UNFCCC)[26] recognised that the increasing concentration of GHG in the atmosphere from anthropogenic sources is causing climate change and its adverse effects are a common concern for humankind. Parties agreed for the first time in 2009 that the increase in global temperature should be below 2°C above pre-industrial temperature.[27]

Paradoxically, the same nations have failed for two decades to achieve an effective, legally binding agreement to reduce global GHG emissions. The Kyoto Protocol formalised the strict divide between developed and developing countries.[28] The developing countries justified this position on the basis of historical emissions and the principle of common but differentiated responsibilities.[29] However, the rigid division impacted on the viability of an effective second commitment period of the Kyoto Protocol, and resulted in the impasse at Copenhagen.[30]

<https://www.iea.org/newsroom/news/2017/march/iea-finds-co2-emissions-flat-for-third-straight-year-even-as-global-economy-grew.html>; ibid.

[26]   United Nations Framework Convention on Climate Change, opened for signature 9 May 1992, 1771 UNTS 107 (entered into force 21 March 1994) (*'UNFCCC'*).

[27]   Conference of the Parties, United Nations Framework Convention on Climate Change, *Report of the Conference of the Parties on Its Fifteenth Session, Held in Copenhagen from 7 to 19 December 2009 – Addendum – Part Two: Action taken by the Conference of the Parties at Its Fifteenth Session*, UN Doc FCCC/CP/2009/11/Add.1 (30 March 2010) ('COP 15') para 1.

[28]   Kyoto Protocol to the United Nations Framework Convention on Climate Change, opened for signature 11 December 1997, 2303 UNTS 148 (entered into force 16 February 2005).

[29]   On the principle of common but differentiated responsibilities, see Christopher D. Stone, 'Common but Differentiated Responsibilities in International Law' (2004) 98(2) *The American Journal of International Law* 276.

[30]   COP 15, above n 27.

Over 20 years after the creation of the UNFCCC, at the 21st Conference of the Parties (COP21) in 2015, the Parties reached a historical agreement, known as the Paris Agreement.[31] The Paris Agreement aims to hold the increase in the global average temperature to below 2°C above pre-industrial levels. Furthermore, the Parties agree to pursue efforts to limit the temperature increase to 1.5°C above pre-industrial levels.

In order to reach this goal, 195 countries will communicate their intended nationally determined contribution (INDCs), with the exception of least developed countries and small island developing States, which will communicate their strategies, plans and actions for low GHG development. Developed countries have also agreed to finance at least USD 100 billion per year, to meet the needs and priorities of developing countries.

The model for international cooperation adopted by the Paris Agreement is based on fragmented action that reflects national circumstances, with leadership expected to be taken by Parties with the greatest responsibility and highest capacity. Thus, the common but differentiated responsibility principle has been reframed in a way that ensures universal participation while respecting local differences. The Paris Agreement opened for signature on 22 April 2016 and entered into force on 4 November 2016. It has been ratified by 139 Parties of 197 Parties to the UNFCCC.[32]

3.1 Domestic Climate Change Policies to Meet INDCs

A great effort is now required from all Parties who have communicated their INDCs to adopt policy instruments at the domestic level that will lead to cost-effective GHG emission reductions. The past decades have seen a range of both traditional (non-market-based) and relatively new (market-based) policy instruments being implemented in several jurisdictions to mitigate climate change. Approaches to deal with externalities

---

[31] Paris Agreement to the United Nations Framework Convention on Climate Change, opened for signature 26 April 2016, UNTS I-54113 (entered into force 4 November 2016).

[32] Number of countries that ratified the Paris Agreement by March 2017.

include, among others, systems for environmental liability,[33] taxation[34] and cap-and-trade schemes.[35]

Due to the complexity of climate change and the limitations of a single instrument to promote the internalisation of emissions costs by polluters, it is likely that cost-effective climate change mitigation will require a mix of one or more market-based instrument combined with non-market forms of environmental regulation.[36] Carbon taxes and ETSs are occupying an increasing space in this policy mix as ideal instruments to address the climate change externality in a cost-effective way.[37] However, the devil is in the detail. Whether or not these instruments will fulfil their intended outcomes depends on how these schemes are designed.

3.2 Carbon Taxes and the Challenges of Determining the Marginal Cost of GHG Emissions

In the 1960s, Pigou proposed that taxes fixed at the amount corresponding to a negative externality, can equalise the private and social marginal costs, leading to the internalisation of the costs by the economic

---

[33] Steve Shavell, *Economic Analysis of Accident Law* (Harvard University Press, 1987); Guido Calabresi, *The Costs of Accidents. A Legal and Economic Analysis* (Yale University Press, 1970).

[34] Arthur Pigou, *The Economics of Welfare* (Macmillan, 4th edn, 1962).

[35] John H. Dales, 'Land, Water and Ownership' (1968) 1(4) *The Canadian Journal of Economics* 791. For a comprehensive analysis and comparison of a range of command and control and market-based instruments, see Stefan Weishaar, *Emissions Trading Design* (Edward Elgar Publishing, 2014) 10–29.

[36] OECD, *The Economics of Climate Change Mitigation: Policies and Options for Global Action Beyond 2012* (2009) 23.

[37] World Bank Group, ECOFYS and Vivid Economics, 'State and Trends of Carbon Pricing' (2016); European Commission, 'EU action against climate change. EU emissions trading – an open scheme promoting global innovation' (2004). In 2004, the European Commission predicted that the cost of meeting its Kyoto target through the implementation of the EU ETS would be between EUR 2.9 billion and EUR 3.7 billion annually, which is equivalent to less than 0.1 per cent of the EU's GDP. In contrast, the cost to meet the same levels of emission reductions in the absence of the EU ETS could reach up to EUR 6.8 billion a year. However, see Robert Stavins, 'The problem of the Commons: Still Unsettled after 100 Years' (2011) 101 *American Economic Review* 8170, 95. Stavins demonstrated that although aggregate social costs are minimised by the use of market instruments, these systems can be more costly for individual firms, which will incur the abatement cost and still pay taxes on residual emissions.

agent.[38] In theory, an optimal pigouvian tax is set at a rate that is equal to the marginal social damage generated by a particular activity, leading to a Pareto-efficient level of activity.[39] However, in practice, estimating the marginal net damage produced by polluters can be challenging.[40]

As the value of marginal net damages is often unknown, Baumol and Oats propose an alternative approach, consisting of the selection of (somewhat arbitrary) standards for an acceptable environment, followed by the imposition of taxes at sufficient levels to achieve these standards.[41] This approach provides practical feasibility to the use of carbon taxes as a regulatory approach for climate change mitigation.[42]

---

[38] Pigou, above n 35; Janet E. Milne and Mikael Skou Andersen, 'Introduction to Environmental Taxation Concepts and Research' in Janet E. Milne and Mikael Skou Andersen (eds), *Handbook of Research on Environmental Taxation* (Edward Elgar, 2012) 153, 17.

[39] Pigou, ibid.; William J. Baumol and Wallace E. Oates, 'The Use of Standards and Prices for Protection of the Environment' (1971) 73(1) *The Swedish Journal of Economics* 42, 43. Baumol and Oates explained that:

> The optimal tax level on an externality generating activity is not equal to the marginal net damage it generates initially, but rather to the damage it would cause if the level of the activity had been adjusted to its optimal level. (...) If there is little hope of estimating the damage that is currently generated, how much less likely it is that we can evaluate the damage that would occur in an optimal world which we have never experienced or even described in quantitative terms.

[40] Ibid., 43. Baumol and Oates described the difficulties in measuring marginal social damage:

> However, it is hard to be sanguine about the availability in the foreseeable future of a comprehensive body of statistics reporting the marginal net damage of the various externality-generating activities in the economy. The number of activities involved and the number of persons affected by them are so great that on this score alone the task assumes Herculean proportions. Add to this the intangible nature of many of the most important consequences – the damage to health, the aesthetic costs – and the difficulty of determining a money equivalent for marginal net damage becomes even more apparent.

In the case of carbon taxes, the intricacies become even further aggravated by the complexities of climate change.

[41] Ibid., 44–45.

[42] Ibid. The authors recognised that this approach 'represents what we consider to be as close an approximation as one can generally achieve in practice to the spirit of the Pigouvian tradition'. Also see Milne and Andersen, above n 38, 18.

Generally, carbon taxes set a fixed price for every tonne of carbon dioxide equivalent $(CO_2\text{-e})$[43] emitted by an activity during a specified amount of time, which might be the respective financial year. One of the key criticisms to carbon taxes when comparing it with ETSs is that a carbon tax is not connected to a mandatory emission cap or reduction target. While there is uncertainty regarding the exact levels of emissions reductions, participants know the cost of carbon well ahead, providing predictability for production.

In theory, emissions reductions should occur as long as the tax rate is higher than the marginal abatement costs; this is considered to be the sufficient level to achieve the desired standard.[44] A strong tax rate is regarded as capable of incentivising businesses to adopt cleaner technology, invest in abatement projects or reduce production.[45]

In 2014, the World Bank estimated that, in order to limit global warming to 2.5°C above pre-industrial levels at the least cost, a global CO_2 price should be set at approximately US$35 per ton or, alternatively, start at approximately US$30 per ton (in 2014 dollars) in 2020, and then rise at around 5 per cent per year.[46] The World Bank report accounted at

---

[43]   As explained in Chapter 2, CO_2-e is a standard metric used to compare the emissions of different GHGs, expressing the warming influence of a particular GHG on the global climate system, based on the radiative forcing of Carbon Dioxide (CO_2).

[44]   Claudia Kettner, Daniela Kletzan-Slamanig and Angela Köppl, 'The EU Emission Trading Scheme: is there a need for price stabilization?' in Larry Kreiser et al (eds), *Environmental Taxation and Green Fiscal Reform*, Critical Issues in Environmental Taxation (Edward Elgar, 2014) vol XIV, 113, 114.

[45]   Mikael Skou Andersen, 'Environmental and Economic Implications of Taxing and Trading Carbon: Some European Experiences' in *The Reality of Carbon Taxes in the 21st Century* (Vermont Law School 2008) 64–65. Andersen suggested:

> One expects carbon-energy taxes to provide incentives in two directions: a demand effect, whereby the demand for energy is reduced as a result of the price-increase caused by the tax; and a substitution effect, whereby carbon-fuels are substituted by low-carbon or carbon neutral fuels to the extent that these are available at lower costs. (...) In other words, we would expect to see changes in energy and carbon intensity as a result of carbon pricing.

[46]   World Bank Group and ECOFYS, 'State and Trends of Carbon Pricing' (2014) 4, 32. Most carbon taxes currently in place are currently below this level, with the exception of the Finnish carbon tax (US$48/$tCO_2$), the Swiss and Norwegian carbon tax (approximately US$68/$tCO_2$) and the Swedish carbon tax at an impressive US$168/$tCO_2$.

the time for 11 national carbon taxes[47] and one subnational carbon tax[48] already implemented worldwide.[49]

Out of those, currently only four are set at levels consistent with the World Bank's threshold: the Swedish carbon tax (US\$131/tCO$_2$), the Swiss carbon tax (US\$86/tCO$_2$), the Norwegian carbon tax (US\$52/tCO$_2$) and the Finnish carbon tax (US\$60/tCO$_2$).[50] Still, most emissions-intensive sectors participating in the European Union Emissions Trading Scheme (EU ETS)[51] are exempt from these carbon taxes, in order to avoid a double carbon-pricing burden, that is, double taxation on the same amount of GHGs emitted.[52] As the following chapters will reveal, it turns out that these sectors are also, to a great extent, protected from a carbon price under the EU ETS.[53] This indicates the complexities of the market instruments and signals the failure of these regulatory instruments, to date, to properly ensure that the climate change externalities are internalised by a number of 'winners', who have consistently benefitted from double carbon pricing exemptions.

Carbon taxes often present lower administration and compliance costs compared to ETSs, as the main institutional arrangements necessary to implement and enforce a new tax are already in place under existing taxation regimes. However, stakeholders tend to prefer regulation over taxation, as the former is more susceptible to pressures from lobbying.

International and/or supranational taxes have their own additional challenges. To illustrate, the difficulties in approving a Community-wide energy tax proposed by the EU Commission tax in the 1990s – considering that fiscal measures require unanimous approved by member states – was a decisive factor in the adoption of the EU ETS, which entered into force in 2005.[54] Unlike a linked ETS, an international carbon

---

[47] Denmark, Finland, France, Iceland, Ireland, Japan, Mexico, Norway, Sweden, Switzerland and the UK.

[48] British Colombia.

[49] World Bank Group and ECOFYS, above n 46, 25.

[50] Group, Ecofys and Economics, above n 37.

[51] On the theory underpinning ETSs see below. See further details on the EU ETS in Chapters 4–6.

[52] World Bank Group and ECOFYS, above n 46, 77.

[53] See Chapters 4–7.

[54] Jean-Philippe Barde and Olivier Godard, 'Economic Principles of Environmental Fiscal Reform' in Janet E. Milne and Mikael S. Andersen (eds), *Handbook of Research on Environmental Taxation* (Edward Elgar, 2012) 33, 47; Denny Ellerman, Frank Convery and Christian De Perthuis, *Pricing Carbon: the European Union Emissions Trading Scheme* (Frank J. Convery, Christian de

tax would raise concerns about the possible implications to countries' sovereignty.

3.3 Emissions Trading Schemes

The atmosphere and the climate system are common pool resources, or commons. That is, these are assets 'that can be used by everyone, for almost any purpose, at zero cost'.[55] The issue of continuous depletion of commons was forcefully depicted in 'The Tragedy of the Commons', where Hardin stressed that circumstances of non-ownership lead to the inexorable outcome of ruin or overuse.[56]

Dales analysed this issue in the context of the use of natural water systems in North America[57] and suggested an explicit ownership system for water management, as an alternative to the general approach of a shadow prices system. Tradable permits schemes have since been generally regarded as an efficient mechanism to deal with water pollution, distribute fishing or hunting quotas, manage wetlands, incentivise waste recycling, and control deforestation, among others.[58]

An early example of such a mechanism is the US sulphur dioxide (SO_2) tradable permits scheme.[59] This nation-wide tradable permits scheme was adopted in 1995 to reduce SO_2 emissions from fossil-fuel burning power plants. It is one of several measures in the US to reduce emissions that are connected to acid rain, acid snow, and/or acid dust.[60]

ETSs are tradable permits schemes aimed at limiting GHG emissions and are also known as Emissions Trading Schemes or Emissions Trading Systems (ETSs). Under an ETS, a central authority, which may be a

---

Perthuis and Emilie Alberola trans, Cambridge University Press, 2010) 50, 58. For further details on the EU ETS, see Chapter 4.

[55] Dales, above n 35, 795.

[56] Garret Hardin, 'The Tragedy of the Commons' (1968) 162 *Science* 1243.

[57] Dales, above n 35.

[58] OECD and IEA, 'Act Locally, Trade Globally: Emissions Trading for Climate Policy' (2005).

[59] Established as a result of the enactment of the *Clean Air Act Amendments of 1990*, 42 USC (1990).

[60] For further details on the SO_2 tradable permits scheme see Richard Schmalensee and Robert Stavins, 'The SO2 Allowance Trading System: The Ironic History of a Grand Policy Experiment' (MIT Center for Energy and Environmental Policy Research, 2012). Also see Denny Ellerman, '*Ex-post* evaluation of tradable permits: the U.S. SO2 cap-and-trade program' (CEEPR, 2003).

government, supranational authority or another delegated agent, sets a limit or cap on the amount of GHGs that may be emitted by a specified number of polluters (participants). Explicit rights to emit CO2-e (emissions permits or allowances) are created at a level that corresponds to the respective cap, with each permit representing one tonne of CO2-e, and distributed among participants.[61]

The ETS market does not develop itself naturally as a result of supply and demand. ETSs are created through extensive government regulation aimed at restricting the right to emit GHGs.[62] Initially, the central authority will determine both the demand and supply of this market. The demand for permits is established by specifying the liable sectors participating in the market, while the supply is determined by the cap-setting.[63]

This artificial creation of a new set of intangible assets is necessarily accompanied by rules on how these assets are issued and traded. Allocation means the issue and distribution of emissions permits to participants, which may take place through either a remunerated transaction (auctioning or for a fixed charge) or a non-remunerated transaction. The free allocation of emissions permits based on historical emission levels is commonly known as 'grandfathering'.[64] While auctioning is the preferred approach as it avoids the political processes of deciding how to allocate free permits to different sectors, and issues to do with subsidisation and competition, free allocation is the most common method.[65]

Once permits are allocated to participants, they can be traded in the market, privately or through an established market platform. From this point, the carbon market should theoretically work like any other market.[66]

---

[61] Legal recognition of allowances as property rights varies according to jurisdiction.

[62] This feature may have consequences for International Economic Law when determining the market baseline in a benefit analysis related to subsidies. For further discussion on this topic, see Chapter 7.

[63] Joseph Kruger, Wallace Oates and William Pizer, 'Decentralization in the EU Emissions Trading Scheme and Lessons for Global Policy' (2007) 1(1) *Review of Environmental Economics and Policy* 112.

[64] Ellerman, Convery and Perthuis, above n 54.

[65] European Commission, 'Green Paper on Greenhouse Gas Emissions Trading within the European Union' (2000) 18.

[66] Christian Egenhofer et al, 'The EU Emissions Trading System and Climate Policy towards 2050: Real incentives to reduce emissions and drive innovation?' (CEPS, 2011) 3.

Participants in an ETS have the choice between reducing emissions, which they will do up to the point where the investment cost equals the permit price, or buy a permit. Where mitigation costs exceed the emissions permit market price, businesses may cover their liability by purchasing the extra emissions permits in the market. Therefore, not only is emissions reduction achieved in an economically efficient manner, but polluters are being continually incentivised to innovate by adopting cleaner technology.[67]

At the end of the given financial year, each participant must hold one emissions permit per tonne of CO_2-e emitted. Participants under the ETS will 'sell permits as long as their market price exceeds their marginal abatement costs; conversely, they will buy permits as long as their market price falls short of their marginal abatement costs'.[68] Where the emissions cap is properly reduced over time, progressive emissions reductions towards medium- and long-term emissions reduction trajectories can be achieved.

While, in theory, ETSs have the potential to generate revenue through the auctioning of emissions permits, similarly to a carbon tax, in practice, due to their vulnerability to political pressures and general concerns with carbon leakage,[69] national ETSs have worked with a large percentage of permits allocated free of cost to liable entities in the early stages of implementation.[70]

The model described above is the most common among existing schemes. As new ETSs are implemented worldwide, with more creative frameworks developed to deal with the practical issues,[71] the perceived distinctions between carbon taxes and ETSs are becoming less noticeable

---

[67] Stephen Smith, 'Environmentally Related Taxes and Tradable Permit Systems in Practice' (OECD, 2007) 3, 7.

[68] OECD, above n 36.

[69] It is not the object of the thesis to exhaust climate policy issues related to carbon taxes. However, the issue of carbon leakage, which is a common issue to carbon taxes and ETSs, is further explained in Chapter 4.

[70] Tatiana Falcão, 'Providing Environmental Taxes with an Environmental Purpose' in Larry Kreiser et al (eds), *Market Based Instruments: National Experiences in Environmental Sustainability* (Edward Elgar, 2013) 4158. Falcão demonstrates that 'the problem derived from this mechanism [ETS] is that (so far) governments have not been able to consistently receive cash funds *they* need in order to finance green actions (…)'.

[71] For example, see the hybrid structure of the former Australian Carbon Pricing Mechanism in Chapter 3.

and the political polarity less acute.[72] Stavins demonstrates that, depending on how these policy instruments are designed, they may resemble each other.[73]

One of the case studies analysed in Chapter 3 is the Australian Carbon Pricing Mechanism (AUS CPM). The scheme was designed as a 'hybrid model', with a three-year period in which permits would be sold for a fixed price in order to provide price certainty and stability during the first years of the scheme.

Other modalities of ETSs also include 'baseline and credit' schemes, where polluters must reduce emissions below a baseline level (rather than an emissions cap) which may be achieved through the use of offset credits from GHG abatement projects. For example, following the repeal of the AUS CPM, the Federal Government has proposed a baseline and credit mechanism, also known as a 'safeguard mechanism'.[74] The baseline will reflect the highest level of reported emissions for a facility over the historical period 2009–10 to 2013–14. Businesses will not pay a carbon price unless – and to the extent in which – their emissions exceed the baseline levels. However, with such low ambition levels, very little can be expected in terms of emissions reductions.

4. THE STRUCTURE OF THIS BOOK

4.1 Chapter 2 Carbon Leakage and Industry Assistance

Chapter 2 discusses the theory of carbon leakage and competitiveness concerns in relation to emissions-intensive and trade-exposed sectors participating in ETSs. Two measures are often considered as alternatives to avoid competitiveness issues and carbon leakage from the implementation of ETSs, that is, border carbon adjustments (BCA) and the free of

---

[72] World Bank Group and ECOFYS, above n 46, 29.

[73] Stavins, above n 38. Stavins pointed out that: 'If allowances are auctioned, a cap-and-trade system looks much like a carbon tax from the perspective of regulated firms. Likewise, if tax revenues are refunded in particular ways, a carbon tax can resemble cap and trade with free allowances.'

[74] Australian Government, *The Emissions Reduction Fund: The Safeguard Mechanism* Department of Environment <https://www.environment.gov.au/climate-change/emissions-reduction-fund/publications/factsheet-erf-safeguard-mechanism>; National Greenhouse and Energy Reporting (Safeguard Mechanism) Rule 2015 (Cth); National Greenhouse and Energy Reporting Amendment (2015 Measures No. 2) Regulation 2015 (Cth); National Greenhouse and Energy Reporting (Audit) Amendment Determination 2015 (No. 1).

cost allocation of permits. While BCAs are not very popular, it is possible that, due to the adoption of free allocation of permits, carbon-pricing schemes have been failing to implement the Polluter Pays Principle.

4.2   Chapter 3 Real World Emissions Trading Schemes: Challenges and Lessons Learnt

Chapter 3 introduces the case studies, providing the reader with a basic understanding of the key elements of each ETS, such as the coverages, emissions caps, governance regimes and links with other schemes. It also reflects on the main achievements and challenges particular to each scheme.

For example, the EU ETS has experienced significant problems with surplus emissions permits, and recent reforms are attempting to provide a much-needed stability to the scheme to enable it to reach its goal of promoting cost-efficient emissions reduction.

Australia has attracted the undesirable distinction of being the only jurisdiction to discard a mandatory carbon price and to move away from its key climate change policy. Despite its short life, the AUS CPM remains a relevant case to be studied due to the innovative framework adopted to prevent issues such as price volatility during the first years of the scheme, building on the lessons learned from the EU ETS.

This promising model did not survive the contentious political debate in the country, which exacerbated misunderstandings about the nature of the scheme (carbon tax or emissions trading scheme), and its impacts on the international competitiveness of the domestic energy-intensive trade-exposed (EITE) industries.

Finally, the NZ ETS is the most distinctive of the three schemes, due greatly to the singularity of New Zealand's economy. The scheme has been resilient and stable, despite significant changes in the country's approach towards international climate change negotiations.

4.3   Chapter 4 Reconsidering the Eligibility Thresholds for the Free Allocation of Permits

Chapter 4 focuses on carbon leakage and free allocation as an industry assistance measure. It develops the theory of carbon leakage and the parameters for economics research.

This chapter argues that jurisdictions linking independent ETSs would benefit from harmonising the free allocation methodologies in order to minimise the competitiveness concerns and to reduce the trade distortions and other impacts inherent to the free allocation system. It proposes a review of the general thresholds in order to assess the exposures to carbon leakage so as to improve the effectiveness and fairness of the ETSs. The two final key recommendations are the removal of the sole trade-exposure factor from the quantitative assessment in the EU ETS and increasing the stringency of all the thresholds to determine emissions-intensity.

4.4 Chapter 5 Free Allocation and Linking Emissions Trading Schemes: The Case for Harmonisation

Chapter 5 examines aspects of the design of the free-allocation methods that might lead to competitiveness distortions. It reviews the data from the first and second trading periods of the EU ETS, when the different Member States had their own separate National Allocation Plans (NAPs).

In the EU ETS context, the different allocation rules generated concerns over the competitiveness of industries subject to the different NAPs. By analogy, key design elements in the legal framework of the EU ETS and the AUS CPM would be problematic from a trade perspective. For example, the uneven benchmarks and output-based allocation *versus* the historical emissions data, which could result in a significant variation of the allocation levels, with the potential to impact trade and distort competition between liable installations under the independent ETSs.

4.5 Chapter 6 The Free Allocation of Permits and the WTO Discipline of Subsidies

The literature has extensively analysed the legal implications of the free allocation system from the perspective of the WTO laws on subsidies.[75] However, the absence of an interdisciplinary approach resulted in a lack of detailed understanding of the functioning of the ETSs, the free allocation methodology and the economic aspects of distributing permits free of cost. Chapter 6 closes the gap between the doctrinal analysis of

---

[75] See, e.g., James Windon, 'The Allocation of Free Emissions Units and The WTO Subsidies Agreement' (2009) 41 *Georgetown Journal of International Law* 1898; Felicity Deane, *Emissions Trading and WTO Law: A Global Analysis* (Edward Elgar Publishing, 2015) 8; Lauren Henschke, 'Going it Alone on Climate Change. A New Challenge to WTO Subsidies Disciplines: Are Subsidies in Support of Emissions Reductions Schemes Permissible Under the WTO' (2012) 11(1) *World Trade Review* 27.

the SCM Agreement, the legal frameworks of these schemes in practice and the economic research data.

Chapter 6 concludes that the free allocation of permits is a subsidy in accordance with the definition in the SCM Agreement and analyses whether it could be a prohibited or actionable subsidy, according to the different thresholds for allocation and the levels of assistance set by each scheme.

In relation to the EU ETS sole emissions-intensity threshold, it seems to have been included in the Directive in order to perpetuate a targeted subsidisation of a small number of enterprises from the cement sector, which were already being favoured by the decentralised NAPs during the first and second trading periods. As such, it is an actionable subsidy and may be challenged if it causes adverse effects on other WTO Members. I recommend the removal of the sole emissions-intensity factor from the EU ETS quantitative assessment. The recent proposal for a directive to amend the EU ETS[76] is partially in line with this recommendation.

4.6   Chapter 7 Summary of the Main Findings

Chapter 7 presents a summarised version of the key findings of this book.

While the EU ETS, the AUS CPM and the NZ ETS have all subsidised emissions-intensive industries, the consequences of this regulatory model have, in general, escaped the scrutiny of legal scholars. The book closes with an important message, that despite formally participating in ETSs, many heavy polluters are not yet paying their fair share of the carbon price.

5.   FINAL REMARKS

Paying the Carbon Price analyses the free allocation of permits methodologies in the ETSs. It demonstrates that the free allocation of permits discriminates between the liable entities under the ETSs, and that it may have undesirable trade impacts. Furthermore, the free allocation of permits may be deemed to be a subsidy subject to the discipline of the SCM Agreement. In this case, affected countries may bring a dispute to the WTO DSB.

---

[76]   Proposal 2015/148 (COD) for a Directive of the European Parliament and of the Council Amending Directive 2003/87/EC to enhance cost-effective emission reductions and low-carbon investments [2015].

The dual focuses of the book determined the choice of an interdisciplinary approach, one which bridged the economic data and the legal interpretations of the SCM Agreement, based on the framework of the ETSs in the case studies.

It should be noted that, between the commencement of the writing of this book in 2011 and its completion in 2016, a number of significant changes in relation to climate change regulations have taken place in the jurisdictions where the case studies were originated. In the first year of writing, the Clean Energy Bills were introduced in Australia, featuring a market instrument known as the Carbon Pricing Mechanism (AUS CPM) as its key instrument for achieving GHG emissions reductions.

The Australian Clean Energy package was approved and a linkage between the AUS CPM and the EU ETS was announced. The AUS CPM functioned for two years and, unfortunately, this work was concluded after the repeal of the Carbon Pricing Mechanism was enacted.

Both the EU ETS and the NZ ETS have also been subject to several amendments. The proposal for amending the EU ETS Directive, discussed in Chapter 3, is of particular importance. In terms of the international negotiations on climate change mitigation, there are reasons for renewed hope due to the entering into force of the Paris Agreement.

2. Carbon leakage and industry assistance

1. INTRODUCTION

In theory, a carbon price triggers an increase in production costs, correcting the climate change externality and driving the economy towards low-emissions production. Under a carbon pricing scheme, the impacts on the profits and, sometimes, to the actual viability of certain businesses may be necessary in order to achieve effective environmental policy outcomes.[1] Therefore, it is not surprising to find that domestic opposition to carbon pricing mechanisms is mostly led by emissions-intensive industries.[2]

Competitiveness concerns and the risk of carbon leakage are largely regarded as obstacles to the implementation of ETSs in many countries,[3] with stakeholders arguing that unilateral carbon policies will place domestic industries in a disadvantageous position in relation to overseas competitors. Carbon leakage concerns are intrinsically connected to the socio-economic impacts from the loss of industrial competitiveness, such as unemployment and deindustrialisation.[4]

This chapter analyses carbon leakage and introduces the concept of free allocation as an industry assistance measure under Emission Trading Schemes (ETS). It starts by addressing the theory of carbon leakage,

---

[1] OECD, 'Linkages Between Environmental Policy and Competitiveness' (OECD, 2010) <http://www.oecd-ilibrary.org/environment/linkages-between-environmental-policy-and-competitiveness_218446820583> 39, 43.

[2] See Aaron Cosbey and Richard Tarasofsky, 'Climate Change, Competitiveness and Trade' (Chatham House, 2007).

[3] Carolyn Fischer and Alan K. Fox, 'The Role of Trade and Competitiveness Measures in US Climate Policy' (2011) 101(3) *The American Economic Review* 258. In Australia it was one of the predominant justifications for the repeal of the carbon pricing mechanism, as demonstrated below.

[4] Stephanie Monjon and Philippe Quirion, 'Addressing Leakage in the EU ETS: Results from the Case II Model' (2009) 2.

setting the parameters for the analysis of carbon leakage in practice developed in Chapter 4.

Two measures are often considered as alternatives to avoid competitiveness issues and carbon leakage from the implementation of ETSs, that is, border carbon adjustments (BCA) and the free of cost allocation of permits. The chapter briefly introduces the topic of BCAs, then moves on to examine the free allocation method. In practice, real-life ETS have been providing targeted assistance and differential treatment to a number of sectors, which has relevant distributional impact. Carbon-pricing schemes have, therefore, been failing to implement the Polluter Pays Principle due to the free allocation of permits methodology.

2. CARBON LEAKAGE THEORY

The IPCC defines carbon leakage as 'the increase in CO_2 emissions outside the countries taking domestic mitigation action divided by the reduction in the emissions of these countries'.[5] The IPCC's definition is broad and covers two main leakage 'channels', that is, the fossil fuel price channel and the competitiveness leakage channel.

2.1 The Fossil Fuel Price Channel

The demand for, and supply of, fossil fuels tends to drop in countries with a stringent carbon policy, with a likely plunge in global energy prices for the fossil fuels. Assuming a continuance of the current state of unequal carbon pricing worldwide, fossil fuel energy consumption would then increase in those countries that chose to free ride.[6]

To illustrate, in 2012 the United States experienced its second-largest decrease in coal demand in five decades due to low gas prices, environmental regulation and a mild winter. China also experienced a weak growth in coal demand in 2012, although its consumption still accounted

---

[5] Intergovernmental Panel on Climate Change, 'Climate Change 2007: Mitigation of Climate Change ' (2007).

[6] OECD, 'Mitigating Climate Change in the Context of Incomplete Carbon Pricing Coverage' in *The Economics of Climate Change Mitigation: Policies and Options for Global Action Beyond 2012* (OECD, 2009); Susanne Dröge et al, 'Tackling Leakage In A World Of Unequal Carbon Prices' (Climate Strategies, 2009) 18; Julia Reinaud, 'Issues Behind Competitiveness and Carbon Leakage: Focus on Heavy Industry' (IEA; OECD, 2008) 31, 4; Tim Denne, 'Impacts of the NZ ETS on Emissions Leakage: Final Report' (COVEC, 2011) 8.

for more than 50 per cent of the global demand, and dominating the world's coal market.[7]

An expansion of the mining capacity in major exporting countries such as Australia and Indonesia, which has not been met by similar growth in demand, resulted in oversupply and low coal prices. However, the decline in demand in the US and China was offset by a growth in demand in India, Russia and other countries, and coal had the largest demand growth among all fossil fuels in 2012.[8]

The fossil fuel price channel is significant, and the least avoidable. It is not limited to trade-exposed industries since it is related to the consumption of fossil fuels across the economy. Denne observed that 'to the extent that emission reductions occur through fuel switching or reductions in energy fuel demand, leakage is an inevitable consequence of any international architecture in which some countries are regulated and others are not'.[9]

Reductions in the consumption of fossil fuel by one country are counterbalanced by an increase in demand in other countries, which do not have carbon-pricing mechanisms in place.[10] The strengthening of international cooperation, such as the cooperation on pricing carbon and increasing the use of renewable energies, are key to minimising the risk of carbon leakage through the fossil fuel channel.

2.2 The Competitiveness Leakage Channel

The competitiveness leakage channel has been a foremost concern for governments implementing an ETS and it has rationalised industry support in the form of the free allocation of emissions permits in the analysed schemes. For example, the ETS Directive defines leakage as the increase in GHG emissions in third countries where industry would not

---

[7] IEA and OECD, 'Coal medium term market report: market trends and projections to 2018' (IEA, 2013).

[8] Ibid. Russia and India are the two largest non-OECD countries using brown coal. The IEA and OECD explained the correlation between India's coal demand and its rapid increase in electricity consumption as being due to ongoing electrification, population growth and increasing GDP per capita. Furthermore, the coal share of the total primary energy consumption has increased in India from 35 per cent in 2000 to 43 per cent in 2011.

[9] Denne, above n 6, ii.

[10] Eric Posner and David Weisbach, *Climate Change Justice* (Princeton University Press, 2010) 32.

be subject to comparable carbon constraints, putting certain energy-intensive sectors and subsectors in the EU, which are subject to international competition, at an economic disadvantage.[11]

An alternative, broader definition considers any relocation of production from countries with a carbon cap to countries or regions that do not have carbon constraints as generating carbon leakage, irrespective of a net increase in emissions. That is, when industries or investment relocates to countries with less stringent carbon policies, there is a decrease in the demand for emissions permits and this reduces the permit prices. A consequent surplus of permits takes place, enabling other sectors to increase their production up to the amount of the cap. According to this definition, emissions produced overseas as a direct result of the relocation of production due to a carbon price would always be additional to the cap and, therefore, increase global net emissions.[12]

In this chapter, a sector-based definition of carbon leakage is adopted. That is, carbon leakage is 'the ratio of emissions increase from a specific sector outside the country (as a result of a policy affecting that sector in the country) over the emissions reduction in the sector (again, as a result of the environmental policy)'.[13]

There is an increasing role for sector-specific modelling and sectoral *ex-post* studies in the analysis of carbon leakage.[14] Economic modelling often identifies more significant leakage rates at the sectoral level rather than economy-wide leakages.[15] Carbon leakage assessment is likely to be more accurate when the underpinning definition is based on the impacts

---

[11] Directive 2009/29/EC of the European Parliament and of the Council of 23 April 2009 Amending Directive 2003/87/EC so as to improve and extend the greenhouse gas emission allowance trading scheme of the Community [2009] OJ L 140/63 (ETS Directive), Preamble para 24. Also see Commission Decision 746/2014/EU of 27 October 2014 Determining, Pursuant to Directive 2003/87/EC of the European Parliament and of the Council, a List of Sectors and Subsectors which are Deemed to be Exposed to a Significant Risk of Carbon Leakage, for the Period 2015 to 2019 [2014] OJ L 308/114.

[12] Ingmar Juergens, Jesús Barreiro-Hurlé and Alexander Vasa, 'Identifying Carbon Leakage Sectors in the EU ETS and Implications of Results' (2013) 13(1) *Climate Policy* 89.

[13] Reinaud, above n 6, 3.

[14] Cf in the context of the definition of competitiveness, Cosbey and Tarasofsky, above n 2, 3 suggested that 'a more useful and legitimate use of the concept of competitiveness is to consider it at the firm or sectoral level. Here it can be simply defined as capture of market share – a state that is maintained in a dynamic contest among firms'.

[15] Reinaud, above n 6, 29.

by particular sectors of the economy, and when the modelling accounts
for the sector specific technological patterns or economic geographies.[16]

Modelling has indicated that industries could potentially lose their
short-term and long-term competitiveness due to the impacts of the
carbon costs relative to their revenues and/or profits.[17] The medium- to
long-term consequence is the shift of investment to third countries where
carbon is not priced.[18]

In the short term, industries could potentially lose international market
share to competitors not facing similar carbon constraints.[19] A shift in the
international trade flow may be noticeable either from the demand side or
the supply side. An example of the former is where the demand for
finished products produced in countries with a carbon price is reduced
due to an increase in the demand for cheaper products from countries
with less stringent carbon constraints. The latter occurs where activities
covered by a carbon price source their components, or other semi-
finished emissions-intensive products, from overseas producers that are
not subject to similar carbon costs.[20]

The loss in market share means a loss in profits, eventually reducing a
company's financial capacity for investment.[21] These consequences are
sector-specific – and sometimes particular to subsectors only – rather
than an economy-wide issue.[22] Several factors can determine a sector or
subsector's vulnerability to loss of competitiveness and carbon leakage,
such as the cost pass-through capacity, the abatement potential and the
regulatory and legal frameworks of a sector.[23]

---

[16]   Dröge et al, above n 6, 16.
[17]   Denne, above n 6, ii.
[18]   Reinaud, above n 6, 5.
[19]   OECD, above n 6.
[20]   Reinaud, above n 6, 6.
[21]   Dröge et al, above n 6, 18.
[22]   See, e.g., Karsten Neuhoff, *Climate Policy after Copenhagen: The Role of Carbon Pricing* (Cambridge University Press, 2011) 199; Reinaud, above n 6, 4. Reinaud suggested that 'none of the simulations focusing on sectoral leakage indicate a leakage rate near 100%: in other words, it is highly unlikely that carbon leakage would wipe out entirely an effort to reduce emissions in an industry'.
[23]   Susanne Dröge and Simone Cooper, 'Tackling Leakage in a World of Unequal Carbon Prices: a Study for the Greens/EFA Group' (Climate Strategies, 2010) 28.

The cost pass-through capacity is related to the 'ability to recover the cost of the carbon constraint, without significantly undermining international competitiveness'.[24] For example, the global aluminium sector is largely reliant on prices set at the London Metals Exchange and the Shanghai Futures Exchange, which means that entities in the sector do not have the advantage of a high pass-through capacity.[25]

An industry's pass-through capacity is dynamic and demands ongoing government assessment.[26] Research has pointed out the following elements as being able to determine a sector's pass-through capability:

(i) *Levels of production cost increase*: an activity's emissions-intensity determines to what extent production costs will increase with the introduction of a carbon price. It varies according to the ratio between the new cost of carbon and the activity's current surplus.[27]

(ii) *Differences in cost structure vis-à-vis non-carbon constrained competitors*: in some cases, the carbon price is only a minor factor impacting on a sector's profitability.[28] Other factors include exchange rates, technology availability, raw material costs, transport costs, productivity and the state of industrial relations, political and economic stability, amongst others.

(iii) *Demand elasticity*: refers to the impacts on demand deriving from the increases in a product's prices. Where demand is inelastic, a sector is able to pass-on the carbon price to its customers without reducing the demand for that product.[29] Demand is often elastic where products are easily substituted, either in the form of imports of the same good (highly traded goods) or in the form of different goods that can serve the same purpose.

---

[24] Reinaud, above n 6, 43; See also OECD, 'The Sectoral Competitiveness Issue: Theoretical Studies' in *The Political Economy of Environmentally Related Taxes* (OECD, 2006) 67.

[25] Reinaud, above n 6, 48–9.

[26] Ibid., 44.

[27] Denne, above n 6, 12.

[28] Tony Wood and Tristan Edis, 'New Protectionism under Carbon Pricing: Case Studies of LNG, Coal Mining and Steel Sectors' (Grattan Institute, 2011). For example, the Grattan Institute showed that a carbon price of A\$40 would not affect investment in the LNG sector in Australia or reduce the production of existing domestic facilities. Therefore, the sector would not be at risk of carbon leakage even under a full carbon price. In spite of the Report's findings, assistance to the LNG industry in Australia is estimated to cost approximately \$A4b between 2012 and 2020.

[29] Reinaud, above n 6, 47.

Data related to the three aforementioned elements are seldom available. Due to an insufficient amount of industry data (e.g., business strategies for operation and investment), governments often have only a rough estimate of a sector's vulnerability when calculating carbon leakage rates. This makes it difficult to counter the political pressure placed upon it by liable entities under a carbon-pricing mechanism.

In practice, the assessment of a sector's cost pass-through capacity has been solely based on the first element and a proxy indicator of the third element. Estimating demand elasticity by country for each product is considered to be an excessively complex task,[30] which is why assessments have considered the degree of competition in the market or 'trade-exposure' as a proxy indicator for the elasticity of demand.[31]

As mentioned, the levels of production cost increases have been primarily measured by the activity's emissions-intensity, disregarding the availability or not of cost-effective abatement measures within a sector due to the complexities that it would add to the valuation. The adoption of abatement measures depends on the availability of affordable and less emissions-intensive inputs, and the adaptability of the sector to lower-carbon technologies and production processes.[32]

Where the carbon price is higher than the abatement costs, industries would have an incentive to shift towards cleaner technologies and reduce the impact of the carbon price. Contrarily, where abatement is not an option, industries will be more or less susceptible to the carbon price, depending on their cost pass-through capacity and the regulatory framework of the sector.

The regulatory framework is determined by the existence of subsidies (e.g., sector specific subsidies and others), trade restrictions, legal and political stability, infrastructure quality and others.[33] Carbon leakage assessment also does not usually account for significant differences that firms within a sector can present in terms of strategic governance,

---

[30] Matthew Bartleet et al, 'Impact of Emissions Pricing on New Zealand Manufacturing: A Short-Run Analysis' (2010) 12.

[31] A remarkable exception is the NZ ETS, as pointed out by Denne, above n 6, 11. Denne explains that New Zealand has adopted the concept of 'potential trade', that is, the notion that 'something could be trade exposed even if it is not traded currently'. Therefore, under the NZ ETS all activities are defined as trade-exposed, unless: (1) there is no international trade of the output of the activity across oceans; or (2) it is not economically viable to import or export the output of the activity.

[32] Dröge and Cooper, above n 23, 30.

[33] Ibid.

technology, resources, among others, which could result in different levels of carbon leakage.[34]

To date, there has not been a demonstrated significant leakage rate in any sector in the compared ETSs, making it 'highly unlikely that carbon leakage would wipe out entirely an effort to reduce emissions in an industry'.[35] In reality, the carbon leakage-exposure rates have been historically overestimated by industry and governments. This topic is given detailed attention in Chapter 4.

3. CARBON LEAKAGE AND BORDER CARBON ADJUSTMENTS

Border carbon adjustments are aimed at levelling the playing field between domestic producers who pay a carbon price through an ETS and overseas producers facing lower or no constraints on their greenhouse gas emissions. BCAs may be implemented through the application of border carbon taxes or by requirements for importers to surrender emissions permits at the border, at a similar amount compared to the carbon costs imposed on domestic industries. In certain cases, the border tax or carbon liability on imports is coupled with an exemption from the domestic carbon price on exported goods.

Much has been written on BCAs to date and it is not the aim of this chapter to reproduce these discussions.[36] The critical point is that BCAs may increase costs for international competitors where products are

---

[34]   OECD, above n 1.

[35]   Reinaud, above n 6, 39. *Contra* Florian Habermacher, 'Is Carbon Leakage Really Low? A Critical Reconsideration of the Leakage Concept' in Larry Kreiser et al (eds), *Carbon Pricing, Growth and the Environment* (Edward Elgar, 2012).

[36]   See, e.g., Kateryna Holzer, *Carbon-related Border Adjustment and WTO Law* (Edward Elgar, 2014); Felicity Deane, *Emissions Trading and WTO Law: A Global Analysis* (Edward Elgar Publishing, 2015); Monjon and Quirion, above n 4; Stephanie Monjon and Philippe Quirion, 'How to design a border adjustment for the European Union Emissions Trading System?' (2010) *Energy Policy* 1; Stephanie Monjon and Philippe Quirion, 'A Border Adjustment for the EU ETS: Reconciling WTO Rules and Capacity to Tackle Carbon Leakage' (2012) *X Annual Conference of the Euro-Latin Study Network on Integration and Trade (ELSNIT): Trade and Climate Change*; Reinaud, above n 6; Frederic Branger and Philippe Quirion, 'Would Border Carbon Adjustments Prevent Carbon Leakage and Heavy Industry Competitiveness Losses? Insights from a Meta-Analysis of Recent Economic Studies' (CIRED, 2013).

imported into a country with carbon constraints, ensuring that the traded products receive equal treatment.[37]

BCAs can be particularly effective in preventing carbon leakage at a sectoral level.[38] Economic modelling suggests that BCAs have the potential to achieve negative leakage rates in the steel (where border adjustments cover exports as well as imports) and aluminium sectors (where border adjustments take into account the indirect costs of electricity production), not only reducing the domestic emissions rate but also reducing global emissions.[39] In the cement sector, Monjon and Quirion demonstrated that a BCA applied to clinker, an intermediate product used in the manufacture of certain types of cement, could produce better outcomes than the free allocation approach, reducing overall clinker production in the EU and incentivising the substitution of clinker to other low-carbon inputs.[40]

Implementing effective BCAs can be challenging due to the administrative, legal and political aspects.[41] Although BCAs have been a constant subject of conjecture in the North American climate policy debate,[42] an example of a BCA can already be found in the EU ETS with the inclusion of international aviation in the scheme, as explained below.

3.1 Administrative Challenges to the Implementation of Border Carbon Adjustments

In theory, the BCAs should impose similar marginal carbon costs on both the domestic and international producers, including direct and

---

[37] Reinaud, above n 6, 87.

[38] See Monjon and Quirionn, above n 36 ('How to design a border adjustment ...'); Dröge et al, above n 6, 57–9.

[39] Monjon and Quirion, above n 4.

[40] Ibid.; Dröge et al, above n 6, 57–9.

[41] The author has previously discussed this topic in Elena Aydos, 'Australia's carbon pricing mechanism' in Larry Kreiser et al (eds), *Carbon Pricing, Growth and the Environment*, Critical Issues in Environmental Taxation (Edward Elgar Publishing, 2012) 261, 272.

[42] Harro Van Asselt and Thomas Brewer, 'Addressing Competitiveness and Leakage Concerns in Climate Policy: An Analysis of Border Adjustment Measures in the US and the EU' (2010) 38 *Energy Policy* 42. In the US, the following proposed bills featured border adjustments: Low Carbon Economy Bill 2007, Climate Security Bill 2008, American Clean Energy and Security Bill 2009. An early draft of the EU Commission's revised Directive proposal also contained provisions for border adjustments, although it was not included in the final proposal.

indirect costs.[43] In a real life ETS scenario, it would be difficult to set the correct adjustment rates as some industry sectors receive free emissions permits while others do not. Market prices for emissions permits also fluctuate and the emissions-intensities and electricity prices vary within sectors and subsectors, and between different regions. Where the adjustment rates fail to impose a similar marginal carbon cost on imported products, the effectiveness of the BCAs to prevent carbon leakage is compromised.[44]

Effective BCAs would be required to cover all products at risk of carbon leakage, including basic materials and manufactured products, which may be challenging.[45] Van Asselt and Brewer suggested that the inclusion of finished products adds great administrative complexities to the implementation of BCAs.[46] A great level of detail would be required, particularly information on imported products, calling into question the feasibility of BCAs.[47]

Furthermore, BCAs should only apply to products facing less or no carbon costs in their own countries of origin. Therefore, at a national level, Governments would have to monitor their trading partners' climate policies and find a measure for comparison between the different policies implemented in developing countries. At an industry level, individual abatement efforts would also have to be monitored and measured.

Finally, in order to protect domestic producers from losses in competitiveness vis-à-vis international competitors, export rebates would be required to mitigate the carbon costs for products exported to countries without similar carbon constraints.[48] The precise estimation of the amounts of the rebates due is challenging, considering that producers may hold emissions permits that are partly purchased at cost levels and partly allocated free of charge. Where rebates are provided at the nationwide average price, some companies would receive compensation above the actual marginal carbon costs, representing export subsidies.[49]

---

[43] Reinaud, above n 6, 88; Julia Reinaud, 'Trade, Competitiveness and Carbon Leakage: Challenges and Opportunities' (Chatham House, 2009).

[44] Reinaud, above n 6, 88.

[45] Ibid., 91. Indeed, effective BCAs would cover, for example, aluminium and steel production, as well as all finished and semi-finished products that contain such materials, for instance vehicles, appliances, and industrial equipment, amongst others.

[46] Van Asselt and Brewer, above n 42, 50.

[47] Reinaud, above n 6, 91.

[48] Ibid., 89.

[49] Ibid. For further details on export subsidies see Chapter 6.

Measuring the climate cost at this level demands complex monitoring and reporting systems both for governments and companies.[50]

3.2 Addressing Carbon Leakage via Allocation of Emissions Permits

There are relevant legal considerations to be taken into account by countries intending to unilaterally impose BCAs, as these measures have the potential to encourage protectionism and trade disputes. Dröge argued that a multilateral process would be required, where the application of a BCA is agreed upon by countries, in order to avoid risking trade conflicts.[51] Garnaut goes further to suggest that a new WTO code must be agreed upon, which would be applicable to climate change policy.[52] Garnaut states that:

> Such a code would provide a framework within which countries could impose border adjustments, and would greatly reduce the likelihood of the imposition of climate change-justified border adjustments degenerating into a trade war. Pending such a global agreement, it would be undesirable for border adjustments to be imposed unilaterally by any country, because of the risks that they would pose to global trade.[53]

The uncertainties around the legality of a measure are primarily related to its compliance with WTO law.[54] In particular, the implementation of BCAs may violate the 'National Treatment'[55] and the 'Most Favoured Nation' provisions of the General Agreement on Tariffs and Trade (GATT).[56]

The 'National Treatment' clause provides that trade measures should not discriminate against foreign products vis-à-vis domestic 'like products'. The 'Most Favoured Nation' clause provides that the rules for 'like imported products' should not favour any importing country over

---

[50]　Ibid., 90.

[51]　Dröge et al, above n 6, 64.

[52]　Ross Garnaut, *The Garnaut Climate Change Review: Final Report* (Cambridge University Press, 2008) 234.

[53]　Ibid., 234.

[54]　OECD, above n 1.

[55]　Marrakesh Agreement Establishing the World Trade Organisation, opened for signature 15 April 1994, 1867 UNTS 3 (entered into force 1 January 1995) annex 1A ('GATT') art III.

[56]　GATT, art. I.

another.[57] In very simplified terms, where products are considered 'like products', the BCAs must be applied to the imported products in the same way that they are applied to domestic products, and must not discriminate between countries and/or producers.

Therefore, a key issue when determining whether BCAs violate the national treatment and/or most favoured nation provisions is whether a product can be differentiated, based on whether a difference is created because it is produced using highly emissions-intensive technology and/or fossil fuel energy as compared to low-carbon technology and/or renewable energy. If this differentiation is acknowledged, a country may adopt a BCA upon the importation of products based on their different pollution levels.

This issue is highly contentious because, in essence, BCAs are non-product-related process and production methods (npr-PPM)[58] targeting emissions-intensive production processes, which most of the time cannot be identified by any physical trace in the final product.[59] Whether the trade restrictions imposed on npr-PPM are WTO compliant is a crucial, and yet unresolved, matter.

The 'product-process' doctrine, considered illegal under the GATT, is the differentiation of products based on non-product-related characteristics, and it was the dominant doctrine until the early 2000s.[60] As the BTAs impose different restrictions on products based on how emissions-intensive their production processes are, or whether or not the producer is internalising a carbon price, it would not be considered WTO consistent as long as the product-process doctrine remains predominant in jurisprudence.[61]

The limitations of the product-process doctrine have been subject to ongoing debate.[62] A different approach seems to be supported in more recent jurisprudence, which considers the measures that differentiate products produced using certain methods, irrespective of who is the

---

[57] For a detailed analysis of BCAs and the GATT provisions see Holzer, above n 36; Deane, above n 36.

[58] Also known as non-incorporated PPMs, these are process and production methods which are linked to the non-physical aspects of a product and do not leave a physical impact on the end product.

[59] Holzer, above n 36, 92.

[60] Ibid., 94.

[61] Ibid., 97.

[62] See, e.g., Steve Charnovitz, 'The Law of Environmental "PPMs" in the WTO: Debunking the Myth of Illegality' (2002) 27 *Yale Journal of International Law* 59.

producer and/or the country of origin, as being WTO consistent.[63] In other words, npr-PPM measures such as the BCAs might be acceptable in the future as long as they are origin and producer-neutral.

3.2.1 Article XX of the GATT

Where a BCA connected to an ETS violates a provision of GATT, there is still a possibility of recourse to the environmental exceptions of Article XX(b) and/or (g) of the GATT, which state that:

> Subject to the requirement that such measures are not applied in a manner which would constitute a means of arbitrary or unjustifiable discrimination between countries where the same conditions prevail, or a disguised restriction on international trade, nothing in this Agreement shall be construed to prevent the adoption or enforcement by any contracting party of measures: (...)
>
> (b) necessary to protect human, animal or plant life or health; (...)
>
> (g) relating to the conservation of exhaustible natural resources if such measures are made effective in conjunction with restrictions on domestic production or consumption (...) .[64]

The list of general exceptions in Article XX of the GATT is extensive.[65] In order for the exception to apply, a measure must fulfil the legitimate objective stipulated in the paragraph as well as the requirement in the chapeau.

The continued release of GHGs into the atmosphere will lead to further warming of the climate system,[66] threatening people's health and life,

---

[63] Holzer, above n 36, 96. Also see Panel Report, *Canada – Certain Measures Affecting the Automotive Industry*, WTO Doc WT/DS139/R, WT/DS142/R (11 February 2000) (*Canada–Autos*).

[64] GATT, art XX.

[65] Holzer, above n 36.

[66] Intergovernmental Panel on Climate Change, 'Climate Change 2013: The Physical Science Basis – Technical Summary' (2013) <www.ipcc.ch> 2, 60. The IPCC assessment selected four different Representative Concentration Pathways (RCP) scenarios from the published literature on which to base its projections. Under such different scenarios, the warming of the global surface temperature may range between least 1.5°C–4°C above pre-industrial levels by the end of the twenty-first century. Also see Intergovernmental Panel on Climate Change, 'Climate Change 2014: Synthesis Report. Summary for Policymakers.' (2015) 8. The IPCC concluded that:

> Continued emission of greenhouse gases will cause further warming and long-lasting changes in all components of the climate system, increasing the

endangering marine species and many other ecosystems. There is climatological certainty in the urgency of the need to reduce GHG emissions. However, whether a BCA would be deemed to be a 'necessary' measure to achieve this outcome is unclear.[67]

In contrast, depending on its design, a BCA may fulfil the legitimate objective in Article XX(g) of the GATT. For example, a requirement for companies to surrender permits or offset credits when importing goods into a country is a measure that 'relates' to the conservation of exhaustible natural resources, such as clean air and natural ecosystems.[68] Furthermore, as the importing country has a domestic ETS in place, the BCA is made effective in conjunction with similar emissions restrictions imposed on domestic production.[69]

Once established that a BCA fulfils the legitimate objective stipulated in at least one of the paragraphs of Article XX, the judiciary would analyse the measure against the conditions of the chapeau of Article XX.[70] That is, the measure must not be applied in a manner which would constitute a means of arbitrary or unjustifiable discrimination between countries where the same conditions prevail, or be used to disguise an improper purpose with a legitimate purpose.[71]

---

likelihood of severe, pervasive and irreversible impacts for people and ecosystems. Limiting climate change would require substantial and sustained reductions in greenhouse gas emissions which, together with adaptation, can limit climate change risks.

[67] Holzer, above n 36, 151. Also see Appellate Body Report, *European Communities – Measures Affecting Asbestos and Asbestos-Containing Products*, WTO Doc WT/DS135/AB/R, AB-2000-11 (12 March 2001), where the conditions to meet the necessity test were met.

[68] See Appellate Body Report, *United States – Standards for Reformulated and Conventional Gasoline*, WTO Doc WT/DS58/AB/R, AB-1998-4 (12 October 1998) (*US – Gasoline*), where the US imposed certain standards on gasoline to protect clean air. Also see Appellate Body Report, *United States – Import Prohibition of Certain Shrimp and Shrimp Products*, WTO Doc WT/DS2/AB/R, AB-1996-1 (29 April 1996), where the measure imposed by the US aimed at protecting endangered species (i.e., sea turtles).

[69] Holzer, above n 36.

[70] GATT, art XX.

[71] For an analysis of the WTO jurisprudence on the provision of the chapeau of art XX, see Lorand Bartels, 'The Chapeau of the General Exceptions in the WTO GATT and GATS Agreements' (2015) 109(1) *The American Journal of International Law* 95. Bartels proposed that the test for 'discrimination' under the chapeau should be an economic test and for an application of purpose based tests to determine whether that discrimination can be justified. For example, the

Interestingly, one of the guiding principles of the UNFCCC reproduces the language of the chapeau of Article XX of the GATT, reinforcing that 'measures taken to combat climate change, including unilateral ones, should not constitute a means of arbitrary or unjustifiable discrimination or a disguised restriction on international trade'.[72] While the provision may be interpreted as a 'hint to make use of exceptions to the international trade rules',[73] it also clearly emphasises the responsibility that members have of not abusing this right.[74]

Van Asselt, Brewer and Mehling understand that, in order to pass the condition in the chapeau, a BCA should take into account the existence of carbon pricing measures in other countries.[75] Different treatments must be provided to countries according to their commitments under the UNFCCC and their levels of economic development.[76] In this case, the WTO member imposing the BCA would have to demonstrate that the measure is necessary to the conservation of exhaustible natural resources in its own jurisdiction, rather than a measure to improve the levels of environmental protection in the other WTO member.[77]

It is important to emphasise that this issue remains unresolved and that there might be some difficulties in demonstrating that a BCA meets the requirement in the chapeau of Article XX. This may be the case, for example, where the BCA liability on imports is coupled with an

---

discriminatory measures required by a WTO-legal regional trade agreement would be justifiable, following this approach.

[72] United Nations Framework Convention on Climate Change, opened for signature 9 May 1992, 1771 UNTS 107 (entered into force 21 March 1994) art 3.5.

[73] Holzer, above n 36, 147.

[74] In *US – Gasoline,* the standards imposed on gasoline were found to be primarily aimed at the conservation of exhaustible natural resources and thus falling within the scope of art XX(g). However, the measure was found to constitute 'unjustifiable discrimination' against Venezuelan gasoline and a 'disguised restriction on international trade' under the chapeau of art XX.

[75] Harro van Asselt, Thomas Brewer and Michael Mehling, 'Addressing Leakage and Competitiveness in US Climate Policy: Issues Concerning Border Adjustment Measures' (Climate Strategies, 2009) 55.

[76] Holzer, above n 36, 177.

[77] See, Panel Report, *European Communities – Conditions for the Granting of Tariff Preferences to Developing Countries,* WTO Doc WT/DS246/R (1 December 2003). The Panel found that the EC could not take domestic measures to improve the health situation in another WTO member (i.e., India).

exemption on exported goods.[78] Deane also pointed out that, as a BCA would be implemented to replace free allocation of permits, the policy may be deemed to be protectionist rather than conservationist.[79]

3.2.2 The EU ETS and international aviation

Due to their controversial feasibility and legality, BCAs have not been widely implemented in connection to ETSs. One recent exception is worth discussing, that is, the inclusion of international commercial aviation emissions under the EU ETS.

In November 2008, the Directive 2003/87/EC[80] (ETS Directive) was amended to take in European and non-European aircraft operators as liable entities starting from 1 January 2012, in relation to all international flights to, from and within the European Union.[81] The extension of liability to non-European airlines operating flights to, from and within the EU qualifies the measure as a BCA.[82]

The measure was opposed by many countries, with China banning airlines from complying with the measure[83] and the US exempting domestic airlines from liability under the EU ETS.[84] The Air Transport Association of America brought a claim to the European Court of Justice (ECJ) challenging the measure. The Court upheld the extension of liability under the EU ETS to non-European aircraft operators, finding a

---

[78] Gary Clyde Hufbauer, Steve Charnovitz and Jisun Kim, *Global Warming and the World Trading System* (Peterson Institute for International Economics, 2009) 69.

[79] Deane, above n 36, 200.

[80] Directive 2003/87/EC of the European Parliament and of the Council of 13 October 2003 Establishing a Scheme for Greenhouse Gas Emission Allowance Trading within the Community and Amending Council Directive 96/61/EC [2003] OJ L 275/32 ('ETS Directive').

[81] Directive 2008/101/EC of the European Parliament and of the Council of 19 November 2008 amending Directive 2003/87/EC so as to include aviation activities in the scheme for greenhouse gas emission allowance trading within the Community [2009] OJ L 8/3.

[82] Holzer, above n 36, 52; Lorand Bartels, 'The WTO Legality of the Application of the EU's Emission Trading System to Aviation' (2012) 23(2) *The European Journal of International Law* 429.

[83] Barbara Lewis and Valerie Volcovici, 'Insight: U.S., China Turned EU Powers Against Airline Pollution Law' (2012) <//www.reuters.com/article/2012/12/10/us-eu-airlines-climate-idUSBRE8B801H20121210#Drb1Yz7Q8WepdLKB.99>.

[84] Suzanne Goldenberg, 'Obama Fails First Climate Test by Rejecting EU Aviation Carbon Regime' (2012) <http://www.theguardian.com/world/2012/nov/28/obama-fails-climate-test-aviation>.

sufficient territorial nexus with emissions caused by flights that arrive at or depart from an EU airport.[85]

The ECJ did not have jurisdiction to assess a possible violation of WTO law. However, in the case of a dispute being taken to the WTO judiciary, it is likely that the measure would be deemed to violate the provisions of the GATT.[86]

The provision extending liability under the EU ETS to aircraft operators was suspended for flights to and from non-European countries in 2012[87] and an amendment of the ETS Directive was made effective limiting the liability for the aviation sector to emissions from flights within the European Economic Area during the period between 2013 and 2016.[88] This occurred following an agreement reached by the International Civil Aviation Organization (ICAO) Assembly to develop a global market-based mechanism addressing international aviation emissions by 2016 and apply it by 2020.[89]

4. ADDRESSING CARBON LEAKAGE VIA ALLOCATION OF EMISSIONS PERMITS

The free of cost allocation of permits to carbon-leakage exposed sectors is preferred by stakeholders and has been widely implemented in practice, as a measure to mitigate carbon leakage, partly due to its perceived WTO compliance. Ironically, Chapter 6 demonstrates that the free allocation of permits, in certain circumstances, may be deemed to be an actionable or even a prohibited subsidy and may be challenged at the WTO level.

In order to best understand how policymakers have addressed carbon leakage via allocation of emissions permits, one must first review the

---

[85]   *Air Transport Association of America and Others v Secretary of State for Energy and Climate Change* (C-366/10) [2011] ECR I-1133 para 124.

[86]   Holzer, above n 36, 184; Bartels, above n 71.

[87]   Commission Decision 377/2013/EU of 24 April 2013 Derogating Temporarily from Directive 2003/87/EC Establishing a Scheme for Greenhouse Gas Emission Allowance Trading Within the Community [2013] OJ L 113/1.

[88]   Regulation 421/2014 of 16 April 2014 amending Directive 2003/87/EC Establishing a Scheme for Greenhouse Gas Emission Allowance Trading within the Community, in View of the Implementation by 2020 of an International Agreement Applying a Single Global Market-Based Measure to International Aviation Emissions [2014] OJ L 129/1.

[89]   European Commission, *Climate Action* <http://ec.europa.eu/clima/policies/transport/aviation/index_en.htm>.

structure of a domestic ETS. In general, ETS legislation will provide for a central authority – which may be a government, supranational authority or another delegated agent – to set a limit to the amount of GHGs that may be emitted by a specific number of businesses, known as an emissions cap.[90] Explicit rights to emit CO_2-e (emissions permits or allowances) are created at a level that corresponds to the respective cap, with each permit representing one tonne of CO_2-e. Legal recognition of allowances as property rights varies according to jurisdiction.[91]

Importantly, the ETS market does not develop itself naturally as a result of supply and demand. ETSs are created through extensive government regulation, aimed at restricting the right to emit GHGs.[92] Initially, the central authority will determine both the demand and supply of this market. The demand for permits is established by specifying the liable sectors participating in the market, while the supply is determined by the cap-setting.[93] The scarcity of permits is key to insure a positive market price and to provide the right incentives for businesses to abate.[94]

The artificial creation of a new set of intangible assets, the emissions permits or allowances, is necessarily accompanied by rules on how these

---

[90] The emissions cap may be absolute or relative, e.g., as a limit to the emissions per unit of output or per unit of GDP. See Stefan Weishaar, *Emissions Trading Design* (Edward Elgar Publishing, 2014) 99. For example, following the repeal of the carbon pricing mechanism in Australia, explained in further detail in Chapter 3, the Federal Government has proposed a baseline and credit mechanism, also known as a 'safeguard mechanism'. The baseline will reflect the highest level of reported emissions for a facility over the historical period 2009–10 to 2013–14. Businesses will not pay a carbon price unless – and to the extent in which – their emissions exceed the baseline levels. With such low ambition levels, very little can be expected in terms of emissions reductions. See Australian Government, *The Emissions Reduction Fund: The Safeguard Mechanism* Department of Environment <https://www.environment.gov.au/climate-change/emissions-reduction-fund/publications/factsheet-erf-safeguard-mechanism>; National Greenhouse and Energy Reporting (Safeguard Mechanism) Rule 2015 (Cth); National Greenhouse and Energy Reporting Amendment (2015 Measures No. 2) Regulation 2015 (Cth); National Greenhouse and Energy Reporting (Audit) Amendment Determination 2015 (No. 1).

[91] See Chapter 6 for further details.

[92] This feature may have consequences for International Economic Law when determining the market baseline in a benefit analysis related to subsidies. For further discussion on this topic, see Chapter 6.

[93] Joseph Kruger, Wallace Oates and William Pizer, 'Decentralization in the EU Emissions Trading Scheme and Lessons for Global Policy' (2007) 1(1) *Review of Environmental Economics and Policy* 112.

[94] Weishaar, above n 90, 101.

assets are issued and traded. Allocation means the issue and initial distribution of emissions permits to participants. Once permits are allocated to participants, they can be traded in the market, privately or through an established market platform. From this point, the carbon market should theoretically work like any other market.[95]

At the end of the given financial year, liable entities or participants must hold one emissions permit per tonne of CO_2-e emitted. Participants will be sellers where their marginal abatement cost is lower than the market price for permits and will be buyers where their marginal abatement cost is higher than the market price for permits.[96] Where the emissions cap is properly reduced over time, progressive emissions reductions towards medium- and long-term emissions reduction trajectories can be achieved.

4.1 The Initial Allocation of Emissions Permits

The debate on the ideal method for allocation of emissions permits has largely focused on the dichotomy between periodical auctioning and the free allocation of permits.[97] Businesses have historically lobbied for free allocation, while economists prefer the auctioning of permits.[98] Legal scholars have, in general, been distanced from this debate.[99]

---

[95] Christian Egenhofer et al, 'The EU Emissions Trading System and Climate Policy towards 2050: Real incentives to reduce emissions and drive innovation?' (CEPS, 2011) 3.

[96] OECD, *The Economics of Climate Change Mitigation: Policies and Options for Global Action Beyond 2012* (2009) 23.

[97] Lawrence H. Goulder and Ian W.H. Parry, 'Instrument Choice in Environmental Policy' (2008) 2(2) *Review of Environmental Economics and Policy* 152. Free of cost allocation may be based on the participants' historical emission levels, practice also known as 'grandfathering', or based on production technology standards, also known as benchmarking. As detailed in Chapter 5, the EU ETS adopted grandfathering during phases I and II and introduced benchmarking after phase III. For more details, see Chapter 5.

[98] See, e.g., Cameron Hepburn et al, 'Auctioning of EU ETS Phase II Allowances: how and why?' (2006) 1.

[99] But see James Windon, 'The Allocation of Free Emissions Units and The WTO Subsidies Agreement' (2009) 41 *Georgetown Journal of International Law* 189; Lauren Henschke, 'Going it Alone on Climate Change. A New Challenge to WTO Subsidies Disciplines: are Subsidies in Support of Emissions Reductions Schemes Permissible under the WTO' (2012) 11(01) *World Trade Review* 27. Also see Chapter 6, which analyses the implications of free allocation from a WTO perspective.

The preference for free allocation among businesses is foreseeable and there are good arguments to support this perspective. In theory, the trading of emissions permits in an ETS will have the same environmental outcome whether emissions permits are initially auctioned or given away free of cost to participants, as long as the overall allocation (emissions cap) is stringent and the monitoring and enforcement procedures are effective.[100] Also, in theory, the overall cost of achieving the aggregate emission reductions under an ETS is minimised (cost-effectiveness) independent of the initial allocation of permits.[101] Therefore, free allocation has been largely regarded as an alternative to address competitiveness concerns while maintaining incentives to reduce emissions.

However, apart from the effectiveness argument, there are other factors to be taken into consideration when deciding the method for initial allocation of permits. First, a key advantage of ETSs, as a market-based instrument, is compromised by free allocation, that is, the capability of the ETSs to deliver emissions reductions with the least economic impacts while generating revenue.[102]

Secondly, there are relevant distributive effects of different allocation methods. While auctioning allows for the generation of government revenue, which can then be recycled to benefit the general public or the environment, free allocation has the effect of distributing rents to the polluting businesses participating in the ETS. Concurrently, there is an increase in the abatement costs to other sectors in the economy, flowing on to sectors not covered by the ETS and, ultimately, households. In fact, at times, free allocation may make polluters better off due to the implementation of the ETS.[103] This occurs where certain sectors of the

---

[100] European Commission, 'Green Paper on Greenhouse Gas Emissions Trading within the European Union' (2000); Goulder and Parry, above n 97, 155. But see Hepburn et al, above n 98.

[101] See Robert Hahn and Robert Stavins, 'The effect of allowance allocations on cap-and-trade system performance' (2011) 54 *Journal of Law & Economics* S267 132; Stefano Clò, *European Emissions Trading in Practice: An Economic Analysis* New Horizons in Environmental and Energy Law series (Edward Elgar, 2011).

[102] Tatiana Falcão, 'Providing Environmental Taxes with an Environmental Purpose' in Larry Kreiser et al (eds), *Market Based Instruments: National Experiences in Environmental Sustainability* (Edward Elgar, 2013) 41.

[103] Goulder and Parry, above n 97, 164. Also see Reinaud, above n 6.

economy benefit from windfall profits[104] or receive an over-allocation of tradable permits.[105]

There are also distributional impacts within ETS participants, where different sectors are treated favourably or unfavourably discriminated against in the allocation process.[106] The disparity of treatment can impact industry's competitiveness due to the availability, or not, of cash flows in the form of readily saleable permits (liquidity),[107] which in its turn can affect entry and exit behaviour.[108]

Thirdly, in practice, free allocation neutralises the desired market signal from the carbon price,[109] mitigating incentives for assisted sectors to invest in cleaner means of production and undermining the incentives for less carbon-intensive industries.[110]

Finally, auctioning promotes an equitable treatment of participants under an ETS and mitigates the process of the race for rents that inevitably occurs under free allocation.[111]

During the consultation process for determining the framework for the ETS the European Commission expressed a preference for the periodic auctioning of permits to participants.[112] However, stakeholders were successful in securing the free allocation of the vast majority of permits.[113]

---

[104] Reinaud, above n 6, 71, 78; Janet E. Milne and Mikael Skou Andersen, 'Introduction to Environmental Taxation Concepts and Research' in Janet E. Milne and Mikael Skou Andersen (eds), *Handbook of Research on Environmental Taxation* (Edward Elgar, 2012) 1555; Garnaut, above n 52, 330.

[105] See Chapters 4 and 5.

[106] Beat Hintermann, 'Allowance Price Drivers in the First Phase of the EU ETS' (2009) *CEPE Working Paper* . See Chapters 4 and 5 for a detailed analysis.

[107] Hahn and Stavins, above n 101, 274.

[108] Ibid., 132, 274.

[109] Milne and Andersen, above n 104.

[110] OECD, above n 6, 88. Also see Carolyn Fischer, Richard Morgenstern and Nathan Richardson, 'Carbon Taxes and Energy-Intensive Trade-Exposed Sectors: Impacts and Options' in Ian Parry, Adele Morris and Roberton Williams III (eds), *Implementing a US Carbon Tax: Challenges and Debates* (Routledge, 2015) who argue that 'exempting certain firms or sectors would almost certainly leave untapped some relatively inexpensive options for cutting emissions in these sectors'.

[111] See below detailed discussion on the application of the Polluter Pays Principle to the issue of free allocation.

[112] European Commission, above n 100, 18.

[113] For further details see Chapter 5.

4.1.1 Real-life allocation measures

While literature has extensively discussed the pros and cons of free of cost allocation versus auctioning, real-life ETSs have adopted variations to the theoretical model, often combining the two methodologies.

One example is the Australian Carbon Pricing Mechanism (AUS CPM), implemented on 1 July 2012 and repealed on 1 July 2014. In order to prevent extreme price fluctuation in the first years of the scheme, the AUS CPM adopted an innovative method for initial allocation of permits. It provided for the sale of permits for a fixed price during the first three years, with auctioning starting from the fourth year onwards. Combined with the phased approach for the selling of permits, an overly generous free allocation method was put in place, to provide targeted assistance to sectors considered EITE.[114] Chapters 3, 4 and 5 discuss the AUS CPM in detail. For now, it is sufficient to point out that, depending on the sector's emissions-intensity, businesses would receive a generous amount of permits free of charge, while businesses in other sectors would have to purchase their permits, initially for a fixed price and later via auctioning.

Another example is the EU ETS. As mentioned above, during phases I and II of the EU ETS, the free allocation method was adopted, with almost 100 per cent of permits initially allocated free of cost. In 2008, a review of the ETS Directive changed the allocation method to be adopted from phase IIII onwards. Community-wide and fully-harmonised rules for initial allocation were adopted, with the free of charge allocations decreasing annually and expected to phase out by 2027.[115]

Therefore, rather than using one standard allocation methodology, ETSs have been adopting a mix of auctioning and free allocation, where the latter is used to provide targeted assistance to emissions-intensive trade-exposed (EITE) sectors. Different sectors are being treated favourably or unfavourably in the allocation process, often based on successful lobbying from a particular sector.

Chapters 4 and 5 explore the issues deriving from free allocation in real-world ETSs. From a legal perspective, countries adopting these mixed methodologies appear to have based the choice on a misconception, that is, the incorrect assumption that the allocation of targeted free

---

[114]   CE Act ss 5 (definition of 'fixed charge year'), 93. See Commonwealth of Australia, 'Strong Growth, Low Pollution: Modelling a Carbon Price' (2011), in especial Clean Energy Future scenario. See Chapter 3 for detailed information on the AUS CPM.

[115]   See Chapter 5.

allocation of permits is a domestic measure, one which does not conflict with the World Trade Organisation (WTO) law.[116]

In fact, while there is support in the literature for border carbon adjustments as the preferred instrument to deal with carbon leakage,[117] these measures are not the standard approach, primarily due to concerns that such adjustments would be challenged at the WTO. However, real-world ETSs are increasingly providing targeted assistance to EITE sectors, dissociating themselves from the old dichotomy 'auctioning versus free allocation'. Allocation of permits is no longer a matter of simple regulatory decision and there may be significant legal implications from a WTO perspective.

4.1.2 Free allocation and the linking of emissions trading schemes
Chapter 1 briefly discussed the role of linking ETSs after the Paris Agreement. One of the anticipated consequences of linking ETSs is the harmonisation of the carbon price across the linked schemes[118] and the increase in the ability of policymakers to address carbon leakage.[119] However, in terms of carbon leakage, a number of studies indicate that linking may not be the ideal instrument to address short-term leakage concerns.[120]

Whether linking reduces carbon leakage in practice will depend on the specific sector and which countries are adopting similar carbon price constraints. Carbon-leakage related benefits from linking may also occur in the absence of linking agreements, as long as the relevant countries adopt similarly stringent carbon pricing schemes. Still, inasmuch as linking is considered a means to an ultimate goal of achieving a global carbon market structure, it is a valid long-term solution to carbon leakage and competitiveness concerns.

In terms of the free allocation of emissions permits, the distributional impacts of free allocation explained earlier may be perpetuated across

---

[116]   Marrakesh Agreement Establishing the World Trade Organization, opened for signature 15 April 1994, 1867 UNTS 3 (entered into force 1 January 1995).

[117]   See, e.g., Damien Demailly and Philippe Quirion, 'Leakage from Climate Policies and Border-tax Adjustment: Lessons from a Geographic Model of the Cement Industry' (2005).

[118]   Aki Kachi et al, 'Linking Emissions Trading Systems: A Summary of Current Research' (2015) 1.

[119]   World Bank Group, ECOFYS and Vivid Economics, 'State and Trends of Carbon Pricing' (2016).

[120]   Andreas Tuerk et al, 'Linking carbon markets: concepts, case studies and pathways' (2009) 9(4) *Climate Policy* 341, 344. Dröge et al, above n 6, 14.

linked ETSs.[121] Targeted free allocation in one ETS is likely to provide preferential treatment for certain sectors, which could have trade implications.[122] There are advantages from harmonising the free allocation methodology which must be carefully considered by countries linking ETSs.[123]

5. DOES FREE OF COST ALLOCATION VIOLATE THE POLLUTER PAYS PRINCIPLE?

Literature has often mentioned that the auctioning of emissions permits is fundamental to the implementation of the Polluter Pays Principle.[124] When discussing the framework of the EU ETS, the European Commission stated that free allocation may promote an unfair distribution of resources and may not ensure that the polluter internalises the social cost of its activities. The Commission viewed the free allocation mechanism as a violation of the Polluter Pays Principle.[125]

Principles, contrarily to legal rules, do not dictate a specific outcome ('all-or-nothing').[126] Instead, they provide standards for the interpretation and application of the law.[127] The Polluter Pays Principle tends to set outer limits, where conduct falling outside its scope is in breach of the principle.[128]

---

[121] See William Blyth and Martina Bosi, 'Linking Non-EU Domestic Emissions Trading Schemes with the EU Emissions Trading Scheme' (OECD International Energy Agency, 2004) 26; Dallas Burtraw et al, 'Linking by Degrees: Incremental Alignment of Cap-and-Trade Markets' (2013) 1.

[122] Reinaud, above n 6. *Contra* Tuerk et al, above n 120.

[123] See Chapters 4 and 5. Also see Kachi et al, above n 118, 8.

[124] The author would like to thank Ms. Amy Elton's research assistance for her help in relation to this section of the manuscript. See, e.g., Michael Grubb and Karsten Neuhoff, 'Allocation and competitiveness in the EU emissions trading scheme: policy overview' (2006) 6(1) *Climate Policy* 7.

[125] European Commission, above n 100, 18.

[126] Ronald Dworkin, *Taking Rights Seriously* (Harvard University Press, 1977) 128, 26–7; Robert Alexy, *A Theory of Constitutional Rights* (Oxford University Press, 2009) 50–56.

[127] Dworkin, ibid.; Alexy, ibid.

[128] See, e.g., Philippe Sands, *Principles of International Environmental Law* (Cambridge University Press, 2003) 280; Philippe Sands et al, *Principles of International Environmental Law* (3rd edn, 2012) 228. In principle, a variety of measures can be validly used to apply the Polluter Pays Principle, from command and control mechanisms to market-based instruments. It is the details of the regulatory framework of these measures that will determine whether or not

The outer boundaries of the Polluter Pays Principle are determined by how the principle is understood. There are different interpretations of the Polluter Pays Principle, with conflicting accounts of how these interplay. The first interpretation is a purely economic understanding, sometimes called the 'efficiency interpretation': the internalisation of environmental and social costs of preventing and controlling pollution by the polluter.[129] The second interpretation requires that the cost of pollution be borne equitably by polluters. This is referred to as the 'equity interpretation'.[130]

The final part of this chapter discusses how each interpretation interferes in the analysis of whether the free allocation of permits is in accordance with the Polluter Pays Principle. But first, we will provide a brief history of the Polluter Pays Principle.

5.1 Brief History of the Polluter Pays Principle

The idea that a polluter should be held responsible for pollution costs has been long contemplated.[131] Most modern legal systems have established their own laws to reflect the responsibility of a polluter to pay for the costs of pollution. For example, under US Tort law, the polluter is required to pay damages to the injured party.[132] This was confirmed in

---

they will fall outside the scope of the principle. Also see Edwin Woerdman, Stefano Clò and Alessandra Arcuri, 'European Emissions Trading and the Polluter-Pays Principle: Assessing Grandfathering and Over-Allocation' in Michael G. Faure and Marjan Peeters (eds), *Climate Change and European Emissions Trading: Lessons for Theory and Practice* (Edward Elgar Publishing, 2008) 128, 130.

[129]   See, e.g., Michael G. Faure and David Grimeaud, 'Financial Assurance Issues of Environmental Liability' (Maastricht University and ECTIL, 2000) 21.

[130]   Clò, above n 101.

[131]   See Kenneth P. Green, January, 2015, 'Polluter Pays Principle' in *Salem Press Encyclopedia of Science* (2015). Green demonstrates that, while the Polluter Pays Principle is a relatively new concept, laws of different legal systems have reflected an agenda to hold polluters responsible for the costs of pollution damage for centuries. For example, prior to 348 BC, Plato constructed one version of the Polluter Pays Principle to circumstances involving water pollution. This law required an accused found guilty of 'injuring the water' to pay damages and purify the water.

[132]   *Trail Smelter Case* (United States, Canada) 16 April 1938 and 11 March 1941. *III, 1920, referring to Story Parchment Company v Paterson Parchment Paper Company* (1931), 282 U.S. 555. Also see R. Miller and R. Brapties *Transboundary Harm in International Law: Lessons from the Trail Smelter Arbitration* (Cambridge University Press, 2006).

the Trail Smelter Case, an early case of transboundary environmental harm caused by Canada to the US.[133]

Domestic laws that hold the polluter responsible for the costs of damage reflect an agenda to ensure equity, encourage corporate social responsibility, and serve social justice. In holding polluters responsible, they are encouraging diligence in relation to the creation of pollution in the first place. This broad justice and equity framework that underlies polluter responsibility was evident long before the modern conception of the Polluter Pays Principle.

However, it was only after the endorsement of the Polluter Pays Principle by the Organization of Economic Cooperation and Development (OECD)[134] that the Polluter Pays Principle was incorporated as a general principle in international environmental law. The OECD adopted the Polluter Pays Principle in the Council Recommendation on Guiding Principles Concerning International Economic Aspects of Environmental Policies 1972, stating:

> The principle to be used for allocating costs of pollution prevention and control measures to encourage rational use of scarce environmental resources and to avoid distortions in international trade and investment is the so-called 'Polluter-Pays Principle'. This principle means that the polluter should bear the expense of carrying out the above mentioned measures decided by public authorities to ensure that the environment is in an acceptable state. In other words, the cost of these measures should be reflected in the cost of goods and services which cause pollution in production and/or consumption. Such measures should not be accompanied by subsidies that would create significant distortions in international trade and investment.[135]

In 1992, the Rio Declaration on Environment and Development incorporated the principle within the list of general rights and obligations of States in relation to the environment, stating that:

> National authorities should endeavour to promote the internalization of environmental costs and the use of economic instruments, taking into account the approach that the polluter should, in principle, bear the cost of pollution,

---

[133] *Trail Smelter Case*, ibid. *III*, 1905–82.

[134] Organization of Economic Cooperation and Development (OECD) established 1960. Includes 35 member countries. <http://www.oecd.org/>.

[135] OECD, Council Recommendation on Guiding Principles Concerning International Economic Aspects of Environmental Policies (1972) [4].

with due regard to the public interest and without distorting international trade and investment.[136]

Other international conventions mention the Polluter Pays Principle as a guiding principle or aim of international environmental law. For example, the Treaty on the Functioning of the European Union[137] and the International Convention on Oil Pollution Preparedness, Response and Co-operation, which reiterates the relevance of the Polluter Pays Principle in several recommendations.[138]

While the Polluter Pays Principle is generally purported to be a goal of the international community, it is rarely enforced internationally.[139] In addition to the lack of enforcement, there is still a level of controversy around the definition and application of the Polluter Pays Principle in practice. In terms of domestic legislation, a number of jurisdictions have internalised the Polluter Pays Principle as a principle of international environmental law. However, it is outside the scope of this chapter to deliver an account of the internalisation of The Polluter Pays Principle in different jurisdictions.[140]

5.2   Free Allocation and the Equity Dimension of the Polluter Pays Principle

While first contemplations of polluter responsibility were centred upon the need to ensure fairness and just compensation, as mentioned above, the modern notion of the Polluter Pays Principle was established in an economic forum and so it is no surprise that economic considerations have since demarcated its scope. In fact, Faure and Grimeaud state that

---

[136]   Rio Declaration on Environment and Development, UN Doc A/CONF.151/5/Rev.1 (12 August 1992) Principle 16.

[137]   Treaty on the Functioning of the European Union, opened for signature 7 February 1992, [2009] OJ C 115/199 (entered into force 1 November 1993).

[138]   International Convention on Oil Pollution Preparedness, Response and Cooperation, 1990 (with annex and procès verbal of rectification). Concluded at London on 30 November 1990 Vol 1891, 1-32194, 79, 233–4.

[139]   Jonathan Remy Nash, 'Too Much Market? Conflict Between Tradable Pollution Allowances and the "Polluter Pays" Principle' (2000) 24 *Harvard Environmental Law Review* 445, 469.

[140]   In terms of European Community Law, the principle was incorporated in art 130R(2) of the Treaty Establishing the European Economic Community, opened for signature 25 March 1957, 298 UNTS 11 (entered into force 1 January 1958).

the Polluter Pays Principle is 'probably the most "economic" of all environmental principles'.[141]

The Polluter Pays Principle has been interpreted by economists as an efficiency principle for allocating costs.[142] This reading of the principle tends to exclude equitable considerations. In the 2008 analytical report on the Polluter Pays Principle, the OECD supported the efficiency interpretation, stating:

> The Polluter-Pays Principle is not a principle of equity; it is designed not to punish polluters but to set appropriate signals in place in the economic system so that environmental costs are incorporated in the decision-making process and hence arrive at sustainable development that is environment-friendly. The aim is to avoid wasting natural resources and to put an end to the cost-free use of the environment as a receptacle for pollution. A degree of environmental pollution will certainly persist, and the consumer will bear the cost initially charged to the polluter. But use of the Polluter-Pays Principle will secure economic efficiency and will reduce distortions in international trade and investment to a minimum.[143]

Thus, when applying the principle to the analysis of free allocation, an efficiency interpretation could possibly suggest that an ETS will be conforming to the Polluter Pays Principle regardless of whether emissions permits are initially auctioned or given away free of cost to participants, as long as the emissions cap is stringent and the monitoring and enforcement procedures are effective.[144] Following this line of reasoning, it does not matter whether the polluter receives allowances free of cost and/or whether the polluter absorbs most of the environment costs or passes it on to consumers.[145] In either case, the polluter will still

---

[141]   Faure and Grimeaud, above n 129, 21.

[142]   OECD, *The Polluter Pays Principle: Definition, Analysis, Implementation,* OCDE/GD(92)81 (OECD Publishing, 2008) 24. The OECD's interpretation is that:

> The Polluter-Pays Principle, as defined in para 4 of the 'Guiding Principles', states that the polluter should bear the expenses of preventing and controlling pollution 'to ensure that the environment is in an acceptable state'. The notion of an 'acceptable state' decided by public authorities, implies that through a collective choice and with respect to the limited information available, the advantage of a further reduction in the residual social damage involved is considered as being smaller than the social cost of further prevention and control.

[143]   Ibid., 9.

[144]   See Clò, above n 101, 107. *Contra* Nash, above n 139.

[145]   OECD, above n 142, 25.

forfeit opportunity costs[146] and the appropriate economic signals will be in place to ensure that environmental costs are incorporated by the market.

An alternative interpretation of the Polluter Pays Principle focuses on an interdisciplinary perspective, which takes into account the economic dimension of the principle without disregarding other goals of law.[147] This interpretation of the Polluter Pays Principle conceives the existence of two dimensions to the principle, an efficiency and an equity dimension, the latter referring to the notion of a just or fair distribution of costs.[148]

While there is some variation on how the literature sees the relationship between equity and cost-efficiency,[149] Woerdman, Clò and Arcuri provide an insightful approach. The authors consider the efficiency interpretation to be the core and the equity criterion to be an extension of the Polluter Pays Principle.[150]

According to this interpretation, the free allocation of permits does not confirm to the Polluter Pays Principle. Free allocation has the practical effect of allotting rents to polluters participating in an ETS, at the expense of other sectors in the economy, at times making polluters better off due to the implementation of the scheme. This wealth transfer from the public to the polluter, which takes place under free allocation of allowances, is inherently unfair. As such, free allocation can be interpreted to violate the extended dimension of the Polluter Pays Principle.[151]

6. CONCLUSION

Carbon leakage language is often used to express economic concerns, such as a loss in productive capacity and jobs availability due to distortions to the local industry's competitiveness. Finding the point of balance between preventing unfair competition and maintaining the incentive for domestic industry to adopt abatement measures can be challenging for countries unilaterally adopting a carbon price policy.

---

[146]   Woerdman, Clò and Arcuri, above n 128, 133.
[147]   Ibid. 101.
[148]   Ibid., 131; Clò, above n 101, 104.
[149]   Woerdman, Clò and Arcuri, above n 128, 131. Also see Nash, above n 139, 498.
[150]   Woerdman, Clò and Arcuri, ibid. Also see Clò, above n 101.
[151]   Woerdman, Clò and Arcuri, ibid., 135–6.

Concerns over competitiveness distortions and carbon leakage have justified a widespread adoption of the free allocation of permits. It appears that the theoretical foundations of this allocation methodology can be traced back to an understanding that the way in which permits are initially distributed does not affect market efficiency. However, there are other relevant elements to be taken into consideration when deciding between auctioning and free allocation, such as the capacity for revenue generation, the distributive impacts of free allocation which arguably may be enhanced in the case of linking ETSs and the lessening of incentives for less carbon-intensive industries under free allocation.

Free allocation violates the extended equity interpretation of The Polluter Pays Principle. As a broad and overarching principle of climate justice, the Polluter Pays Principle shapes the norms of society by prescribing that the costs of pollution must be internalised.[152] Free allocation provides an unfair advantage to the polluting businesses participating in an ETS, at the expense of other sectors in the economy, including households. Where an equity interpretation is given to the Polluter Pays Principle, free allocation is found to be inconsistent with the extended dimension of the Polluter Pays Principle.

From a legal perspective, the key argument in favour of free allocation has been to avoid a violation of WTO law that the implementation of the BCAs would otherwise lead to. This issue is examined in detail in Chapter 6, where it is demonstrated that the free allocation methodology may also be inconsistent with WTO law.

---

[152] Nash, above n 139, 480.

3.   Real world emissions trading schemes: challenges and lessons learnt

1.   INTRODUCTION

In 2016 the World Bank reported the existence of 40 nation-wide carbon-pricing initiatives and over 20 subnational carbon-pricing initiatives.[1] The total coverage of carbon pricing in 2016 was calculated at 7 gigatons of carbon dioxide equivalent ($GtCO_2e$) or 13 per cent of global greenhouse gas (GHG) emissions.[2]

While carbon-pricing schemes are multiplying, they vary in their legal frameworks and design features, which is to be expected given the geographic, economic, legal and political aspects of each jurisdiction. This chapter compares the design features of three emissions trading schemes (ETSs): the European Union Emissions Trading System (EU ETS), the Australian Carbon Pricing Mechanism (AUS CPM) and New Zealand's Emissions Trading Scheme (NZ ETS). By comparing key elements of each ETS, such as their coverages, emissions caps, governances and links with other schemes, it provides a valuable insight into the challenges of implementation faced by governments when adopting ETSs.

The AUS CPM was dismantled in June 2014, long before the publishing of this book. Still, it remains a relevant case to be studied due to its unique features. To various degrees, the design, implementation and/or sustainability of all three schemes have been compromised due to the political pressure of lobby groups. In the case of Australia, the political debate went as far as to cause the repeal of the AUS CPM.

---

[1]   World Bank Group, ECOFYS and Vivid Economics, 'State and Trends of Carbon Pricing' (2016) 22.
[2]   Ibid.

2. A ROLLER COASTER: THE EUROPEAN UNION EMISSIONS TRADING SYSTEM

On 13 October 2003, the European Parliament and the Council of the European Union adopted Directive 2003/87/EC[3] (ETS Directive), establishing a Community-wide Emissions Trading System, known as the EU ETS. The EU ETS was the first carbon dioxide (CO_2) trading market in the world, and it is still the largest, currently covering 31 jurisdictions[4] with significant distinctions, such as differences in languages, economies, political structures and emissions reductions commitments.

The EU ETS was implemented in three different stages. A first trading period, known as the trial phase, commenced on 1 January 2005 and ended on 31 December 2007, three years prior to the Kyoto Protocol's first commitment period. The second trading period commenced on 1 January 2008 and ended on 31 December 2012, coinciding with the first Commitment period of the Kyoto Protocol. The EU ETS entered its third trading period on 1 January 2013, which is expected to last eight years, until 31 December 2020.[5]

The short time for preparation prior to the commencement of the EU ETS, its continental coverage, and the largely decentralised system adopted in the first two trading periods all created implementation challenges. An ongoing issue faced by the EU ETS has been the problem of surplus emissions permits, known as European Union Allowances (EUAs). The surplus problem and the other complexities faced by the EU ETS are further explained below.

2.1 Coverage under the Emissions Trading System

During the trial phase, the EU ETS exclusively covered CO_2 emissions. Sectoral coverage was also limited to large power and heat producers and a number of large energy-intensive industrial activities.[6] Still, over

---

[3] Directive 2003/87/EC of the European Parliament and of the Council of 13 October 2003 Establishing a Scheme for Greenhouse Gas Emission Allowance Trading within the Community and Amending Council Directive 96/61/EC [2003] OJ L 275/32 (ETS Directive).

[4] Countries from the European Economic Area (EEA) that is, 28 EU Member States plus Iceland, Liechtenstein and Norway.

[5] ETS Directive, art 13(1).

[6] Ibid., annex I. Production capacity thresholds in place. Industrial activities included oil refining, the production and processing of ferrous metals, cement and lime, and ceramics including bricks, glass, pulp, paper and board.

10,000 installations across Europe were liable under the EU ETS, corresponding to nearly half of the total EU CO_2 emissions and 40 per cent of the total EU greenhouse gas (GHG) emissions.

The ETS Directive was later amended to include, from the third trading period onwards, other GHGs, such as perfluorocarbons (PFCs) and Nitrous Oxide (N_2O), and new sectors, such as the production of aluminium and several chemical substances.[7] The transport, agricultural and service sectors, as well as buildings, are not presently included in the scheme.

2.1.1 Problems arising from generic definitions

A general definition of combustion plants[8] adopted by the ETS Directive[9] in the first trading period resulted in discrepancies between the Member States, with the same type of installation being covered in some Member States but not in others. Issues culminated in the decision of the Commission that 'a consistent interpretation and coverage of combustion installations across the Member States in the second trading period was vital in order to avoid significant distortions of competition throughout the Internal Market'.[10]

2.1.2 The aviation sector

In November 2008, the ETS Directive was amended to include aviation activities in the scheme starting from 1 January 2012, including all international flights that arrive at, or depart from, an EU airport, covering around 45 per cent of the EU's GHG emissions.[11] The extension of liability to the non-European airlines and international flights to and from non-European countries consists of a border adjustment measure.[12]

---

[7] Ibid.

[8] Combustion plants with a rated thermal input exceeding 20 MW.

[9] ETS Directive, art 3 definition of combustion. The Directive provided that 'combustion' means any oxidation of fuels, regardless of the way in which the heat, electrical or mechanical energy produced by this process is used, and any other directly associated activities, including waste gas scrubbing.

[10] Communication from the Commission COM/2005/703 Further guidance on allocation plans for the 2008 to 2012 trading period of the EU Emission Trading Scheme [2005] para 35.

[11] Directive 2008/101/EC of the European Parliament and of the Council of 19 November 2008 amending Directive 2003/87/EC so as to include aviation activities in the scheme for greenhouse gas emission allowance trading within the Community [2009] OJ L 8/3.

[12] See Chapter 2.

A number of the legal and political challenges followed the inclusion of aviation in the EU ETS, leading to the suspension of the provision in relation to flights to and from non-European countries in 2012.[13] Following the temporary suspension, the ETS Directive was amended, limiting the liability of the aviation sector to the emissions from flights within the European Economic Area (EEA) in the period between 2013 and 2016.[14]

Discussions for the inclusion of emissions from flights outside the EEA were initiated under the auspices of the International Civil Aviation Organization (ICAO) and, in October 2016, ICAO's Assembly reached a historical agreement. Assembly Resolution A39-3, sets the general framework for a voluntary market-based mechanism called the Carbon Offsetting and Reduction Scheme for International Aviation (CORSIA), aimed at offsetting emissions from international civil aviation.[15] By 12 October 2016, 66 States accounting for more than 86.5 per cent of international aviation activity have declared their intention to participate in the voluntary scheme,[16] including all EU ETS Members.[17] The CORSIA scheme will commence in 2021.

Given the success of the negotiations under the auspices of ICAO, the EU ETS will proceed with its approach of covering the aviation sector in relation to flights exclusively within the EEA post-2016.[18]

---

[13]   Commission Decision 377/2013/EU of 24 April 2013 Derogating Temporarily from Directive 2003/87/EC Establishing a Scheme for Greenhouse Gas Emission Allowance Trading Within the Community [2013] OJ L 113/1.

[14]   Regulation 421/2014 of 16 April 2014 amending Directive 2003/87/EC Establishing a Scheme for Greenhouse Gas Emission Allowance Trading within the Community, in View of the Implementation by 2020 of an International Agreement Applying a Single Global Market-Based Measure to International Aviation Emissions [2014] OJ L 129/1. An agreement was reached between the EU and the International Civil Aviation Organization (ICAO) in order to develop a global market-based mechanism addressing international aviation emissions by 2016 and apply it by 2020.

[15]   Resolution A39-3, Adopted at the 39th Session of the Assembly, Consolidated statement of continuing ICAO policies and practices related to environmental protection – Global Market-based Measure (MBM) Scheme, ICAO (Montréal, 27 September–6 October 2016).

[16]   International Civil Aviation Organization, *Carbon Offsetting and Reduction Scheme for International Aviation (CORSIA)* ICAO Environment <http://www.icao.int/environmental-protection/Pages/market-based-measures.aspx>.

[17]   European Commission, *Reducing Emissions from Aviation* <https://ec.europa.eu/clima/policies/transport/aviation_en>.

[18]   Ibid.

2.2   First Ride: Early Surplus Issues

The first trading period of the EU ETS was aimed at establishing the ETS market infrastructure and provide the EU with a 'learning-by-doing'[19] opportunity to prepare for the second trading period (from 1 January 2008 until 31 December 2012). This was particularly important as the second trading period would overlap with the first commitment period of the Kyoto Protocol.

The ETS Directive originally provided that each Member State would develop a national allocation plan (NAP) determining the national emissions cap and the methodology for initial allocation of EUAs for the period.[20] The general criteria to be observed by Member States were provided in Annex III.[21] The decentralised, bottom-up process of national decision-making coexisted with the Commission's role of coordination and guidance in the creation of the NAPs. Essentially, it meant that the European Commission would review the Member States' NAPs and could reject them in part, or in whole, on the basis of incompatibilities with the criteria listed in the Directive.[22]

Hence, the emissions cap in the EU ETS pilot phase corresponded to the sum of the 25 national caps (27 with the accession of Romania and Bulgaria in 2007). The final EU-wide cap was not defined until all the NAPs were accepted, which did not occur until after the start of the first trading period.[23] In the first allocation phase, 15 NAPs were 'conditionally approved' or 'approved with technical changes' resulting in a total reduction of the emissions caps of 4.3 per cent of the proposed annual amounts, equivalent to 100 million tonnes per year.[24]

---

[19]   European Commission, 'Green Paper on greenhouse gas emissions trading within the European Union' (COM/2000/0087 final, European Commission, 8 March 2000) 10. In 2000, the Commission analysed that 'there would be considerable benefits in terms of "learning-by-doing" that would ensure that the Community was better prepared for the start of international emissions trading from 2008 under the Kyoto Protocol'.

[20]   ETS Directive, art 9(1). Chapter 4 further develops the general allocation methodology adopted in the first trading period of the EU ETS.

[21]   Ibid., annex III.

[22]   Ibid., art 9(3).

[23]   The last NAP approved by the Commission was the Greek NAP, approved on 20 June 2005.

[24]   See Denny Ellerman, Frank Convery and Christian De Perthuis, 'The European Carbon Market in Action: lessons from the First Trading Period' (2008) 42; Denny Ellerman, 'The EU's Emissions Trading Scheme: A Prototype Global System?' (MIT, 2009) 8.

Despite Annex III criteria calling for the compatibility of a Member State's cap with its obligations under the burden-sharing agreement and the Kyoto Protocol, in practice the emissions caps were set largely based on the expected business as usual (BAU) emissions.[25] The non-existence of reliable emissions data within the ETS sectors and the short deadlines to be met by Member States contributed to overly generous emissions caps in most ETS Member States.[26] Improvements in energy and carbon efficiency also contributed to the low verified emissions in Eastern European countries.[27]

2.2.1 Impacts of uncertainty of emissions projections on EUA prices

The first trading period of the EU ETS suffered from uncertainties in relation to emissions projections, permit prices and, even, instabilities related to the permanence of the scheme.[28] In the first year of the EU ETS and until late April 2016, most of the participants expected a global shortage of allowances.[29] Consequently, EUA prices stayed above the marginal abatement costs and were passed on, imposing substantial costs on consumers. Furthermore, the dominant players, such as the power and heat producers in the UK and Germany, may have set the prices artificially above the abatement costs in order to maximise their own windfall profits, while they were receiving free of cost EUAs.[30]

In May 2006, the volume of the surplus permits was made public and the EU ETS experienced a severe permit price crash.[31] Following the release of verified emissions, showing an unexpected 4.3 per cent allowance surplus, the EUA price experienced a decline of €10/EUA in

---

[25] See Ellerman, Convery and Perthuis, ibid., 36.

[26] Ibid., 36–9.

[27] Ibid., 45.

[28] Michael Grubb, 'Strengthening the EU ETS: Creating a Stable Platform for EU Energy Sector Investment' (University of Cambridge Centre for Mitigation Research, 2012) on the enduring nature of uncertainties around emission projections and other factors in an ETS. Also see Chapter 3 on the experiences of the EU ETS and former AUS CPM.

[29] Beat Hintermann, 'Allowance Price Drivers in the First Phase of the EU ETS' (2009) *CEPE Working Paper*, 24. Ellerman, Convery and Perthuis, above n 24.

[30] Hintermann, ibid., 26.

[31] Ellerman, Convery and Perthuis, above n 24. Ellerman, Convery and De Perthuis note that 'until the release of the 2005 verified emissions data in April 2006, the EU-wide cap was not viewed as being too lax. If anything, the higher than expected EUA prices and analyst forecasts suggested the opposite'.

only two days and reached 0.2 Euros t/CO_2 by the end of 2007.[32] The over-allocation issue was further aggravated by the impossibility of banking emissions permits for use in the subsequent trading period.[33]

The trial period ended with a surplus of emissions permits, mainly located in the Eastern European countries.[34] Consequently, it failed to achieve a sufficiently stringent emissions cap and to establish strong price signals. The task of improving the market's efficiency through more rigid cap-setting was assigned to the second trading period.[35] The issue of surplus permits has been ongoing and led to structural reforms of the EU ETS in 2014 and 2015.

2.3 Second Ride: The Emissions Trading System in Crisis

The second trading period of the EU ETS overlapped with the first commitment period of the Kyoto Protocol, which meant that the emissions caps had to be consistent with the EU's Kyoto AAUs.[36] In addition, new rules were required for the use of the Joint Implementation (JI) mechanism and Clean Development Mechanism (CDM) credits for compliance under the EU ETS.

In 2004, Directive 2004/101/EC[37] amended the ETS Directive to allow the use of JI and CDM credits up to a percentage of the allocation of the allowances of each installation to be specified by each Member State in

---

[32] See Denny Ellerman, Frank Convery and Christian De Perthuis, *Pricing Carbon: the European Union Emissions Trading Scheme* (Frank J. Convery, Christian de Perthuis and Emilie Alberola trans, Cambridge University Press, 2010); Regina Betz and Misato Sato, 'Emissions Trading: Lessons Learnt From the 1st Phase of the EU ETS and Prospects for the 2nd Phase' (2006) 6 *Climate Policy* 351, 352; Ellerman, Convery and Perthuis, above n 24.

[33] Raphael Trotignon And Anais Delbosc, 'Allowance Trading Patterns During The Trial Period: What Does the CITL Reveal? ' (Mission Climate, 2008), 4.

[34] A description of the surplus permits distributed by Member States is found in Ellerman, Convery and Perthuis, above n 24, 46.

[35] Betz and Sato, above n 32.

[36] Ellerman, Convery and Perthuis, above n 24, 49.

[37] Directive 2004/101/EC of the European Parliament and of the Council of 27 October 2004 Amending Directive 2003/87/EC Establishing a Scheme for Greenhouse Gas Emission Allowance Trading Within the Community, in respect of the Kyoto Protocol's Project Mechanisms [2004] OJ L 338/18 (Linking Directive).

its NAP. The percentages should be consistent with the Member State's obligations under the Kyoto Protocol.[38]

In 2005 and 2006, the Commission released two guidance communications in order to assist with the creation of the allocation plans for the second trading period (NAP2). The first Communication, in December 2005, contained early traces of the harmonisation process which was further adopted in the third trading period. In the Communication, the Commission stated that:

> In general, Member States and stakeholders also stress a preference for increasing harmonisation of allocation rules. The Commission considers it necessary to achieve more coherence in the second trading period, to the extent that the divergent progress by Member States towards their individual Kyoto targets allows for. In addition, further harmonisation is desirable beyond 2012. The Commission will consider these issues in the context of the strategic review of the EU ETS.[39]

The release of the verified emissions data for 2005 in May 2006, revealing lower BAU emissions than initially estimated, urged the Commission to review the cap-setting method. In November 2006, the Commission released a second Communication and confirmed that the 'aggregate 2005 emissions, at just over 2 billion tonnes, were significantly below the annual average allocation for the first period of close to 2.2 billion tonnes'.[40]

In an attempt to set more stringent caps for the second trading period, the Commission decided that the 2005 verified emissions figures would be the point of reference for the second period caps, unless exceptional circumstances justified the adjustment of the 2005 data. A carbon intensity improvement factor of 0.5 per cent per annum was adopted, making up for a 2.5 per cent cap reduction during the five-year period

---

[38]   ETS Directive, art 11a (1), annex III (12).

[39]   An example of the coherence desired by the Commission is the uniform definition of combustion installations adopted by the Commission in 2005, to be applied by all Member States (Communication from the Commission COM/ 2005/703, above n 10, para 36).

[40]   Communication from the Commission to the Council and to the European Parliament COMM/2006/275, on the Assessment of National Allocation Plans for the Allocation of Greenhouse Gas Emission Allowances in the Second Period of the EU Emissions Trading Scheme Accompanying Commission Decisions of 29 November 2006 on the National Allocation plans of Germany, Greece, Ireland, Latvia, Lithuania, Luxembourg, Malta, Slovakia, Sweden and the United Kingdom in accordance with Directive 2003/87/EC [2006] 2.

from 2005 to 2010.[41] The Commission also set a formula to calculate
JI/CDM credits, ensuring consistency across the EU.[42]

The Commission assumed a greater role in the cap-setting process
during the second trading period. Under the new rules, only four Member
States had their original NAP2s approved, i.e., Denmark, France, the
United Kingdom and Slovenia.[43] Excluding data from new installations,
the NAP2 total for the EU27 was 11.8 per cent below the NAP1 totals
and 5.2 per cent below the average first-period emissions.[44]

However, the early analysis of NAP2 concluded that the national
allocation plans were set too high relative to the emissions projections.[45]
Betz and Sato suggested that in many Member States, the national caps
and allocations of permits were excessive when compared to 2005
emissions, the historic trends and the country-level projections.[46] Anger,
Böhringer and Oberndorfer also reported that in NAP2, 'due to a
generous allowance allocation to covered industries, the induced emissions abatement is rather limited'.[47]

Kyoto credits[48] became eligible under the EU ETS and participants
used this option beyond the initial predictions.[49] Finally, a third factor
was added to the already generous NAP2 and the excessive use of offset
credits, which was the 2008 global financial crisis. With the financial
crisis and the consequent decrease of industrial production in many
Member States, the demand for EUAs plummeted.[50]

---

[41]   Ibid., 5.
[42]   Ibid., 9–10.
[43]   Ellerman, Convery and Perthuis, above n 24, 54.
[44]   Ibid.
[45]   Karsten Neuhoff et al, 'Emission Projections 2008–2012 Versus National
Allocation Plans II' (2006) 6(4) *Climate Policy* 395.
[46]   Betz and Sato, above n 32.
[47]   Niels Anger, Christoph Böhringer and Ulrich Oberndorfer, 'Public Interest vs. Interest Groups: Allowance Allocation in the EU Emissions Trading
Scheme' (2008) <ftp://ftp.zew.de/pub/zew-docs/dp/dp08023.pdf>, 1.
[48]   Certified Emission Reduction credits (CERs) and Emission Reduction
Units (ERUs).
[49]   Frank Convery and Luke Redmond, 'The European Union Emissions
Trading Scheme: Issues in Allowance Price Support and Linkage' (2013) *Annual
Review of Resource Economics* 1.
[50]   Ross Garnaut, 'Garnaut Climate Change Review Update: Progress
Towards Effective Global Action on Climate Change' (Commonwealth of
Australia, 2011) 6. Garnaut stated that:

    The Great Crash of 2008 has pushed the developed countries of the northern
    hemisphere onto a lower long-term growth trajectory. It has left most of

Prices fell considerably between mid-2008 and early 2009. From 2009, the EU ETS experienced an increasing cumulative surplus of EUAs and Kyoto credits compared to emissions. In 2012, the Commission reported a surplus of 955 million EUAs / international credits between 2008 and 2011.[51]

The surplus continued to rise, and in 2012 the EU ETS had the largest gap between annual supply and demand in its history. The sovereign debt crisis in 2011 also contributed to a decrease in the demand for EUAs. Consequently, after a period of price-stability between mid-2009 and early 2011, the average price for EUAs dropped from 29 Euros/t in 2008 to 7.30 Euros/t in 2012,[52] reaching close to zero by the time the ETS entered its third trading period in early 2013.

The literature demonstrates that the ETS led to some abatement in the first two periods, as measured by intensity improvements.[53] However, what levels of abatement may be attributed exclusively to the ETS remains difficult to estimate. Egenhofer et al argue that 'there are indications based on case studies and interviews that the CO_2 price generated by the ETS has influenced business and investment decisions',[54] but this would also not be consistent across sectors.

2.4 Third Ride: Reforms and Attempts to Save the Emissions Trading System

The ETS Directive was again amended in 2009, effective from the third trading period onwards, adopting a centralised system for cap-setting and emission allocations. The former individual NAPs were replaced by a Community-wide emissions cap. The emissions cap for 2013 was based

---

Western Europe and the United States with an awful legacy of unemployment, public sector debt and financial vulnerability that has sapped the confidence of communities and weakened the influence and power of even the most able leaders.

[51] European Commission, 'Report from the Commission to the European Parliament and the Council: The State of the European Carbon Market in 2012' (European Commission, 2012) 30, 4.

[52] Emil Dimantchev et al, 'Carbon 2013: at a Tipping Point' (Point Carbon, 2013), 2.

[53] Johanna Arlinghaus, 'Impacts of Carbon Prices on Indicators of Competitiveness: A Review of Empirical Findings' (OECD, 2015).

[54] Christian Egenhofer et al, 'The EU Emissions Trading System and Climate Policy towards 2050: Real Incentives to Reduce Emissions and Drive Innovation?' (CEPS, 2011), v.

on the NAP2 caps (period from 2008–12), with a separate cap applicable for aviation.

The emissions cap (except for the aviation cap) has been set to decrease annually by a linear factor of 1.74 per cent, up to 2020.[55] However, a proposal is in place to increase the linear factor to 2.2 per cent per year from 2021 (fourth trading period), in order to assist the EU to reach its 2030 GHG reduction target of at least 40 per cent compared to 1990.[56]

The third trading period also started with a large surplus of allowances, including the EUAs banked from the second trading period (the reasons for this surplus are explained above), further imports of international credits, the early auctioning of phase three EUAs and other phase three EUAs sales.[57] The Commission predicted that, without action, an overall surplus of more than 2 billion allowances could be carried forward in most of phase three, most likely undermining the ability of the EU ETS to meet more stringent emission reduction targets cost-effectively.[58]

Furthermore, the price crisis in the EUA in 2013 also brought serious concerns with regard to the future of the EU ETS. In April 2013, the EU ETS allowances price fell to €2.81, reaching a record low and escalating rumours of the possible end of the EU ETS.

As a short-term measure, the Commission decided to 'back-load' the supply of phase three EUAs. The Commission decided to postpone the auctions of 900 million EUAs scheduled for 2013, 2014 and 2015 until

---

[55] ETS Directive, art 9.

[56] European Council, 'Council conclusions 169/14 of 23 and 24 October 2014' (2014) <http://www.consilium.europa.eu/uedocs/cms_data/docs/pressdata/en/ec/145397.pdf>; Proposal 2015/148 (COD) for a Directive of the European Parliament and of the Council Amending Directive 2003/87/EC to enhance cost-effective emission reductions and low-carbon investments [2015]. In order to achieve the 40 per cent reduction target by 2030, the EU Commission has calculated that the EU ETS sectors will have to reduce their emissions by 43 per cent and the non-EU ETS sectors will have to reduce emissions by 30 per cent compared to 2005. The 43 per cent reduction target translates into a declining cap of 2.2 per cent per annum from 2021 onwards.

[57] European Commission, above n 51, 4; Proposal for a Directive of the European Parliament and of the Council Amending Directive 2003/87/EC to Enhance Cost-Effective Emission Reductions and Low Carbon Investments [2015] COM/2015/0337 final/2.

[58] Ibid.; also see Convery and Redmond, above n 49.

2019–20, when it expected that the demand would have picked up.[59] Rather than a definite solution to the issue of the surplus, the measure aimed at providing a temporary boost to the allowance prices and must be followed by other measures.[60] The back-loading strategy proved successful, with a reduction to approximately 1.78 billion surplus permits in 2015, against estimates of a surplus at least 40 per cent higher in the absence of the measure.[61]

In order to further correct the supply-demand imbalance in the mid- to long-term, six non-exclusive policies were suggested in 2012 by the Commission and were broadly discussed:

(i) increasing the EU reduction target to 30 per cent in 2020;
(ii) retiring a number of allowances in phase three;
(iii) early revision of the annual linear reduction factor;
(iv) extending the EU ETS coverage to other sectors of the economy;
(v) limiting access to international credits; and/or
(vi) adopting discretionary price management mechanisms, such as a carbon price floor.[62]

The proposals were not received unanimously across the EU Members. Among the supporters of structural changes to the ETS, preferences went to measures that removed permits permanently from the market – e.g., through an early revision of the linear reduction factor[63] or by an

---

[59] Regulation 176/2014 of 25 February 2014 amending Regulation (EU) No. 1031/2010 in particular to determine the volumes of greenhouse gas emission allowances to be auctioned in 2013–20 [2014] OJ L 56/11.

[60] See Nicolas Koch et al, 'Politics Matters: Regulatory Events as Catalysts for Price Formation Under Cap-and-Trade' (2015) 1. The authors explain that the decision to back-load allowances caused a price decline rather than the expected increase, due to the low confidence of the market participants in the measure.

[61] European Commission, Structural Reform of the EU ETS <https://ec.europa.eu/clima/policies/ets/reform_en>.

[62] European Commission, above n 51, 7–10.

[63] The Netherlands, 'Consultation on Structural Options to Strengthen the EU Emissions Trading System' (2013) <http://ec.europa.eu/clima/consultations/articles/0017_en.htm>; European Commission, *Consultation on structural options to strengthen the EU Emissions Trading System* European Commission <http://ec.europa.eu/clima/consultations/0017/index_en.htm>; Nicolas Berghmans, Oliver Sartor and Nicolas Stephan, 'Reforming the EU ETS: Give it some Work!' (2013) (28) *Climate Brief: Focus on the Economics of Climate Change* 1.

exceptional retirement of permits in phase three.[64] However, Member
States such as Poland were strictly opposed to any unilateral intervention
and such proposals were rejected.[65]

A legislative proposal for a 'market stability reserve' was approved by
the European Parliament on 7 July 2015 and by the Council on 6 October
2015.[66] The market stability reserve will operate from 1 January 2019. It
is a mechanism to adjust the annual volume of permits auctioned, by
either adding permits to the reserve or releasing them for future auction,
in situations where the total number of allowances in circulation is
outside a certain predefined range.

The adjustment in the volume of auctions is triggered when an
imbalance in the supply and demand of EUAs is detected, which occurs
whenever the total surplus is higher than 833 million allowances, in
which case EUAs would be added to the reserve, or where the total
surplus is below 400 million allowances, in which case EUAs would be
released from the reserve for future auctioning.

A more comprehensive proposal for a Directive to amend the ETS
Directive has also been presented by the European Commission for the
post-2020 period. Alongside the market stability reserve, the proposed
faster reduction of the annual emissions cap at an annual rate of 2.2 per
cent from 2021 onwards, mentioned above, is also expected to lead to a
reduction of the existing surplus. Furthermore, the Commission is
proposing the review of rules for the free allocation of units to carbon
leakage exposed sectors.

2.5 Reporting and Surrendering Obligations and the Consequences of Non-Compliance

Participants under the scheme are known as 'operators', that is, those
who operate and control the 'installations' where listed activities are

---

[64] Finland, 'Consultation on Structural Options to Strengthen the EU
Emissions Trading System' (2013) <http://ec.europa.eu/clima/consultations/
articles/0017_en.htm>; Christian De Perthuis and Raphaël Trotignon, 'The
European CO2 Allowances Market: Issues in the Transition to Phase III' (2012).

[65] Polish Ministry of the Environment, 'Consultation on Structural Options
to Strengthen the EU Emissions Trading System' (2013) <http://ec.europa.eu/
clima/consultations/articles/0017_en.htm>.

[66] Proposal 2014/0011 (COD) Concerning the Establishment and Operation
of a Market Stability Reserve for the Union Greenhouse Gas Emission Trading
Scheme and Amending Directive 2003/87/EC [2014].

carried out, including aircraft operators, from 1 January 2012.[67] The operators hold a 'greenhouse gas emissions permit' and are responsible for the monitoring and reporting of emissions in relation to activities covered by the ETS in each calendar year.[68]

The EU ETS compliance cycle encompasses the following stages: first, within three months of the end of the calendar year (by 31 March), the operator prepares the annual emissions report, seeks verification (by an accredited verifier) and submits the verified report to the competent authority. Then, by 30 April, the operator must surrender a number of permits equal to the total emissions from that installation during the preceding calendar year. These permits are subsequently cancelled.[69]

An excess emissions penalty is applicable in the case of failure to surrender the correct number of eligible permits.[70] During the trial period, the penalty imposed for each unit shortfall was €40 for each tonne of carbon dioxide equivalent emitted by that installation for which the operator has not surrendered allowances, that is above 100 per cent of the average EUAs market price throughout the period. From the second trading period the monetary penalty increased to €100.[71] The monetary penalty does not release the operator from the obligation to surrender an amount of allowances equal to those excess emissions when surrendering allowances in relation to the following calendar year.[72]

In the first two trading periods, the monitoring, reporting and enforcement were decentralised, with each constituent Member State establishing and maintaining a national registry.[73] The decentralisation of the

---

[67] ETS Directive, art 3(e) (definition of 'installation') (f) (definition of 'operator').

[68] Ibid., art 4, 6(1)(2)(e).

[69] Ibid., art 12(3).

[70] See *Bundesrepublik Deutschland v Nordzucker AG* (C-148/14) [2015] ECR I-287. The European Court of Justice ruled that an operator would not be subject to the excess penalty where it is established that the operator had mistakenly understated its emissions and surrendered insufficient permits. However, see *Billerud Karlsborg AB and Billerud Skärblacka AB v Naturvardverket* (C-203/12) [2013] ECR I-664. In this case, the Court ruled that the excess penalty is due, irrespective of the reason for the non-surrendering, even where operators hold a sufficient number of allowances on the date.

[71] ETS Directive, art 16(3), (4).

[72] Ibid.

[73] Ibid., art 19(1).

compliance mechanism faced unexpected events, such as the EU ETS being used for laundering money and other criminal activities in 2009.[74]

From 1 January 2012, a Community-wide registry was created for the maintenance of the holding accounts opened in the Member State and the allocation, surrender and cancellation of allowances are now centralised at Community level.[75] Nevertheless, Member States remain responsible for the inspection and sanctioning and for checking for compliance with the MRV process.[76]

2.6 Links to Other Schemes

Since its implementation, the EU ETS has created a unilateral link with the Kyoto Protocol mechanisms. During the trial phase, the liable entities were allowed to use CER credits only. In the second trading period, entities could use CER and ERU credits up to a percentage of the cap specified by the Member States.[77] The limits imposed by Member States on the use of CDMs and JIs during the second trading period averaged 13.5 per cent at the EU level. The leftover CDM and JI credits from the second trading period were validated to use in the third trading period until 2020, subject to a cap.[78] The EU ETS will be linked with the Kyoto Protocol mechanisms until 2020.

The ETS Directive also provides that the scheme may be linked with other regional, national or subnational emissions trading schemes through the mutual recognition of allowances.[79] Under this provision a full bilateral linking with the AUS CPM was announced for 2018, only to be cancelled due to the repeal of the Australian scheme, as discussed below. A link between the EU ETS and the soon to be implemented nationwide Chinese ETS could be expected in the future.

---

[74] Jonathan Verschuuren and Floor Fleurke, 'Entracte: Report on the Legal Implementation of the EU ETS at Member State Level' (Tilburg Sustainability Center, 2012). Verschuuren and Fleurke state that 'the instances of fraud and criminal activities in the past have been addressed through tightened rules under market abuse and anti-money laundering legislation'.

[75] ETS Directive, art 19(1).

[76] Verschuuren and Fleurke, above n 74.

[77] ETS Directive, art 11a(1).

[78] Ibid., art 11a(2).

[79] Ibid., art 25.

3. WHAT WENT WRONG? A SHORT-LIVED CARBON PRICE IN AUSTRALIA[80]

After two years of a functioning AUS CPM, Australia's Prime Minister Tony Abbott delivered his campaign promise of abolishing the scheme. A legislative package, also known as the 'carbon tax repeal legislation', passed in the House of Representatives and the Senate and received Royal Assent on 17 July 2014, dismantling the AUS CPM. The legislation entered into effect from 1 July 2014.

Despite its short life, the AUS CPM remains a relevant case to be studied. Indeed, its innovative framework was designed to prevent issues such as price volatility during the first years of the scheme.

Regrettably, its promising model was not enough to prevent constant political resistance. The political debate centred particularly on the nature of the scheme (carbon tax or emissions trading) and the impacts on the international competitiveness of domestic energy-intensive trade-exposed (EITE) industries. Both aspects are discussed below.

3.1 'Labor' and Birth of a Pricing Mechanism

In 2008, the Australian Labor Party (ALP) government proposed the introduction of an emissions trading scheme known as the Carbon Pollution Reduction Scheme (CPRS).[81] A thorough policy development process was put in place, starting with a Green Paper on ETS design issues in July. This was followed by the release of a comprehensive report on the impacts of climate change on the Australian economy commissioned by the Commonwealth, known as the Garnaut Review, and the Treasury modelling and a White Paper in December.[82] The legislation package failed to obtain support within the Parliament and was abandoned by the Labor Party.

---

[80] See Elena Aydos, 'What Went Wrong? Lessons from a Short-Lived Carbon Price in Australia' in Leonardo de Andrade Costa, Ana Alice De Carli and Ricardo Lodi Ribeiro (eds), *Tributacao e Sustentabilidade Ambiental* (FGV Editora, 2015) 75.

[81] Carbon Pollution Reduction Scheme Bill 2009 (Cth) ('CPRS Bill').

[82] Department of Climate Change, 'Carbon Pollution Reduction Scheme: Green Paper' (2008); Commonwealth of Australia, 'Australia's Low Pollution Future: The Economics of Climate Change Mitigation' (2008); Department of Climate Change, 'Climate Change Carbon Pollution Reduction Scheme: White Paper' (2008).

Three years later, in July 2011, the Australian Federal Government released a Clean Energy Action Plan and legislative package.[83] The main feature of the action plan was the introduction of a price on carbon through the Carbon Pricing Mechanism (AUS CPM). In November 2011, the legislative package was passed in Parliament, and received Royal Assent in December 2011.[84] The AUS CPM commenced on 1 July 2012, near the end of the first commitment period under the Kyoto Protocol.

The AUS CPM covered CO_2 equivalent (CO_2-e) emissions (i.e., carbon dioxide, methane, nitrous oxide and perfluorocarbons from aluminium smelting) from stationary energy, non-legacy waste,[85] transport,[86] industrial processes and fugitive emissions, except from decommissioned coal mines. While land use activities were left out of the AUS CPM, a range of abatement and carbon sequestration projects in the land sector were eligible under a domestic voluntary offsets crediting scheme, the Carbon Farming Initiative (CFI), further described below.

The AUS CPM was a relatively small scheme. Only the biggest polluters in Australia, with a threshold of 25,000 tonnes of CO_2-e per year or more of the covered emissions, were included as participants in the AUS CMP (approximately 360 entities).[87] A lower threshold applied to landfill facilities in order to prevent waste being diverted from large landfill facilities into facilities below the threshold.[88] Natural gas retailers

---

[83]   Australian Government, 'Securing a Clean Energy Future: The Australian Government's Climate Change Plan' (2011).

[84]   Clean Energy Act 2011 (Cth) ('CE Act'); Clean Energy Regulator Act 2011 (Cth); Climate Change Authority Act 2011 (Cth); Australian National Registry of Emissions Units Act 2011 (Cth); Clean Energy (Charges – Customs) Act 2011 (Cth); Clean Energy (Charges – Excise) Act 2011 (Cth); Clean Energy (Consequential Amendments) Act 2011 (Cth); Clean Energy (Household Assistance Amendments) Act 2011 (Cth); Clean Energy (Unit Issue Charge – Auctions) Act 2011 (Cth); Clean Energy (Unit Issue Charge – Fixed Charge) Act 2011 (Cth); Clean Energy (Unit Shortfall Charge – General) Act 2011 (Cth); Clean Energy (Tax Laws Amendments) Act 2011 (Cth).

[85]   Legacy waste is waste accepted by the landfill prior to the introduction of the AUS CPM (CE Act 2011 s 32). Legacy waste is not covered by the AUS CPM but is eligible for abatement projects under the Carbon Farming Initiative. Carbon Farming Initiative Act 2011 (Cth) ss 53(1)(b), 55(1)(b).

[86]   Rail, domestic aviation and shipping.

[87]   CE Act s 20(4); Clean Energy Regulator, *LEPID for the 2013–14 Financial Year* (30 June 2015) Australian Government <http://www.cleanenergy regulator.gov.au/Infohub/CPM/Liable-Entities-Public-Information-Database/LEPID-for-the-2013-14-financial-year>.

[88]   CE Act, s 23(10).

were also included in relation to the potential GHG emissions embodied in the amount of gas supplied.[89]

Despite its small size, around 60 per cent of Australia's emissions were covered by the AUS CPM. The Australian government was not as innovative as New Zealand,[90] and ended up not including the transport and forestry sectors in its scheme. However, the legislation on fuel tax and synthetic GHGs imposed an equivalent carbon price on some business transport emissions, the non-transport use of liquid and gaseous fuels (except natural gas) and synthetic GHGs.[91] Combining all these instruments, around two-thirds of Australia's emissions were directly or indirectly covered by a carbon price.[92]

3.2 An Innovative Pricing System

An innovative feature of the scheme was the adoption of a phased approach to pricing, starting with a fixed price, with flexibility increasing over time.[93] During the first three years of the scheme, known as the fixed charge years (from 1 July 2012 until 30 June 2015), GHG emissions permits, known as Australian Carbon Units (ACUs), were either allocated for free to eligible participants or issued for a fixed price, having the practical effect of a carbon tax. The price of ACUs was $23 per tonne of CO_2-e in the financial year 2012–13 and $24.15 per tonne in the financial year 2013–14.[94]

---

[89] Ibid., s 33.

[90] See Section 4 below.

[91] There are seven main Greenhouse gases (GHGs) in the atmosphere: Carbon dioxide (CO_2), Methane (CH_4), Nitrous oxide (N_2O), Hydrofluoro-carbons (HFCs), Perfluorocarbons (PFCs), Sulphur hexafluoride (SF_6) and Nitrogen trifluoride (NF_3). The first three GHGs occur naturally in the atmosphere, while HFCs, PFCs, SF_6 and NF3 are synthetic. As mentioned above, the AUS CPM covered exclusively CO_2, CH_4, N_2O and PFCs from aluminium smelting.

[92] Explanatory Memorandum, Clean Energy Bill 2011 (Cth) 33 ('coverage of the carbon price').

[93] CE Act, s 5 (definition of 'fixed charge year'; definition of 'flexible charge year'). Also see Elena Aydos, 'Australia's Carbon Pricing Mechanism' in Larry Kreiser et al (eds), *Carbon Pricing, Growth and the Environment*, Critical Issues in Environmental Taxation (Edward Elgar Publishing, 2012) 261, 262; Peter Sopher, Anthony Mansell and Clayton Munnings, 'Australia' (EDF IETA, 2014).

[94] CE Act, ss 5 (definition of 'fixed charge year'), 93. See Commonwealth of Australia, 'Strong Growth, Low Pollution: Modelling a Carbon Price' (2011), in especial Clean Energy Future scenario. Also see World Bank Group and ECOFYS, 'State and Trends of Carbon Pricing' (2014) 30. The World Bank

During the fixed charge years, emissions were not capped. Instead, the amount of ACUs issued to liable entities was limited to the equivalent of the participant's emissions, minus any eligible units[95] surrendered by the entity for each financial year.[96] Once issued, the units were automatically surrendered via electronic transaction. Consequently, there was no trading of ACUs within the two years of the functioning of the AUS CPM.[97]

From 1 July 2015 onwards, the Clean Energy Act provided for the commencement of the flexible charge years, with the auctioning of ACUs.[98] A carbon pollution cap would limit the number of ACUs auctioned and allocated free of cost.[99] The scheme would effectively work as a cap-and-trade system, with ACUs being freely traded in the market by participants and/or non-participants of the scheme.[100]

As mentioned *supra*, flexibility was meant to increase gradually. Disregarding the recommendation of the Garnaut Review against the use of price ceilings and floors,[101] a safety mechanism was integrated into the first three flexible charge years. In the financial years beginning on 1 July 2015, 1 July 2016 and 1 July 2017, the liable entities would have the option of purchasing carbon units for a fixed charge, set by regulations.[102] The issue of carbon units for a fixed charge would work as a price ceiling.

---

report on carbon pricing estimates that CO_2 prices should be approximately \$35 per ton in order to compensate for damages or, alternatively, 'a global CO_2 price starting at about \$30 per ton (in current dollars) in 2020 and rising at around 5 per cent a year would be roughly in line with ultimately containing mean projected warming to 2.5°C at least cost'.

[95]   Apart from with ACUs, the scheme may allow liable entities to meet compliance requirements by surrendering other units, such as offset credits from the forestry sector. For further details and a description of eligible credits under the AUS CPM see Section 3.6 below.

[96]   CE Act, s 100(3)(4).

[97]   Ibid., s 100(7).

[98]   Ibid., ss 4, 5 (definition of 'flexible charge year').

[99]   Further details on the carbon pollution cap are discussed below, Part 3.3.

[100]   CE Act, s 14.

[101]   Ross Garnaut, *The Garnaut Climate Change Review: Final Report* (Cambridge University Press, 2008) 335. Garnaut argued that 'while politically expedient, the introduction of a price ceiling or floor on permits would damage greatly the normal operation of the scheme'. A price ceiling would possibly undermine firm commitments on the levels of emissions and dampen the incentives for the development of secondary markets. Price floors could increase the levels of mitigation, although at a higher total adjustment cost.

[102]   CE Act, s 100(1).

The original design of the AUS CPM also included a price floor (AU$15, rising annually by 4 per cent) in the first three flexible charge years,[103] but this feature was removed as part of the agreement to link the AUS CPM with the EU ETS. The removal of the price floor was enacted by an amendment to the Clean Energy Act,[104] and was justified on the basis of the need to 'reduce the complexity of the linking arrangement and ensure the convergence of Australian and EU carbon prices'.[105] Remarkably, a price floor has been recently recommended as part of a necessary structural reform to stabilise the surplus and price issues in the EU ETS, as further discussed below.[106]

3.3 Emissions Cap

A pollution cap was to be set to best reflect Australia's medium- and long-term targets for reducing net greenhouse gas emissions and the different possible trajectories towards it.[107] In order to provide the flexibility for adaptations to possible changes in Australia's reduction targets over time, the caps were to be set by Regulations.[108]

The cap for the first five years of the flexible period, starting on 1 July 2015, was to be tabled in each House of Parliament no later than 31 May 2014.[109] Regulations would declare the carbon pollution cap for the following years with at least five years before the end of the relevant flexible charge year. For example, for the financial year starting on 1 July 2020, the carbon pollution cap would be declared no later than 31 June 2016.[110]

Default carbon caps were also provided for, to observe the goal of reducing pollution caps over time. In the absence of regulations declaring the cap, the default carbon pollution cap for the flexible charge year beginning on 1 July 2015 was to be equivalent to the total emissions numbers for the eligible financial year beginning on 1 July 2012, minus

---

[103] Explanatory Memorandum, Clean Energy Bill 2011 (Cth) 32.
[104] CE Act, s 111(5).
[105] Explanatory Memorandum, Clean Energy Legislation Amendment (International Emissions Trading and Other Measures) Bill 2012 and related Bills (Cth) 4.
[106] Grubb, above n 28. Also see European Commission, above n 51.
[107] CE Act, s 14(2).
[108] Ibid., s 14.
[109] Ibid., s 16.
[110] Ibid.

38,000,000 tonnes.[111] The default carbon pollution caps for the following flexible charge years (beginning on or after 1 July 2016) were to be equivalent to the carbon pollution cap number for the previous flexible charge year, minus 12,000,000 tonnes.[112]

Thus, through an updated cap every five years, the AUS CPM framework allowed the government the flexibility to review emissions reduction targets in future international commitments.[113] Furthermore, reliable emissions data from the first fixed charge years and the mechanisms for periodical reviews of the cap would provide certainty to the liable entities and minimise issues with price volatility once the ACUs were auctioned, as was experienced in the first two trading periods of the European Union Emissions Trading Scheme (EU ETS).[114]

3.4 Reporting and Surrendering Obligations and the Consequences of Non-Compliance

During the two fixed-charge years of the AUS CPM, the reporting and surrendering of obligations followed a two-stage approach. By 15 June, participants provided the Regulator with an estimate of the *interim emissions number* for the year and surrendered the required number of units to cover its interim emissions numbers.[115] The final emissions number was reported by 31 October in the year following the compliance year.[116] By 1 February participants were required to surrender the remaining carbon units to cover the final emissions number.[117]

With the repeal of the AUS CPM effective from 1 July 2014, the participants were required to report final emissions numbers by 31 October 2014 and acquit their final carbon price liability for 2013–14 by 2 February 2015. Failure to comply with interim emissions obligations and/or final emissions liabilities triggered a unit shortfall charge.[118] In

---

[111]   Ibid., s 17(2).
[112]   Ibid., s 18(2).
[113]   See Sopher, Mansell and Munnings, above n 93, 8.
[114]   ACUs were issued exclusively for the purpose of compliance with emissions obligations, with no trading and/or banking allowed. Thus, by the end of the fixed charge years the government would have a precise estimate of the companies' business as usual emissions.
[115]   CE Act, ss 125, 126.
[116]   Ibid., ss 119, 120.
[117]   Ibid., s 126.
[118]   Ibid., s 134(2).

case a unit shortfall charge remained unpaid after the due date, a penalty was also applied at the rate of 20 per cent of the amount unpaid per annum.[119]

3.5 Governance

The institutional arrangements in place for the holding and transferring of ACUs discussed in this section are relevant for the analysis of whether ACUs may be deemed to be goods (intangible assets) for the purposes of the Agreement on Subsidies and Countervailing Measures (SCM Agreement)[120] discussed in Chapter 6. It is worth noting that, in Australia, ACUs were given the legal status of personal property.[121]

The participants under the AUS CPM were required to maintain an account with the Australian National Registry of Emissions Units (Registry).[122] The Registry is an electronic system created to comply with Australia's commitments under the Kyoto Protocol, allowing legal entities to register and transfer Kyoto units.[123] With the implementation of the AUS CPM and the Carbon Farming Initiative (CFI),[124] the Registry was expanded to account for the issuance, holding, transfer and surrender of ACUs, Australian Carbon Credit Units (ACCUs) from the CFI, Kyoto units and international prescribed units.

A statutory body named the Clean Energy Regulator administered the AUS CPM, the CFI and the Registry.[125] The ACUs and ACCUs were issued by the Regulator on behalf of the Commonwealth through an electronic entry in the Registry, consisting of the identification number of a carbon unit.[126] All transfers of units between Registry accounts or between a Registry account and a foreign Registry were electronic.[127]

---

[119]   Ibid., s 135(1)(a)(b).

[120]   Marrakesh Agreement Establishing the World Trade Organization, opened for signature 15 April 1994, 1867 UNTS 3 (entered into force 1 January 1995) Annex 1A ('Agreement on Subsidies and Countervailing Measures').

[121]   CE Act, s 103 provided that 'a carbon unit is personal property and, subject to sections 105 and 106, is transmissible by assignment, by will and by devolution by operation of law'.

[122]   Ibid., s 93(4).

[123]   Australian National Registry of Emissions Units Act 2011 (Cth) s 9; Carbon Credits (Consequential Amendments) Act 2011 (Cth).

[124]   See Section 3.6 below for further information on the CFI.

[125]   Australian National Registry of Emissions Units Act 2011 (Cth).

[126]   Ibid., s 98.

[127]   Ibid., s 104.

The carbon price repeal legislation provided for the Regulator's continuing powers and transitional provisions so that liabilities incurred in relation to 2012–13 and 2013–14 would be collected and obligations enforced. Any remaining ACUs must be cancelled by the Regulator after the final surrender deadline for the compliance year 2013–14.[128]

Finally, an independent statutory body, the Climate Change Authority, was established on 1 July 2012 to assess progress towards meeting national targets, provide advice on pollution caps and undertake reviews of the scheme.[129] The proposed abolition of the Climate Change Authority, by the Abbott government, was subject to a separate Bill introduced into Parliament in November 2013 and was subsequently rejected by the Senate in March 2014.[130]

3.6 Links to Other Schemes

The legal framework of the AUS CPM was developed with a clear view to allow future links with domestic and international offset schemes and with existing and emerging independent carbon markets.[131] The AUS CPM was linked from its commencement to the national CFI scheme and would be linked to international schemes from 2015 onwards.

Contrary to the provisions in the CPRS Bill, the AUS CPM did not cap emissions from deforestation and it did not cover the agriculture sector. Instead, these activities were eligible under the CFI, a voluntary offset crediting mechanism for abatement and carbon sequestration projects in the land-use sector.[132]

---

[128]   Clean Energy Legislation (Carbon Tax Repeal) Act 2014 (Cth) Pt 3.

[129]   Climate Change Authority Act 2011 (Cth).

[130]   Climate Change Authority (Abolition) Bill 2013.

[131]   Garnaut, above n 101, 324, 338. The integration of international markets was one of many recommendations in the Garnaut Review:

> An emissions trading scheme must be able to coexist and integrate with international markets for emissions entitlements as well as with other financial, commodity and product markets in the domestic and international economy. This requires that there be no barriers to the appropriate transmission of information within and between markets.
>
> (...)
>
> Determining strategic and policy parameters for linking with other permit markets should be a role for the Commonwealth Government.

[132]   Carbon Farming Initiative Act 2011 (Cth). Also see Carbon Farming Initiative Amendment Act 2014 (Cth). The CFI has been amended and now operates under the 'Emissions Reduction Fund', which is independent to the

The CFI generated ACCUs to compensate for two types of offset projects, that is, the abatement and sequestration activities recognised under the Kyoto Protocol (Kyoto-ACCUs) and non-Kyoto projects, such as soil carbon, revegetation and cessation of logging in native forests.[133] The latter non-Kyoto ACCUs were to be sold in the international and domestic voluntary markets and purchased by the government through a 'Carbon Farming Initiative non-Kyoto Carbon Fund'. Non-Kyoto ACCUs were not eligible for compliance under the AUS CPM.

During the fixed price years of the AUS CPM, participants were allowed to meet up to 5 per cent of their liability for the relevant year though the surrendering of Kyoto-ACCUs.[134] ACCUs purchased or surrendered in excess were bankable. After 1 July 2015, there would be no limits to the surrendering of ACCUs, which was expected to increase the flexibility within the scheme and strengthen the CFI.

International units, such as those from CDM and JI projects, were not eligible during the fixed charge years of the AUS CPM. With the commencement of the flexible charge years, Kyoto units would be eligible to meet up to 50 per cent of the participants' liability for the relevant year.[135]

In September 2011, Australia and the EU agreed to regular 'senior official talks on climate change' (SOT). In December 2011, the 'Terms of Reference for the Australia-Europe Senior Official Talks on Climate Change' were released, explaining that 'the talks will (...) examine the

---

AUS CPM. For further information on how the CFI functioned when linked to the AUS CPM, see Celeste Black, 'Linking Land Sector Activities to Emissions Trading: Australia's Carbon Farming Initiative' in Larry Kreiser et al (eds), *Carbon Pricing, Growth and the Environment*, Critical Issues in Environmental Taxation (Edward Elgar, 2012) vol XI, 184.

[133] CE Act, s 5 (definition of 'eligible Australian carbon credit unit'). Non-Kyoto compliant Australian carbon credit units derived from emissions sources and sinks that would have been credited with a Kyoto ACCU if the abatement had occurred before the end of the relevant accounting period for the Kyoto Protocol first commitment period (31 December 2012 for reforestation and avoided deforestation activities, or 30 June 2012 for all other activities) or any other type of ACCU prescribed in regulations.

[134] Ibid., s 125(7).

[135] Ibid., ss 121, 123A(8).

mechanics of linking Australia's Carbon Pricing Mechanism with the EU's Emissions Trading Scheme'.[136]

The negotiations under the auspices of the Australia-Europe SOT advanced rapidly, and on 28 August 2012 the linking of the EU ETS and Australia's CPM was announced. GHG emissions permits from the EU ETS (European Union Allowances) were to be eligible to be used for compliance under the AUS CPM from July 2015 until July 2018 ('one-way link'). From 1 July 2018 a two-way link would be put in place, with mutual recognition of carbon units between the two ETSs.[137]

The Clean Energy Act was amended to provide for the linking of the AUS CPM with the EU ETS. Between 2015 and 2020, participants were to be allowed to meet up to 50 per cent of their annual liability with eligible units from their EU ETS and Kyoto units, that is, assigned amount units (AAU), certified emission reductions (CER), emission reduction units (ERU) or removal units (RMU), with a limit of 12.5 per cent of Kyoto units.[138]

While the participants of the AUS CPM would benefit from reduced compliance costs, a considerable cash flow from Australia to the EU was to be expected due to the ongoing issue of surplus permits under the EU ETS, as discussed below. It was expected that ACU prices would converge with the international price and the market value of ACCUs would also be impacted.[139]

---

[136]   Australian Government, 'Australia and Europe strengthen collaboration on carbon markets' (2011) <http://www.climatechange.gov.au/ministers/hon-greg-combet-am-mp/media-release/australia-and-europe-strengthen-collaboration-carbon>.

[137]   Australian Government, 'Australia and European Commission agree on pathway towards fully linking Emissions Trading Systems' (2012) <http://www.climatechange.gov.au/en/media/whats-new/linking-ets.aspx>.

[138]   CE Act, s 123 A, as amended by Clean Energy Legislation Amendment Act 2012 (Cth); Clean Energy Legislation Amendment (International Linking) Regulation 2013 (Cth).

[139]   Elena Aydos, 'Levelling the Playing Field or Playing on Unlevel Fields: the Industry Assistance Framework under the European Union ETS, the New Zealand ETS, and Australia's CPM' in Larry Kreiser et al (eds), *Market Based Instruments: National Experiences in Environmental Sustainability*, Critical Issues in Environmental Taxation (Edward Elgar Publishing, 2013) vol XIII, 135; Fitsum G. Tiche, Stefan E. Weishaar and Oscar Couwenberg, 'Carbon Leakage, Free Allocation and Linking Emissions Trading Schemes' (2013) *University of Groningen Faculty of Law Research Paper Series*.

Efforts to link the AUS CPM and the New Zealand ETS were also carried out.[140] However, the negotiations never reached an agreement for the effective linking of the ETSs, given the repeal of the AUS CPM in 2016.

3.7 Death of the Carbon Price

Australia is a highly vulnerable country to the effects of climate change and, paradoxically, one of the highest per capita emitters in the world.[141] The debate around the AUS CPM has been monopolised by a small group of emissions-intensive industries interested in postponing the economic transition towards a low carbon economy. Yet, the repeal of the AUS CPM cannot be attributed to poor design or implementation issues.

Indeed, the AUS CPM had a solid beginning and the potential to achieve its environmental goals without serious harm to the economy. Despite the overly-generous industry assistance model analysed in Chapters 4 and 5, the scheme introduced a number of distinctive features and managed to avoid many of the issues faced by the EU ETS.[142]

In only the two years of its existence, the AUS CPM demonstrated the potential to reach meaningful emissions reductions and did not harm the economy.[143] The assistance to the EITE sectors was quite substantial, with 104,203,895 ACUs allocated free of cost under the Jobs and Competitiveness Program in the 2012–2013 financial year (worth AUS$23.00 per unit) and 97,834,540 ACUs allocated free of cost in the 2013–2014 financial year (worth AUS$23.15 per unit).[144]

---

[140] Australian Government, 'Australia and New Zealand advance linking of their emissions trading schemes' (2011) <http://www.climatechange.gov. au/ministers/hon-greg-combet-am-mp/media-release/australia-and-new-zealand-advance-linking-their>.

[141] Jos Olivier et al, 'Trends in Global CO2 Emissions' (2013); Collaborative Economics, 'Green Innovation Index: International Edition' (Next 10, 2015).

[142] See EU ETS above.

[143] Marianna O'Gorman and Frank Jotzo, 'Impact of the Carbon Price on Australia's Electricity Demand, Supply and Emissions' (Centre for Climate Economic & Policy, 2014). O'Gormann and Jotzo conclude that 'the carbon price has worked as expected in terms of its short-term impacts'. In economic terms, the Treasury modelling predicted that 'the Australian economy will continue to prosper as we reduce emissions'. See also Paul Twomey, *Obituary: The Carbon Price* UNSW Australia <http://newsroom.unsw.edu.au/news/business/obituary-carbon-price>.

[144] Chapter 4 argues that the transitional assistance to EITE sectors is an expensive and, most of the time, unnecessary subsidy.

Two factors decisively contributed to the 'demise' of the newly established carbon price: the lack of both political leadership and consistent long-term strategic goals in relation to climate action, and the power of a group of emissions-intensive sectors whose interest was to postpone the transition towards a low-emissions economy in Australia, despite the generous assistance packages that these sectors secured within the scheme.[145] Arguably the way in which the media covered the impacts of climate change and presented the CPM, as against the economic interest of the mining industry, also played a role in the decline of the AUS CPM.[146]

A variety of strategies to deal with climate change have been discussed over the years in Australia. Different policies at Federal and State levels have been introduced, not always as a coordinated and continuous process. At the Federal level, both the centre-left ALP and the Liberal-National Coalition (an alliance of centre-right parties) have adopted inconsistent approaches towards climate action over the last decade.

Australia was one of the countries to immediately ratify the United Nations Framework Convention on Climate Change (UNFCCC) at the Rio Earth Summit, under a Labor Federal government.[147] In 1998, the Howard Liberal-National Coalition Government negotiated and signed the Kyoto Protocol to the UNFCCC.[148] However, Prime Minister Howard subsequently refused to ratify the Kyoto Protocol, arguing that the Protocol would harm the economy, which was consistent with the argument of the US.

---

[145] For further information on the assistance to EITE sectors, see Chapters 4 and 5.

[146] Wendy Bacon, 'Sceptical Climate Part 2: Climate Science in Australian Newspapers' (Australian Centre for Independent Journalism, 2013) <http://sceptical-climate.investigate.org.au/part-2/>; Wendy Bacon, 'A Sceptical Climate: Media coverage of climate change in Australia' (Australian Centre for Independent Journalism, 2011); Wendy Bacon and Chris Nash, 'Playing the Media Game: The Relative (in)visibility of Coal Industry Interests in Media Reporting of Coal as a Climate Change Issue in Australia' (2012) 13 *Journalism Studies* 243.

[147] United Nations Framework Convention on Climate Change, opened for signature 9 May 1992, 1771 UNTS 107 (entered into force 21 March 1994) (UNFCCC).

[148] Kyoto Protocol to the United Nations Framework Convention on Climate Change, opened for signature 11 December 1997, 2303 UNTS 148 (entered into force 16 February 2005). Also see: Parliament of Australia, 'Hill Signs Historic Agreement to Fight Global Warming' (1998) <http://parlinfo.aph.gov.au/parlInfo/search/display/display.w3p;query=Id%3A%22media%2Fpressrel%2FP1205%22>. Australia signed the Kyoto Protocol on 29 April 1998.

In the 2007 Federal elections, climate change was once again at the centre of the political agenda, with both leaders promising to introduce an emissions trading scheme if elected.[149] The Leader of the Labor Opposition, Kevin Rudd, stated during his campaign that climate change was the 'great moral challenge of our generation' and promised to 'forge a national consensus on climate change'.[150]

The first official act of the newly elected Prime Minister Rudd was to formally ratify the Kyoto Protocol,[151] and commit to GHG emissions reductions equivalent to 108 per cent of 1990 levels over the first commitment period (2008–12). As part of the development process of a domestic policy to adopt an emissions trading scheme, in July 2008, the Carbon Pollution Reduction Scheme (CPRS) Green Paper was released.[152]

An independent report inspired by the Stern Review,[153] known as the Garnaut Review,[154] was launched shortly after the CPRS Green Paper. Following a consultation period, the CPRS White Paper was also released.[155]

In late 2009, the Labor Government introduced into Parliament three packages of legislation to implement Australia's first emissions trading scheme (CPRS Bills). Sopher and Mansell explained the political process that led to the failure in obtaining the requisite support for the legislation package in the Senate:

> The Government had sufficient votes in the House of Representatives, and it seemed likely that the Opposition parties under the leadership of moderate MP Mr. Malcolm Turnbull would support the bills. However, six days before the Senate vote, Mr. Turnbull lost the Opposition leadership to Mr. Tony Abbott who opposed the bills. Consequently, Opposition Senators and non-Labor Senators (including the Green Party) joined to vote down the CPRS on various grounds: that it would harm Australian competitiveness and exports; that emissions would merely 'leak' abroad to competitor economies; and, that its environmental ambition was not sufficient. Mr. Abbott began an aggressive new political attack on the ETS as 'a great big new tax'.[156]

---

[149] Sopher, Mansell and Munnings, above n 93.
[150] Twomey, above n 143.
[151] Ratification came into force on 11 March 2008.
[152] Department of Climate Change, above n 82 (green paper).
[153] Nicholas Stern, *The Economics of Climate Change: The Stern Review* (Cambridge University Press, 2006).
[154] Garnaut, above n 101.
[155] Department of Climate Change, above n 82 (white paper).
[156] Sopher, Mansell and Munnings, above n 93, 2.

After a second failed attempt in 2010, Prime Minister Rudd deferred the CPRS legislation until the end of the first commitment period of the Kyoto Protocol in 2012. The decision to postpone the CPRS Bills, one of the core promises of the election campaign, cost Prime Minister Rudd his position as Leader and Prime Minister.[157]

Prior to the federal elections in August 2010, the new Labor Leader and Prime Minister Gillard famously stated that there would be no carbon tax under her government.[158] In July 2011, the Gillard Government released a Clean Energy Action Plan, followed by a draft of the Clean Energy legislative package.[159] In November 2011, the legislative package was passed in Parliament, receiving Royal Assent in December 2011. The main feature of the action plan was the introduction of the AUS CPM.

As previously explained, one of the distinctive features of the AUS CPM is the phased approach to pricing, starting with a fixed price which had practical effects similar to a carbon tax. From the moment legislation was introduced into Parliament, Opposition Leader Tony Abbott persistently stated that the AUS CPM was a 'bad tax based on a lie'.[160] Once again, Labor seemed to have failed to deliver a campaign promise in the public's eyes.

3.8 Carbon Tax or ETS – Did It Really Matter?

The debate around the nature of the carbon price, and whether former Prime Minister Gillard did break a campaign promise, had undisputable impacts on the political process leading to the repeal of the AUS CPM. Arguably, this is as far as the relevance of this debate goes.

Undoubtedly, the choice of a policy instrument to reduce GHG emissions is both conceptual and political. As demonstrated in Chapter 2, the theoretical foundations of carbon taxes and ETSs are, in reality, distinct, and the choice of the best market-based instrument for climate change mitigation still polarises the literature to date.[161]

---

[157] Ibid.

[158] Ibid.

[159] Australian Government, above n 83.

[160] *The Canberra Times*, 'Tony Abbott's speech on the carbon tax' (2011) <http://www.canberratimes.com.au/environment/tony-abbotts-speech-on-the-carbon-tax-20110914-1wopf.html>.

[161] See, e.g., Tatiana Falcão, 'Providing Environmental Taxes with an Environmental Purpose' in Larry Kreiser et al (eds), *Market Based Instruments:*

The AUS CPM was designed as a 'hybrid model', based on Garnaut's principled approach.[162] The fixed price years were meant to provide both price certainty and stability during the first years of the scheme. As already pointed out, the framework of the AUS CPM did not differ substantially from the CPRS.

While the CPRS Green Paper mentioned Garnaut's approach, a transitional fixed price was not yet regarded as a central element in a future Australian ETS.[163] Following public consultation, the CPRS White Paper report was published. A provisional fixed price was clearly considered as a viable policy option at this time, as stated in policy position 14.8.[164]

The phased approach was eventually incorporated in the AUS CPM legislation.[165] Today, it remains an innovative model and a flexible solution to common issues, such as the lack of reliable emissions data and price fluctuations, which may be experienced in the first years of a new emissions trading scheme.

In Australia's case, the National Greenhouse and Energy Reporting scheme (NGER) had already been in place since 2007, providing a national framework for the reporting of GHG emissions, energy production and energy consumption.[166] The main aims of the fixed pricing period were to provide stability and predictability for the participants and the Government, and to give businesses time to get used to the new system and to understand the functioning of the scheme and their obligations.[167]

Thus, despite having the initial effects of a carbon tax, the AUS CPM was unequivocally designed to create a new market which would eventually link to other independent carbon markets. The artificial creation of a new set of assets (ACUs) was accompanied by rules on how these assets were issued and would be traded from July 2015. As mentioned above, the asset nature of the ACUs was reinforced by a legal

---

National Experiences in Environmental Sustainability (Edward Elgar, 2013) 41. Also see World Bank Group and ECOFYS, above n 94.

[162] Garnaut, above n 101.

[163] Department of Climate Change, above n 82 (green paper), 163. The Green Paper stated that 'the Garnaut review considers the option of a transitional price control (fixing the price) for the period 2010–2012 but expresses a preference for an unconstrained system coupled with the early acceptance of European Union Emissions Trading Scheme allowances instead'.

[164] Department of Climate Change, above n 82 (white paper).

[165] Carbon Pollution Reduction Scheme Bill 2009 (Cth) s 89.

[166] National Greenhouse and Energy Reporting Act 2007 (Cth).

[167] Explanatory Memorandum, Clean Energy Bill 2011 (Cth) 30.

status of personal property.[168] Once the scheme transitioned into the flexible charge years, the carbon market would gradually work like any other ETS.

Following the repeal of the AUS CPM, on 12 October 2015 the Federal Government tabled the relevant legislative instruments in both Houses of Parliament to adopt a baseline and credit mechanism, also known as the 'safeguard mechanism'.[169] The safeguard mechanism was due to begin operation on 1 July 2016 and covers a small number of high emissions-intensive businesses.[170] The safeguard mechanism is outside the scope of this chapter. Nevertheless, it is relevant to note that the baselines will reflect the highest level of reported emissions for a facility over the historical period 2009–10 to 2013–14, which means that very little can be expected in terms of emissions reductions from this scheme.

With renewed expectations of reaching an international legally binding agreement for global GHG mitigation under the auspices of the UNFCCC by 2015, Australia is 'swimming against the tide'. The political contexts in this case are indicative of the need for public education on the current state of scientific knowledge, the economic impacts of climate change, as well as on the existing and future investment opportunities for a low carbon economy.

4. SMALL AND RESILIENT: THE NEW ZEALAND EMISSIONS TRADING SCHEME

The NZ ETS was the first national ETS to be implemented in the Australasian region, and is now the longest lasting. Despite changes in the Government's approach to climate change policy and New Zealand's opt-out from the second phase of the Kyoto Protocol, the NZ ETS remains the main policy instrument to achieve the country's national emissions reduction targets.

---

[168] CE Act, s 103 providing that 'a carbon unit is personal property and, subject to sections 105 and 106, is transmissible by assignment, by will and by devolution by operation of law'.

[169] National Greenhouse and Energy Reporting (Safeguard Mechanism) Rule 2015 (Cth); National Greenhouse and Energy Reporting Amendment (2015 Measures No. 2) Regulation 2015 (Cth); National Greenhouse and Energy Reporting (Audit) Amendment Determination 2015 (No. 1).

[170] Australian Government, *The Emissions Reduction Fund: The Safeguard Mechanism* Department of Environment <https://www.environment.gov.au/climate-change/emissions-reduction-fund/publications/factsheet-erf-safeguard-mechanism>.

The uniqueness of the NZ ETS legal framework makes it an interesting case for study. Some of the distinctive features of the scheme are the lack of a carbon cap in the first years of the ETS, the extent to which it has been open for linking with the global carbon market, the coverage of the forestry and transport sectors and, particularly important for this chapter, the details of its industry assistance.

The distinctiveness of the NZ ETS may be attributed to the country's comparatively small level of industrial activity,[171] its predominantly agricultural-based economy and the presence of hydropower energy generation. Therefore, the analysis of the NZ ETS may provide possible lessons for small, agriculture-based economies interested in adopting ETSs in the future.

As demonstrated below, the NZ ETS has been indirectly linked to the EU ETS from its commencement. The geographical proximity and volume of trade between New Zealand and Australia made the two jurisdictions obvious candidates for a future link between the NZ ETS and the AUS CPM. Nevertheless, the negotiations for a direct link were not successful prior to the infamous repeal of the latter.

4.1 Coverage

Different GHGs and sectors have been included under the NZ ETS in its various stages. Currently, the NZ ETS covers CO_2, HFCs, PFCs, SF_6, CH_4 and N_2O[172] emissions. The activities facing surrendering obligations under the NZ ETS are forestation, transport, stationary energy, waste, selected industry sectors (iron or steel, aluminium, clinker or burnt lime, glass and gold)[173] and the import, manufacture and/or use of specified synthetic GHGs.

A unique feature of the NZ ETS is that, upon its commencement on 1 January 2008, it covered CO_2 emissions resulting from the deforestation of pre-1990 forests.[174] Post-1989 forest landowners and, from 1 January 2013, pre-1990 offsetting forest landowners[175] were given the

---

171 See Environmental Protection Authority, '2014 Emissions Trading Scheme Report' (2014), reporting that on 30 June 2015 the NZ ETS included a total of 329 participants.
172 Liability is limited to reporting in relation of N_2O emissions.
173 Climate Change Response Act 2002 (NZ) Sch 3 Pt 4 sub-pt 1 (CCR Act).
174 Ibid., Sch 3 Pt 1.
175 Ibid., Sch 3 Pt 1A.

option to enter the scheme and become entitled to receive New Zealand Units (NZUs) from forestry removal activities.[176]

There are significant challenges to including land use, land-use change and forestry (LULUCF) activities in an emissions trading scheme, particularly in relation to the accountability of emissions and removals.[177] Under the NZ ETS, both post-1989 forest owners and pre-1990 offsetting forest landowners, who opted to join the scheme and receive NZUs from forestry removal activities, are liable for emissions in the event of either the harvesting or deforestation of those lands.

The NZ ETS is the only scheme of the three case studies which, since 1 July 2010, imposes liability on CO_2 emissions from the domestic transport sector.[178] The liability falls on liquid fossil fuel suppliers and includes emissions from the petrol, diesel, aviation gasoline, jet kerosene, light fuel oil and heavy fuel oil used in New Zealand.[179]

There are five large fuel importers and suppliers participating in the NZ ETS: BP, Caltex, Gulf, Mobil and Shell.[180] The emissions from fuel for exportation and the fuel used for international aviation and marine transport are exempt from the scheme.

The stationary energy sector, including the use of gas and coal in electricity generation and in the direct production of industrial heat as well as geothermal energy, joined on 1 July 2010 (with mandatory reporting from 1 January 2010). Liability falls on coal importers, coal miners, natural gas importers, natural gas miners, users of geothermal fluid for generating electricity or industrial heat, facilities that use the combustion of used oil or waste oil for generating electricity or industrial heat, the combustion of used tyres or waste for generating electricity or industrial heat, and petroleum refiners (minimum thresholds apply).[181]

---

[176]   Ibid. sch 4 pt 1.

[177]   Garnaut, above n 101.

[178]   CCR Act, Sch 3 Pt 2. Mandatory reporting by the transport sector has been in place since 1 January 2010.

[179]   Ibid.

[180]   Ministry for the Environment, New Zealand Government, *Liquid Fossil Fuel Suppliers' Obligations: Reporting Emissions and Surrendering NZUs* (21 December 2012) Climate Change Information <http://www.climatechange. govt.nz/emissions-trading-scheme/participating/fossil-fuels/obligations/>.

[181]   Ministry for the Environment, New Zealand Government, *Energy's Obligations: Reporting Emissions and Surrendering NZUs* (3 December 2012) Climate Change Information <http://www.climatechange.govt.nz/emissions-trading-scheme/participating/energy/obligations/index.html>.

From 1 January 2014 onwards, the use of crude oil or other liquid hydrocarbons, where any prescribed threshold is met, will join the NZ ETS.[182]

Selected industry sectors entered the scheme as mandatory participants from 1 July 2010 (mandatory reporting from 1 January 2010). These include the production of iron or steel, aluminium (resulting in the consumption of anodes or the production of anode effects), clinker or burnt lime (resulting in the calcination of limestone), glass (using soda ash) and gold (where emissions per annum exceed 5,000 tonnes).[183]

In 1 January 2013, importers and manufacturers of HFCs and PFCs, and large users of SF_6 joined the NZ ETS (mandatory reporting from 1 January 2011).[184] Those who export or remove HFCs or PFCs may voluntarily participate in the scheme. Importers of HFCs and PFCs in goods and motor vehicles are not covered by the NZ ETS. Instead, they will face a carbon price through a levy administered by the New Zealand Transport Agency (levy on motor vehicles) and the New Zealand Customs Service (levy on all other goods that contain HFCs and PFCs).[185]

Landfill operators were given the option to voluntarily report on methane emissions from 1 January 2011.[186] Mandatory reporting for disposal facilities[187] started from 1 January 2012, and from 1 January 2013 the sector joined the NZ ETS as mandatory participants with liability to surrender units. Small and remote landfills are exempt from surrender and reporting obligations under the ETS. However, this exemption is not available for new facilities.[188]

From January 2012, the agricultural sector has faced mandatory reporting obligations on its biological emissions. Biological emissions comprise of methane emissions from ruminant animals and animal waste and nitrous oxide emissions from urine, dung and nitrogen fertiliser. Participants with reporting obligations in the agricultural sector are meat processors, dairy processors, fertiliser manufacturers and importers, and live animal exporters.

---

[182]   CCR Act, Sch 3 Pt 3 sub-pt 2.
[183]   Ibid., Sch 3 Pt 4 sub-pt 1.
[184]   Ibid., sub-pt 2.
[185]   Ibid., Pt 7.
[186]   Ibid., s 218.
[187]   Ibid., Pt 1 s 4 (definition of 'disposal facility').
[188]   Ministry for the Environment, 'A Guide to Landfill Methane in the New Zealand Emissions Trading Scheme' (2011).

The agricultural sector was originally due to join the ETS with surrender obligations from 2015. However, the initial date has been reviewed, and there is currently no legislated date for when biological agricultural emissions will face obligations to surrender NZUs under the ETS. Nevertheless, the sector is eligible to receive free of cost NZUs as an assistance towards the increased electricity price due to the carbon price.

4.2 Emissions Cap

Originally, the legal framework of the NZ ETS did not provide for an emissions cap. The basis for emission reductions was New Zealand's commitments under the Kyoto Protocol first trading period and voluntary commitments under the UNFCCC after 2013.

During the first commitment period of the Kyoto Protocol, in order to keep within reduction targets, government 'backed' NZUs issued with an equivalent amount of approved international units, for example, through the retirement of NZ AAUs from the first Kyoto commitment period or other international units. That is, the scheme was linked to the Kyoto emissions trading scheme.

A review of the NZ ETS in 2012 altered several aspects of the scheme, including the introduction of a new power for the government to sell New Zealand units by auction and to set an overall cap.[189] The cap would be valid for a period of five years and may be reviewed periodically.[190]

Due to the crediting system for emissions abatement in the forestry sector, the cap may not limit the issue of forestry-NZUs above cap levels. However, where the overall allocation, including all types of NZUs, exceeds the cap, the issue of new NZUs for auctioning would not be allowed.[191]

4.3 Reporting and Surrendering Obligations and the Consequences of Non-Compliance

A person who carries out an activity covered by the NZ ETS is called a 'participant'. The Participants are liable to surrender NZUs to cover the emissions released as a result of such activity.[192] Similarly to the EU ETS, the compliance cycle is based on the calendar year.

---

[189]   CCR Act, s 30GA.
[190]   Ibid.
[191]   Ibid., s 30GA(5)(b).
[192]   Ibid. pt 4 s 54.

Participants must submit an emissions report by 31 March of the following calendar year in relation to an eligible financial year and are liable to surrender emissions permits or pay a fixed price of \$25 per tonne to cover their direct GHG emissions or the emissions associated with their products by 31 May.[193] Post-1989 forest landowners report their emissions or removals and surrender units once every five years.

A penalty applies in cases where a participant fails to surrender the required number of units. The penalty consists of the surrender of the number of NZUs required and the payment of an excess emissions penalty of NZ\$30 for each unit that the entity failed to surrender by the required date.[194] The excess emissions penalty may be reduced up to 100 per cent if the participant voluntarily discloses the failure to surrender or repay units before receiving a penalty notice.[195]

In the surrendering period of the NZ ETS,[196] the NZUs credited to the forestry sector were the predominant type of permit surrendered.[197] This changed dramatically from 2011 onwards, with the use of forestry units dropping to only 2.36 per cent in 2014, while 96.8 per cent of liability was met with international units, above all ERUs, and accounted for 73.87 per cent of all surrendered units in 2014.[198] With the regulations in 1 December 2014[199] prohibiting the use of Kyoto units after 30 May 2015, the NZU will soon regain its status as the principal unit of trade in the NZ ETS.

---

[193] Participants from the transport, energy and industry sectors initially benefited from a transitional measure which required them to surrender only one eligible emission unit for every two tonnes of CO_2-e produced and/or buy one NZU for a fixed price for every two tonnes of CO_2-e produced. The transitional arrangement was provided by s 222A(2) of the CCR Act and removed by provision of the Climate Change Response (Emissions Trading and Other Matters) Amendment Act 2012 (NZ) which repealed s 222A(2) of the CCR Act.

[194] CCR Act, s 134.

[195] Ibid., s 135.

[196] From 1 July 2010 until 31 December 2010.

[197] Ministry for the Environment, 'Report on The New Zealand Emissions Trading Scheme' (2011) 9. In 2010, 64 per cent of units surrendered (5,314,161 units) were NZUs given to foresters in the ETS Environmental Protection Authority, 'The New Zealand Emissions Trading Scheme'. ETS 2014 – Facts and figures' (2014).

[198] Environmental Protection Authority, 'The New Zealand Emissions Trading Scheme. ETS 2014 – Facts and figures' (2014).

[199] Climate Change (Unit Register) Amendment Regulations 2014 (NZ) SR 2014/364.

4.4 Linking with Other Schemes

The NZ ETS was initially open to a global carbon market. In its first years, a direct unilateral link with the Kyoto ETS and Kyoto units was in place. Participants under the NZ ETS were allowed to meet their liability with RMUs, ERUs and certain types of CERs. This created an indirect link between the EU ETS and the NZ ETS through the common use of Kyoto credits.[200]

There were no quantitative restrictions on the use of Kyoto credits. However, qualitative limits were set on the use of offset credits, including the exclusion of CERs derived from forestry and nuclear power projects, CERs and ERUs generated under CDM projects which destroy HFC-23 and N_2O (from 2013) and CERs and ERUs generated from selected large-scale hydropower projects.[201]

From 2011 onwards, there was a predominant use of international units to meet compliance under the NZ ETS, reaching 95 per cent of units surrendered in 2012.[202] As mentioned above, the lack of an emissions cap was counterbalanced by government 'backed' NZUs issued with an equivalent amount of approved international units, for example through the retirement of NZ AAUs from the first Kyoto commitment period.

During the 2012 Review process, the Government expressed concerns about the 'real risk that New Zealand will end up holding more international units than it requires to meet its international obligations',[203] with the inadvertent consequence of an unnecessary flow of funds offshore. In 2013 New Zealand announced that it would not participate in a second phase of the Kyoto Protocol. Following this decision, regulations were put in place to exclude Kyoto units from the NZ ETS. Participants had until 31 May 2015 to use these units.[204] From 1 June 2015, Kyoto units could no longer be surrendered to meet emissions

---

[200] For further details on the functioning of the indirect links between ETSs, see Chapter 3.

[201] Ministry for the Environment, *Regulations Banning the Use of Certain International Units in the ETS* (17 December 2012) Climate Change Information, New Zealand <http://www.climatechange.govt.nz/emissions-trading-scheme/building/regulatory-updates/restricting-cers.html>.

[202] Environmental Protection Authority, 'The New Zealand Emissions Trading Scheme. ETS 2012 – Facts and figures' (2012).

[203] Ministry for the Environment, 'Updating the New Zealand Emissions Trading Scheme' (Consultation document, New Zealand Government, April 2012) 7.

[204] Climate Change (Unit Register) Amendment Regulations 2014 (NZ) SR 2014/364.

obligations and NZUs became the predominant means to meet compliance under the NZ ETS.[205]

It is worth mentioning that a tentative direct linking between the AUS CPM and the NZ ETS was discussed between the two jurisdictions. However, the negotiations for the link were not as successful as between the EU ETS and the AUS CPM, due to fundamental discrepancies with other elements in the schemes, such as the methodology for cap-setting and the unlimited use of international units, as explained above.[206]

5. CONCLUSION

The experience of the EU ETS, particularly due to the price volatility of the EUAs, may well resemble a roller coaster. The primary reason for the far too low prices of the EUAs has been the challenges experienced by the EU ETS since its implementation in 2005, with surplus emissions permits and the prohibition against banking EUAs from the first trading period. Recent reforms are attempting to provide a much-needed stability to the scheme to enable it to reach its goal of promoting cost efficient emissions reductions.

As per the AUS CPM, Australia was the first – and to date the only – jurisdiction to discard a mandatory carbon price and move back from its main climate mitigation policy. However, the choice to include the AUS CPM in the case studies is valid despite its repeal in July 2014. The successful negotiation of a direct linking with the EU ETS, the phased approach to pricing and the likelihood of Australia re-implementing an ETS in the future are factors that confirm the relevance and suitability of the case study.

Finally, the NZ ETS is the most distinctive of the three schemes, significantly due to the singularity of New Zealand's economy. Despite changes in the Government's approaches to international climate change negotiations, the NZ ETS has proven to be resilient and stable. Considering its small size, the current approach of disconnecting from international carbon trading, in the short-term, is likely to further strengthen the effectiveness of the NZ ETS, with NZUs becoming the predominant unit for compliance under the scheme.

The three independent ETSs, in one way or another, interacted with each other. More importantly, the chapter focused on the distinctive

---

[205] Ibid.
[206] Australian Government, above n 140.

aspects that make each of the ETSs worthy of this investigation and provided a critical analysis of the different challenges of implementation faced by each scheme.

4. Reconsidering the eligibility thresholds for the free allocation of permits

1. INTRODUCTION

This chapter discusses how carbon leakage rates have been historically overestimated, giving way to a race for exemptions and compromises which have ultimately reduced the effectiveness of carbon mitigation policies.

The 'free allocation method' has been widely used as a measure to protect domestic industry from carbon leakage in the European Union Emissions Trading System (EU ETS), during the two years of Australia's Carbon Pricing Mechanism (AUS CPM) and in the New Zealand Emissions Trading Scheme (NZ ETS). In the three schemes, policy-makers have yielded to the pressures of industry groups and failed to respond adequately to the consistent conclusions of the independent economic modelling, and the *ex-post* studies examined below, which demonstrate that only a limited number of sectors are exposed to a significant risk of carbon leakage. Furthermore, the experience with the EU ETS demonstrates that certain sectors have been overcompensated for their emissions abatement efforts, originating windfall gains.

While the free allocation of permits remains a political condition for the implementation and preservation of ETSs, this chapter suggests that a review of the general thresholds to assess carbon leakage exposures is warranted, in order to improve the effectiveness and fairness of the ETSs. As best practice approaches, it is recommended the removal of the sole trade-exposure factor from the quantitative assessment in the EU ETS and increased stringency towards all the thresholds determining the emissions-intensities. The recent proposal for a Directive to amend the EU ETS[1] is partially in line with these recommendations, as further explained below.

---

[1] Proposal 2015/148 (COD) for a Directive of the European Parliament and of the Council Amending Directive 2003/87/EC to enhance cost-effective emission reductions and low-carbon investments [2015].

2. STORM IN A TEACUP: FROM MODELLING TO POLICY IN THE EUROPEAN UNION EMISSIONS TRADING SYSTEM[2]

The EU ETS is the longest surviving CO_2 scheme in the world, and has produced data that can be used to assess the actual impacts on industry in phases I and II. Therefore, at this stage, *ex-post* studies can be compared to *ex-ante* estimations.[3]

To understand the allocation system in the EU ETS, it is important to take a step back to the consultation process leading up to the adoption of the ETS Directive, when the European Commission expressed its preference for the periodic auctioning of permits to participants.[4] After the consultation process in 2002, it became clear that a 'blanket' free allocation of permits was a political condition to the implementation of the ETS.[5] As a result, the ETS Directive provided that at least 95 per cent of the European Union Allowances (EUAs) issued would be allocated free of cost in phase I, and that at least 90 per cent of the EUAs issued would be grandfathered in the second trading period.[6]

---

[2]   An early version of the following analysis has been published in Elena Aydos, 'Levelling the Playing Field or Playing on Unlevel Fields: The Industry Assistance Framework Under The European Union ETS, The New Zealand ETS, And Australia's CPM' In Larry Kreiser et al (eds), *Market Based Instruments: National Experiences In Environmental Sustainability*, Critical Issues In Environmental Taxation (Edward Elgar Publishing, 2013) Vol XIII, 135.

[3]   Modelling conducted before the introduction and at the early stages of a new policy, such as the introduction of an ETS, are known as *ex-ante* studies, while *ex-post* research consists of empirical analysis of data collected after implementation.

[4]   European Commission, 'Green Paper on Greenhouse Gas Emissions Trading within the European Union' (2000) 49, 18.

[5]   Denny Ellerman, Frank Convery and Christian De Perthuis, *Pricing Carbon: the European Union Emissions Trading Scheme* (Frank J. Convery, Christian de Perthuis and Emilie Alberola trans, Cambridge University Press, 2010) 42, 61.

[6]   Directive 2009/29/EC of the European Parliament and of the Council of 23 April 2009 Amending Directive 2003/87/EC so as to improve and extend the greenhouse gas emission allowance trading scheme of the Community [2009] OJ L 140/63 (ETS Directive), art 10. For further details on the allocation system during phases I and II, see Chapter 5.

Amendments to the ETS Directive in 2009 provided for a reform in the allocation methodology.[7] The decentralised National Allocation Plans were replaced by a Community-wide emissions cap and fully-harmonised rules for the allocation of EUAs.[8] From the third trading period onwards, auctioning is gradually implemented until it becomes the default system for the allocation of EUAs, which was expected to happen by 2027.[9]

2.1 Carbon Leakage Assessment

In contrast to the assessments from the early economic modelling,[10] there has been no indication of carbon leakage during the first two trading periods of the EU ETS, even for those sectors deemed to be highly emissions-intensive and trade-exposed. For example, there is no evidence of relevant carbon leakage in the steel, cement, aluminium and refineries sectors in the EU between 2005 and 2007.[11]

Chan, Li and Zhang focused on the impact of the EU ETS on the costs, employment and turnover of the power, cement, iron and steel sectors in the EU ETS first trading period and early in the second trading period

---

[7] Directive 2009/29/EC of the European Parliament and of the Council of 23 April 2009 Amending Directive 2003/87/EC so as to improve and extend the greenhouse gas emission allowance trading scheme of the Community [2009] OJ L 140/63.

[8] ETS Directive, art 10a(1).

[9] Ibid., art 10(1).

[10] See, e.g., Paul M. Bernstein, W. David Montgomery and Thomas F. Rutherford, 'Global Impacts of the Kyoto Agreement: Results from the MS-MRT Model' (1999) 21 *Resource and Energy Economics* 375; Mustafa H. Babiker, 'Climate Change Policy, Market Structure, and Carbon Leakage' (2005) 65 *Journal of International Economics* 421; Alan S. Manne and Richard G. Richels, 'The Kyoto Protocol: A Cost-Effective Strategy for Meeting Environmental Objectives?' (1998); Sergey V. Paltsev, 'The Kyoto Protocol: Regional and Sectoral Contributions to the Carbon Leakage' (2001) 22(4) *The Energy Journal* 53.

[11] Julia Reinaud, 'Issues Behind Competitiveness and Carbon Leakage: Focus on Heavy Industry' (IEA; OECD, 2008) 10. However, see Johanna Arlinghaus, 'Impacts of Carbon Prices on Indicators of Competitiveness: A Review of Empirical Findings' (OECD, 2015) 20 for a critique of the limitations of Reinaud's analysis, which is based on aggregate data and does not distinguish the effects of the EU ETS from other trends and shocks that might have occurred at the same time.

(2001–09).[12] The research compared participant and non-participant firms of similar sizes within the same industry sectors. They concluded that the EU ETS did not significantly impact on the unit material costs, employment and turnover in the cement, iron and steel sectors, pointing out the unlikeliness of a shift of production elsewhere.[13] Indeed, the analysis demonstrated that the 'EU ETS is neither detrimental nor profitable for the cement industry' and that there is little evidence to support carbon leakage for the sector.[14]

Branger, Quirion and Chevallier assessed the incidences of leakage in the short-term (operational leakage) using data from phases I and II of the EU ETS. The research concluded that 'net imports of cement and steel have been driven by domestic and foreign demand but not by the CO_2 allowance price, falsifying the claim that the ETS has generated leakage, at least in the short run'.[15] Yet, these sectors received significant assistance through the free allocation of permits during phases I and II of the EU ETS.[16]

More recently, Sartor assessed the empirical evidence of carbon leakage on the EU primary aluminium industry sector between 2005 and the second half of 2011.[17] The EU primary aluminium industry was not directly liable under the EU ETS until 2013, although, being a highly electricity-intensive sector, it faced the indirect carbon costs caused by the increase in electricity costs, while not being eligible to receive a free allocation of EUAs.

The sector suffered from a steady rise in net imports from non-EU ETS countries meeting the EU demand in a period coinciding with the first six years of the EU ETS. However, the empirical data demonstrates that the impacts of an indirect carbon cost on the primary aluminium industry have been less than predicted by the *ex-ante* literature.[18] Other

---

[12]   Hei Sing (Ron) Chan, Shanjun Li and Fan Zhang, 'Firm Competitiveness and the European Union Emissions Trading Scheme' (The World Bank: Europe and Central Asia Region, 2013) 19–23.

[13]   Ibid.

[14]   Ibid., 19.

[15]   Frederic Branger, Philippe Quirion and Julien Chevallier, 'Carbon Leakage and Competitiveness of Cement and Steel Industries under the EU ETS: Much Ado About Nothing' (CIRED, 2013) 3.

[16]   For further information on the free allocation in phases I and II of the EU ETS, see Chapters 5 and 6.

[17]   Oliver Sartor, 'Carbon Leakage in the Primary Aluminium Sector: What evidence after 6½ years of the EU ETS?' (2012) <http://ssrn.com/abstract=2205516>.

[18]   Ibid.

factors seem to have affected the industry more significantly than the rise in the carbon cost, such as the effects of the global financial crisis and the phasing-out of long-term power-supply contracting in EU countries.[19]

The discrepancies between the *ex-ante* and *ex-post* results in phases I and II of the EU ETS might be partially explained by the different assumptions and data used in the early research, resulting in more or less realistic models.[20] It has been suggested that the lack of competitiveness and/or carbon leakage impacts are due to the fact that participants received most of the permits necessary to meet their liabilities free of cost, with some sectors even receiving an over-allocation of permits.[21] However, an *ex-post* study compared firms in Germany who were over-allocated permits with firms that received less than the necessary amount to meet compliance, and concluded that the reduced level of free allocation did not have a significant impact on the competitiveness of the latter.[22] In other words, there is evidence that the free allocation system adopted in the scheme does not completely explain the absence of competitiveness effects.[23]

Even where leakage rates are insignificant, unjustified concerns about losses of competitiveness still prevail, circumstances known as 'false trade-off situations'.[24] Indeed, despite the gradual adoption of auctioning as the default allocation system, sectors deemed to be EITE will continue to receive 100 per cent assistance at least until 2020.[25] The advantages of being identified as an EITE sector are unmistakable.

---

[19]   Ibid., 2.

[20]   Susanne Dröge and Simone Cooper, 'Tackling Leakage in a World of Unequal Carbon Prices: A Study for the Greens/EFA Group' (Climate Strategies, 2010) 28, have argued that several sectors have been deemed to be exposed to carbon leakage due to inadequate choice or indicators and/or too low thresholds in the assessment.

[21]   See, e.g., Reinaud, above n 11, 38.

[22]   Niels Anger and Ulrich Oberndorfer, 'Firm Performance and Employment in the EU Emissions Trading Scheme: An Empirical Assessment for Germany' (2008) 36 *Energy Policy* 12.

[23]   Arlinghaus, above n 11, 17.

[24]   OECD, 'Linkages Between Environmental Policy and Competitiveness' (OECD, 2010) <http://www.oecd-ilibrary.org/environment/linkages-between-environmental-policy-and-competitiveness_218446820583>39, 36, 32.

[25]   Chapter 5 analyses in detail the Community-wide harmonized rules for free allocation of permits in the EU ETS third trading period.

2.2 The EU ETS First Carbon Leakage List

According to the amended ETS Directive, the European Commission undertakes its own impact assessment in order to identify whether a sector or subsector is at risk of carbon leakage.[26] Regrettably, the thresholds for defining EITE sectors in the EU ETS were largely affected by lobbying, both from industries and Member States.[27] Wettestad reported on the 'frenetic lobbying' during late 2007 and early 2008, pointing out that the energy-intensive industries were among the most active and intense industrial actors in the process that led to the definition of the thresholds and the assistance levels to emissions-intensive and/or trade-exposed sectors.[28]

There are three alternative quantitative criteria to determine whether a sector or subsector is exposed to carbon leakage. In addition, the Directive also provides that a qualitative analysis may identify a sector or subsector as vulnerable to carbon leakage, for example, where trade exposure or direct and indirect cost increase rates are close to one of the quantitative thresholds:[29]

(i)   emissions-intensity and trade-exposure threshold: where the additional direct and indirect production costs correspond to at least 5 per cent of the gross value added *and* a trade-intensity above 10 per cent;[30] or

(ii)   sole emissions-intensity threshold: where the additional direct and indirect production costs are at least 30 per cent of gross value added;[31] or

(iii) sole trade-exposure threshold: where activities have a trade-intensity above 30 per cent;[32]

(iv)   trade-intensity for the purposes of (i) and (iii) is defined as the ratio between the total value of the exports to third countries plus the value of the imports from third countries and the total market size

---

[26]   ETS Directive, art 10a (15)–(17).

[27]   Dröge and Cooper, above n 20, 14.

[28]   Jorgen Wettestad, 'EU Energy-Intensive Industries and Emission Trading: Losers Becoming Winners?' (2009) 19(5) *Environmental Policy and Governance* 309, 316.

[29]   ETS Directive, art 10a (15)–(17). Eligibility criteria for new entrants are discussed in Chapter 5.

[30]   Ibid., art 10a(15).

[31]   Ibid., art 10a(16)(a).

[32]   Ibid., art 10a(16)(b).

for the Community (annual turnover plus total imports from third countries).[33]

The European Commission must assess sectors and subsectors deemed to be exposed to a risk of carbon leakage according to the harmonised thresholds and publish the results in a list that is valid for five years. The European Commission has the autonomy to determine the average carbon price that will be used in the assessment.[34]

In December 2009, the European Commission published the first official carbon leakage list, applicable to 2013 and 2014. The list identified 164 sectors and subsectors (out of the total of 258 manufacturing sectors) deemed to be at significant risk of carbon leakage.[35]

2.2.1 Criticisms of the EU ETS carbon leakage list

The European Commission has been openly criticised for having assumed a carbon price of €30/t CO_2, which was considerably above average prices for EUAs during the first two trading periods, and very optimistic estimates of CO_2 prices for the third trading period.[36] Sandbag also demonstrated that in the third trading period of the EU ETS, almost all the manufacturing sectors were 'seeking to qualify for the carbon leakage list and, in some cases, exploiting the rules governing partial cessation'.[37]

In reality, the European Commission list identified an excessive number of activities as being at risk of carbon leakage. Furthermore, while formally only 60 per cent of the ETS sectors are deemed to be at risk of carbon leakage, in practice around 99.55 per cent of ETS activities belong to these sectors and, as such, have been identified as eligible to receive industry assistance.[38] This practice is inconsistent with most economic modelling which has predicted significant leakage rates for

---

[33]   Ibid., art 10a(15)(b) and (16)(b).

[34]   Ibid., art 10a(14).

[35]   Commission Decision 2010/2/EU of 24 December 2014 Determining, Pursuant to Directive 2003/87/EC of the European Parliament and of the Council, a List of Sectors and Subsectors which are Deemed to be Exposed to a Significant Risk of Carbon Leakage, OJ L 1/236.

[36]   Sandbag, 'Slaying the Dragon: Vanquish the Surplus and Rescue the ETS' (Sandbag, 2014) 44.

[37]   Ibid., 44, 32–3.

[38]   Ibid., 36.

only a selected number of sectors/subsectors[39] and, even more significantly, with the *ex-post* studies reviewed in this chapter, which have not confirmed significant competitiveness issues in phases I and II of the EU ETS.

2.2.2 The Cambridge Econometrics assessment of carbon leakage

In 2010, Cambridge Econometrics et al undertook a comprehensive analysis of carbon leakage exposures in relation to sectors liable under the EU ETS. The report concluded that the EC criteria were too broad and included sectors which were not genuinely at risk of carbon leakage.[40] The eligibility criteria adopted by the EU ETS for industry assistance in its 2009 impact assessment[41] was considered robust by Cambridge Econometrics et al, to the extent that additional quantitative criteria could not be firmly recommended.[42] However, the way in which the criteria were applied allowed for the identification of sectors which

---

[39]   See, e.g., Reinaud, above n 11; Susanne Dröge et al, 'Tackling Leakage in a World of Unequal Carbon Prices' (Climate Strategies, 2009) 10; 'EU ETS impacts on profitability and trade: a sector by sector analysis' (Carbon Trust, 2008); Damien Demailly and Philippe Quirion, 'Leakage from Climate Policies and Border-Tax Adjustment: Lessons from a Geographic Model of the Cement Industry' (2005) 47. Demailly and Quirion developed an economic model which, assuming that the representation of international trade was essential to assess competitiveness and carbon leakage, also explicitly accounted for transportation costs. The authors predicted a leakage rate of approximately 20 per cent for the cement sector, based on a carbon price of 15 euros per tonne. Also see Damien Demailly and Philippe Quirion, 'European Emission Trading Scheme and competitiveness: a case study on the iron and steel industry' (2008) 30 *Energy Economics* 2009. Demailly and Quirion estimated small leakage rates for the iron and steel sectors, considered to be both highly emissions-intensive and relatively trade-exposed, supporting a more stringent allocation system for phase II. Also see Terry Barker et al, 'Carbon Leakage from Unilateral Environmental Tax Reforms in Europe, 1995–2005' (2007) 35 *Energy Policy* 6281. Barker et al investigated carbon leakage from unilateral environmental tax reforms other than the EU ETS in six EU Members, concluding that carbon leakage rates were very small and in some cases negative due to technology spillover effects.

[40]   Cambridge Econometrics, Climate Strategies and Entec, 'Assessment of the Degree of Carbon Leakage in Light of an International Agreement on Climate Change: A Report for the Department of Energy and Climate Change' (2010).

[41]   Commission Decision 2010/2/EU, above n 35.

[42]   As explained above, sectors meeting any one of the following thresholds in the European Commission's assessment are deemed to be at risk of leakage: (i) increase in production costs above 5 per cent of gross value added, and extra-EU trade intensity above 10 per cent; (ii) increase in production costs

are not genuinely at risk of carbon leakage. This assessment confirmed previous modelling and concluded that only a small number of sectors which are both highly carbon-intensive and highly trade-exposed are significantly at risk of carbon leakage.[43] In other words, sectors with low carbon costs or low levels of trade intensity face low risks of carbon leakage and should not be eligible for the assistance to EITE sectors.

The Cambridge Econometrics report demonstrated that activities with low carbon costs (below 5 per cent of gross value added) and high trade intensities are less vulnerable, and that trade-exposure alone is not a statistically significant criterion. However, in practice, the application of the sole trade-exposure threshold (trade-intensity above 30 per cent) resulted in the inclusion of 117 sectors.[44]

Two sectors were included based on the sole emissions-intensity threshold, i.e., the manufacture of cement and lime,[45] while 27 sectors met the combined emissions-intensity and trade-exposure threshold described above.[46] That is, of the 164 sectors, nearly 120 sectors in the Commission's 2010 carbon leakage list might not have been genuinely at risk of carbon leakage based on the Cambridge Econometrics criteria.

2.3   The EU ETS Second Carbon Leakage List

In early 2013, a robust assessment of carbon leakage over phases I and II was commissioned by the European Commission in preparation for a new carbon leakage list to be adopted in 2014, for the period of 2015 to 2019.[47] ECORYS et al undertook the research, focusing on energy-intensive sectors such as iron, steel, non-ferrous metals, refineries, cement, lime, pulp and paper. The study did not detect the occurrence of carbon leakage between 2005 and 2012.[48]

In spite of this, the second carbon leakage list adopted by the European Commission was once again liberal, representing nearly 4 billion CO_2

---

above 30 per cent of gross value added; and (iii) extra-EU trade intensity above 30 per cent. These factors were calculated at a €30/t carbon price.

[43]   Cambridge Econometrics, Climate Strategies and Entec, above n 40.

[44]   Commission Decision 2010/2/EU, annex 1(1.4).

[45]   Ibid., annex 1(1.3). See Chapter 6 for an analysis of the sole emissions-intensity threshold as a prohibited subsidy.

[46]   Ibid., annex 1 (1.1).

[47]   Hans Bolscher et al, 'Carbon Leakage Evidence Project: Factsheets for Selected Sectors' (ECORYS, Öko-Institut, Cambridge Econometrics and TNO, 2013).

[48]   Ibid.

emission allowances to be allocated for free up to 2020.[49] From the 245 sectors and 24 subsectors assessed, 175 sectors were deemed to be exposed to a significant risk of carbon leakage.

Robust indicia support the conclusion that the list overestimates the future carbon leakage risk. The European Commission maintained the assumption of a carbon cost of €30/t CO_2, which is substantially above the average price recorded in phases I and II, and is likely to be superior to the average carbon price in the third trading period. Sandbag estimates that nearly 99.55 per cent of manufacturing activities have been defined as carbon leakage exposed and will be eligible to receive 100 per cent of their allowances free of charge.[50]

The Cambridge Econometrics report provided sound evidence to support the elimination of the sole trade-exposure threshold as an eligibility criterion to receive assistance under the EU ETS. The amendment of the ETS Directive accordingly would result in around 120 activities being removed from the EITE list for the following years.[51]

Installations which are not identified as at risk of carbon leakage will continue to receive a percentage of allowances (EUAs) free of charge in phase III as a transitional assistance measure, which is currently provided to phase out by 2027.[52] However, a proposal for an amendment of the ETS Directive is aiming at removing the provision for the phasing out of free allocation by 2027 and maintaining a minimum assistance level to non-EITE sectors of at least 30 per cent until 2030.

2.4 Lessons from Carbon Leakage Assessment in the EU ETS

The lessons from the data at this point are that carbon leakage risks remain real for only a few sectors, which might require the assistance of leakage-mitigating measures. Therefore, the identification of a considerable number of sectors as being exposed to carbon leakage in the past

---

[49] Commission Decision 2014/746/EU of 27 October 2014 Determining, Pursuant to Directive 2003/87/EC of the European Parliament and of the Council, a List of Sectors and Subsectors which are Deemed to be Exposed to a Significant Risk of Carbon Leakage, for the Period 2015 to 2019 [2014] OJ L 308/114.

[50] Sandbag, above n 36.

[51] Reinaud, above n 11, 43. Reinaud explained that 'yesterday may be a poor indication of tomorrow's industry structure and continuous analysis of which factors may have caused what changes in industrial operations on a global basis is needed if governments seek to assess the reality of carbon leakage'.

[52] ETS Directive, art 10a(11).

two official lists by the European Commission is questionable, suggesting that a review of the eligibility assessment criteria should be undertaken.

Any changes to the qualitative thresholds to determine the eligibility for assistance[53] can only take place through the amendment of the ETS Directive. The European Commission seems to have reflected on the lessons above and a proposal for a Directive to amend the ETS Directive and revise the EU ETS after 2020 was presented by the European Commission on 15 July 2015.[54]

The proposed Directive removes the sole trade-exposure and sole emissions-intensity thresholds.[55] It maintains two thresholds which combine emissions-intensity and trade-exposure, where the emissions-intensity is being measured by the amount of CO_2-e (in kilograms) divided by the gross value added, removing the calculation of increased production costs based on an assumption of the EUA prices.[56] The data analysed above supports the changes in thresholds, excluding the sole emissions-intensity and sole trade-exposure thresholds, with one important caveat. The proposed Directive provides a guarantee to all sectors to be excluded from the carbon leakage list after 2020 of a minimum 30 per cent free allocation until at least 2030. While this compromise may be necessary for the political acceptability of the proposal, the analysis above suggests that minimum levels of a 30 per cent free allocation to non-EITE sectors until 2030 may not be consistent with the economic analyses of these sectors.

3. INDUSTRY ASSISTANCE IN THE AUS CPM AND CARBON LEAKAGE ASSESSMENT

The AUS CPM provided for free of cost allocation of Australian Carbon Units (ACUs) exclusively to the EITE sectors and electricity generators.[57] The eligibility criteria for free allocation of ACUs to EITE sectors was

---

[53] These are set by the ETS Directive.
[54] Proposal 2015/148 (COD), above n 1, 1.
[55] Ibid., 1, art 1(6).
[56] Ibid., 1, art 1(6)(1).
[57] Further details on the allocation system under the AUS CPM and the specific eligibility criteria for new entrants are discussed in Chapter 5.

based on the combined thresholds for emissions-intensity and trade-exposure,[58] which is consistent with the best practice approach suggested in this thesis.

The trade-exposure factor was assessed either through a quantitative threshold or a qualitative test. The quantitative threshold determined that activities must have a trade-intensity of greater than 10 per cent in any one of the years 2004–05, 2005–06, 2006–07 or 2007–08.[59] Similarly to the EU ETS criteria, trade-intensity was measured by a ratio of the value of imports and exports to the value of domestic production.

The Government could also adopt a qualitative approach to assess an activity's trade exposure. The qualitative assessment could be implemented where the quantitative trade data is not available for activities, or was not considered accurate by the Government, or where the annual trade share was below the 10 per cent threshold and entities conducting the activity demonstrated a lack of capacity to pass through costs due to the 'potential for international competition'.

The emissions-intensity assessment is based on the weighted average emissions per million dollars of revenue or per million dollars of value added.[60] There are two categories of eligibility, i.e., moderately emissions-intensive and highly emissions-intensive. Moderately emissions-intensive activities have weighted average emissions intensities of between 1,000 tonnes and 1999 tonnes CO_2-e/\$m revenue or between 3,000 tonnes and 5,999 tonnes CO_2-e/\$m value added. Highly emissions-intensive activities have weighted average emissions intensities of at least 2,000 tonnes CO_2-e/\$m revenue or 6,000 tonnes CO_2-e/\$m value added.[61]

---

[58]   Clean Energy Act 2011 (Cth) (*CE Act*) Pt 7.

[59]   Commonwealth of Australia, 'Strong Growth, Low Pollution: Modelling a Carbon Price' (2011). For this purpose, the Government considered data from the Australian Bureau of Statistics International Merchandise Trade Data (2004–05 to 2007–08) in conjunction with domestic production data supplied by firms in the industry.

[60]   The weighted average emissions per unit of product is calculated by dividing the sum of the total emissions from all entities conducting the activity in the relevant time periods by the total output of the product as defined in the activity definition. Value added is measured by a proxy consisting of the revenue less the cost of the most significant non-labour, non-capital inputs. The formula uses the estimates of the weighted average emissions per unit of product for the years 2006–07 to 2007–08 combined with estimates of the revenue (or value added) per unit of product from 2004–05 to the first half of 2008–09. See Commonwealth of Australia, ibid., 22.

[61]   Department of Climate Change, 'Carbon Pollution Reduction Scheme: Green Paper' (2008) 28. The thresholds were based on the policy framework

3.1   Comparing Free Allocation in the AUS CPM and in the EU ETS

Denne compared the EU ETS and the AUS CPM emissions-intensity thresholds in terms of an equivalent percentage of gross value added or of revenue.[62] Assuming a standard emission price of €20/t, the EU system adopts a threshold of approximately 3.3 per cent of gross value added or 1.1 per cent of revenue, while the Australian thresholds ranged between 8.6 per cent (medium emissions-intensive) and 17.1 per cent (highly emissions-intensive) of gross value added or 2.9 per cent (medium emissions-intensive) and 5.7 per cent (highly emissions-intensive) of revenue.

In other words, had the EU emissions-intensity thresholds been adopted by the AUS CPM, a much larger set of industries would have been considered eligible to receive free of cost ACUs. Furthermore, if the sole trade-exposure threshold had been adopted, at least 39 industry sectors would be identified as carbon leakage exposed.[63] Instead, Regulations identified 24 activities as highly emissions-intensive and

---

originally developed for the CPRS, except that the original Government proposal measured emissions-intensity based on weighted average emissions per million dollars of revenue, with no option to use the value added data. The Green Paper criticised the 'value added' metric as it may 'exhibit considerable variability within sectors and over time because of variations in the business cycle and the relative economic performance of entities'. The Government also mentioned that 'calculating value added requires a large amount of information on output levels, product prices, input costs and wages costs, as well as a significant number of additional items' (at 309). Furthermore, under the minimum emissions-intensity threshold to be eligible to receive assistance was more stringent, at 1,500t CO_2-e/$ million revenue. The political pressure during the consultation process was successful in reducing the cut-in point for activities to be classified as medium emissions-intensive to 1,000t CO_2-e/$ million revenue; as well as in adding to the threshold the alternative for qualification based on value added. The new, less stringent thresholds, after the CPRS failed to obtain the required parliamentary support, were then adopted to establish the eligibility of activities with respect to the assistance provided under the Renewable Energy Target scheme and assistance to the EITE sectors under the Carbon Pricing Mechanism.

[62]   Tim Denne, 'Impacts of the NZ ETS on Emissions Leakage: Final Report' (COVEC, 2011) 10, 18.

[63]   Brian Fisher, Anna Matysek and Paul Newton, 'The CPRS and the European Union Emissions Trading Scheme: The Trade Intensity of Australian Industry Sectors' (BAEconomics, 2009) 10.

trade-exposed, and seven activities as medium emissions-intensive and trade-exposed.[64]

3.2 Carbon Leakage Assessment in the AUS CPM

The short period of the scheme's existence did not allow for *ex-post* studies on the impacts of the AUS CPM to industry.[65] In terms of *ex-ante* assessments, in 2011 the Australian Government released the Treasury modelling[66] and update[67] that concluded that a carbon price would not have severe impacts on the economy.[68]

The Treasury modelling noted that more than 90 per cent of the workforce accounted for less than 10 per cent of emissions. Therefore, the broad sectoral effects were predicted to be small compared to other variations, such as productivity, the terms of trade or changing tastes.[69]

The carbon price was estimated to cause a 10 per cent increase in electricity prices, driving significant changes to the energy sector which would make renewable energy more competitive relative to coal.[70] This being so, the Treasury modelling concluded that the impacts on manufacturing output would be small, with some sectors in the economy actually benefiting from the carbon price.[71] While the Treasury modelling stated that some emissions-intensive sectors would require transitional assistance, it did not focus on specific sectors/subsectors of the economy in

---

[64]　Clean Energy Regulations 2011 (Cth) s 401.

[65]　See Marianna O'Gorman and Frank Jotzo, 'Impact of the Carbon Price on Australia's Electricity Demand, Supply and Emissions' (Centre for Climate Economic & Policy, 2014) on the impacts to the electricity sector, which accounted for the greatest share of the emissions covered under the scheme. The research concluded that the AUS CPM did not have unexpected impacts to the sector.

[66]　Commonwealth of Australia, above n 59.

[67]　Ibid.

[68]　The original assumed initial carbon price in the Treasury Modelling was A\$20/t CO_2-e growing at five per cent per year plus inflation, which was slightly lower than the actual carbon price that was initially fixed at A\$23/tCO_2-e. Nevertheless, the Clean Energy legislation provided for an increase of only 2.5 per cent per year. The modelling also predicted a flexible carbon price starting at A\$29/tCO_2-e which would probably have been above the actual carbon price during the flexible period due to the negotiated linking with the EU ETS from 2015 onwards.

[69]　Commonwealth of Australia, above n 59, 85.

[70]　Also see ibid., 96. The estimates were confirmed in the modelling update.

[71]　Ibid., 113. Sectors likely to be impacted included iron and steel production, alumina and aluminium refining. Less emissions-intensive sectors such as

order to inform the appropriate levels of assistance. Modelling on a sectoral level was undertaken in relation to specific sectors/subsectors by the Grattan Institute, as discussed below.

3.3 The Grattan Report on Carbon Leakage and the Political Reality of Industry's Reaction to the CPM

Despite the more stringent eligibility thresholds compared to the EU ETS, independent research demonstrated that the industry assistance under the AUS CPM was still excessive. In 2011, the Grattan Institute analysed the likely impacts of a carbon price of A$23 rising to A$40 on a number of industry sectors in Australia.[72] It concluded that the industry support in the form of the free allocation of permits to the liquefied natural gas (LNG), coal mining and steel industries was unjustified and costly, putting at risk the environmental efficiency of the scheme and unjustifiably increasing the general costs of carbon reduction elsewhere in the economy, including non-participant sectors and households.[73]

While Don Voelte, CEO of the Australian-owned oil and gas producer Woodside, proclaimed that 'gas is good and Australia is penalising it. We don't get it',[74] the Grattan report concluded that even a carbon price of A$40[75] would neither impact on investment in the LNG sector nor reduce the productivity in existing facilities. The report demonstrated that the transitional assistance to the LNG industry, costing approximately $4 billion between 2012 and 2020, was unjustified as the sector would not be at risk of carbon leakage even under a full carbon price.[76]

The Grattan Institute also assessed that the carbon price would be unlikely to affect the financial viability of coal mines in Australia. Furthermore, the transitional assistance to be provided by the Government may inhibit the replacement of high emissions mines by others with lower emissions.[77]

---

printing textiles, clothing and footwear; motor vehicle and part manufacturing; and food manufacturing, would likely become more competitive with the carbon pricing.

[72] Tony Wood and Tristan Edis, 'New Protectionism under carbon pricing: case studies of LNG, coal mining and steel sectors' (Grattan Institute, 2011) 33.

[73] Ibid.

[74] Alexandra Kirk, *Woodside wants LNG Exempt from Carbon Tax* (11 April 2011) ABC News <http://www.abc.net.au/am/content/2011/s3187564.htm>.

[75] This amount is considerably higher than the initial carbon price of A$23/tCO$_2$-e and above the estimated average carbon price for 2020.

[76] Wood and Edis, above n 72.

[77] Ibid., 25.

In April 2011, BlueScope Steel's CEO, Paul O'Malley, stressed that a carbon tax would 'do irreparable damage to the Australian steel industry' and would only be appropriate 'when China, the United States, Japan, Korea, India, Russia, Brazil and others are paying a similar tax'.[78] According to the Grattan Institute, steel production would be vulnerable to a carbon price, although it was not clear whether carbon leakage would occur.[79] Nevertheless, the levels of assistance proposed by the government were excessive (rates were far above the ideal levels) and inappropriate as the best policy would have been the use of border adjustments.[80]

Indeed, the Grattan Institute concluded that the levels of free allocation would generate windfall gains to the steel producers and border adjustments would be a more effective approach to prevent carbon leakage.[81] Even where the free allocation policy was considered adequate, the proposed rates of assistance would protect the steel sector beyond the scope of the Jobs and Competitiveness Program, preventing structural adjustments which would otherwise occur due to the shifts in global steel prices and exchange rates.[82]

While the manufacturing sector was engaged in heavy lobbying to secure protection from the impacts of the carbon price, asserting that 'the Australian carbon tax will hold back export industries, investment and jobs growth',[83] 'non-protected' segments of the economy are often unaware of the distributional consequences of lowering the thresholds of the assistance to EITE industries, which explains the lack of representation against it.[84]

---

[78]   Lauren Wilson, 'Steel Giants Back Howes Over Carbon Tax', *The Australian* (Canberra), 16 April 2011 2011 <http://www.theaustralian.com.au/news/nation/steel-giants-back-howes-over-carbon-tax/story-e6frg6nf-1226039943 407>.

[79]   Wood and Edis, above n 72. The Grattan Institute noted that the profitability of the Australian steel industry had declined over the past years and it may continue declining due to shifts in international steel prices rather than exclusively due to the carbon pricing.

[80]   Ibid.

[81]   Ibid., 3, 27.

[82]   Ibid., 27.

[83]   Rio Tinto, 'Australian Carbon Tax will Hold Back Export Industries, Investment and Jobs Growth' (10 July 2011) Rio Tinto <http://www.riotinto.com/media/media-releases-237_1156.aspx>.

[84]   Ross Garnaut, *The Garnaut Climate Change Review: Final Report* (Cambridge University Press, 2008) 58, 349.

4. CARBON LEAKAGE ASSESSMENT AND INDUSTRY ASSISTANCE IN NEW ZEALAND

In March 2010, the New Zealand Ministry of Economic Development released an Occasional Paper on the impact of emissions pricing on the manufacturing sectors.[85] It concluded that mega and large emitters from the food, beverage and tobacco sectors, petroleum, coal and chemicals sectors, and machinery and equipment sectors, where they are involved in export activities, were the most carbon leakage exposed.[86] Furthermore, the Occasional Paper also concluded that the trade exposure factor is a 'poor predictor of the effects on output'. The authors demonstrated that the overall trade exposure may not be a good guide to measure the impacts of a carbon price on products' gross output.[87]

In a separate research paper, Numan-Parsons, Iyer and Bartleet compared the relative impacts of a carbon price on the manufacturing industry in terms of the quantity of the GDP that is at stake in New Zealand against the impacts on industries located in the US, the EU, the UK, Australia, Germany and the Netherlands.[88] In the analysis, the food processing[89] and beverage industries in New Zealand are featured as being materially at risk of carbon leakage.[90] Given New Zealand's

---

[85]   Matthew Bartleet et al, 'Impact of Emissions Pricing on New Zealand Manufacturing: A Short-Run Analysis' (2010) 35.

[86]   Ibid., 76. This conclusion is in line with the Cambridge Econometrics report mentioned above, which proved that only when both a sector's trade intensity and carbon cost are moderate to high is this sector deemed to be exposed to carbon leakage.

[87]   Ibid., 61.

[88]   Elisabeth Numan-Parsons, Kris Iyer and Matthew Bartleet, 'The Surprising Vulnerability of New Zealand Manufacturing to CO2 Emissions Pricing: The Lessons of an International Comparison' (2010) 40(3) *Economic Analysis and Policy* 313.

[89]   Roughly two-thirds of New Zealand exports pertain to primary industry producers, including the manufacturing industries that process primary products, such as dairy, meat and seafood processing. Also see Bartleet et al, above n 85.

[90]   Numan-Parsons, Iyer and Bartleet, above n 88, 323. The analysis also concluded that New Zealand and Australia's economies are reliant on overall low-technology manufacturing exports compared to other economies, increasing the impact of a carbon price on the share of GDP.

predominantly agricultural-based economy, food manufacturing is a key sector in the economy, contributing approximately 2.21–2.57 per cent of the GDP.[91]

Therefore, despite its comparatively low average electricity emissions factor, due to the large proportion of hydroelectric generation in New Zealand, the study found that a much larger share of GDP is potentially at risk compared to the other analysed jurisdictions.[92] The authors suggested that the results are explained by a remarkable difference between average and marginal electricity emissions factors, noting that the study considered data from the marginal factors for electricity purchased from the grid. The study proposed that the marginal generation source should set the price of electricity and that in New Zealand's case, rather than being determined by its large share of hydroelectricity generation, it is instead represented by a mix of coal and gas.[93]

It is relevant to note that the study overestimated the carbon price at NZ$50/tCO$_2$-e, which turned out to be four times the price cap during the first years of the scheme, ultimately affecting the carbon leakage risk assessment.[94] Indeed, the NZ ETS offered, from its commencement, a transitional fixed price option of $25/tCO$_2$-e. The fixed price, combined with the one-for-two obligation rule available to the liquid fossil fuels, stationary energy and industrial processes sectors between 2010 and 2012, resulted in an effective price cap of $12.5/tCO$_2$-e.

Furthermore, the NZUs were available on the market at considerably lower prices than the fixed price option, resulting in effective carbon prices of $1.3/tCO$_2$-e for the highly EITE sectors and $5.0/tCO$_2$-e for the moderately EITE sectors in 2012.[95] Finally, the threshold adopted to define a sector as being 'at risk' – an average emissions-intensity of 400 KgCO$_2$-e per NZ$1,000 of value added – translated into 'a generous interpretation of "materially" [impacted] especially with emissions prices below $50 per tonne CO$_2$-e'.[96]

---

[91] Note that the primary sector has not been accounted for in this study in estimating the cost impacts on manufacturing industries that process primary products.

[92] Numan-Parsons, Iyer and Bartleet, above n 88, 319.

[93] Ibid., 322. The comparative low average electricity emissions factor is due to the large proportion of hydroelectric.

[94] Bartleet et al, above n 85, 23. Also see Ministry for the Environment, 'Doing New Zealand's Fair Share. Emissions Trading Scheme Review 2011: Final Report' (2011).

[95] Ibid., 44.

[96] Bartleet et al, above n 85, 23.

In contrast, an independent report prepared by COVEC for the Ministry for the Environment concluded that, on an intensity basis, firms located in New Zealand are less at risk than Australian sectors and most overseas sectors, with the only exception being the burnt lime industry.[97] Two of the most at risk sectors, aluminium and steel, were the least emissions-intensive sectors in New Zealand compared to overseas firms.[98]

4.1 Eligibility for Assistance in the NZ ETS

While the New Zealand carbon leakage policy was inspired, to a certain extent, by the then proposed Australian scheme,[99] the result was less stringent eligibility criteria due to the general rule waiving the application of the trade-exposure threshold. The conclusions in the Occasional Paper prepared by the New Zealand Ministry of Economic Development on the inadequacy of the trade exposure threshold to predict the effects on output[100] were not reflected in the policy framework, with the Climate Change Act defining all sectors as trade-exposed, unless determined otherwise.

In other words, while under the former AUS CPM the entity carrying out the activity would have to prove its trade-exposure factor, in the NZ ETS the 'potential' for international competition was assumed. The sole emissions-intensity threshold was justified by the concept of a potential international trade, according to which it is the potential for trade that limits prices, instead of the actual trade, so that 'something could be trade-exposed even if it is not traded currently'.[101]

The only circumstances in which an activity is taken to be manifestly not trade-exposed are where there is no international trade from the output of the activity across oceans, or where it is not economically viable to import or export the output of the activity. Based on the exceptions, the transport and electricity sectors were not considered eligible for assistance.

Apart from that, the emissions-intensity thresholds adopted under the NZ ETS are similar to the Carbon Pollution Reduction Scheme (CPRS) Green Paper structure, and ultimately the eligibility criteria under the former AUS CPM. There are two levels of energy-intensity, calculated by

---

97 Denne, above n 62, 32.
98 Ibid.
99 See, e.g., Bartleet et al, above n 85.
100 Ibid., 61.
101 Denne, above n 62, 11.

tonnes of CO_2-e per NZ$1 million of revenue (the gross value added option has not been adopted), as follows:

(i) activities that emit between 800 and 1,599 whole tonnes of green-house gases (GHG) per $1 million of specified revenue from the activity are considered moderately emissions-intensive;[102] and
(ii) activities that emit 1,600 or more whole tonnes of GHG per $1 million of specified revenue from the activity are classified as highly emissions-intensive.[103]

In 2011, 26 eligible industrial activities (approximately 300 entities) were identified as EITE, and eligible to receive free of cost NZUs.[104] Not only were the main industrial activities (i.e. iron, steel, aluminium, clinker or lime and glass) included in the list, but also entities from the horticultural and other food sectors, such as the production of gelatine, lactose and protein meal.

4.2 Comparing Free Allocation in the EU ETS, AUS CPM and NZ ETS

The comparative analysis above demonstrates that the AUS CPM and NZ ETS emissions-intensity thresholds are similar to one another. However, the firms in New Zealand benefited from the questionable assumption of trade-exposure, whereas the Australian firms would have to prove it.

In contrast, the EU ETS initially adopted comparatively lower emissions-intensity thresholds, with the exception of the sole emissions-intensity threshold based on a production cost increase of 30 per cent of the gross value added.[105] Only two sectors, the manufacture of cement and lime, were deemed to be eligible under the sole emissions-intensity threshold.

As a result, different sectors would have been classified as being at risk of carbon leakage in the EU, New Zealand and Australia. This discrepancy would have impacted on the competitiveness of industry sectors once two or more ETSs were effectively linked. This is particularly true with respect to the European sole trade-exposure threshold

---

[102] Climate Change Response Act 2002 (NZ) s 161C(1)(a).
[103] Ibid., s 161C(1)(b).
[104] Ministry for the Environment, above n 94, 15.
[105] ETS Directive, art 10a(16)(a).

(trade-intensity above 30 per cent), which resulted in the eligibility of 117 sectors for assistance in the EU ETS. The proposed amendment to the EU ETS eligibility thresholds are, therefore, welcome and in line with the conclusions of this chapter.

5. CONCLUSION

The free allocation of permits is still the main industry assistance measure in countries with an ETS in place. Therefore, getting the right system for allocating free of cost permits to industry can be crucial for the success of the domestic policy, and can play an important role in establishing future links between independent ETSs.

Empirical research on carbon leakage demonstrates that the policy responses to carbon leakage adopted by the EU ETS, AUS CPM and NZ ETS have not been consistent with the empirical findings. As a result, Governments have historically been providing free permits to a number of sectors which are not significantly exposed to carbon leakage.

While the independent *ex-post* research has consistently demonstrated the non-occurrence of carbon leakage during phases I and II of the EU ETS, the scheme persists in relying on a costly industrial support system. Even though it may be argued that the empirical evidence from phase I and phase II of the EU ETS is limited in assisting to predict the carbon leakage impacts from phase III onwards, the independent economic modelling demonstrates that the present thresholds are not justifiable. Similar conclusions were stressed by independent research on the assistance under the AUS CPM.

The concepts of emissions-intensity and trade-exposure have been controlled by the political processes, with the policy and legislation not being entirely able to reflect the assessments in the economic modelling and *ex-post* studies. This study's initial conclusion is that transitional assistance must be provided exclusively to the most carbon leakage-exposed sectors, which vary according to domestic and regional disparities.

The identification of an excessive number of sectors as carbon leakage exposed must be avoided. Among the possible areas for improvement, the removal of the sole thresholds for trade-exposure and emissions-intensity is a pressing one.

The European Commission's proposal to review the eligibility thresholds in order to exclude the sole emissions-intensity and sole trade-exposure thresholds is a step in this direction. However, the compromise offered by the European Commission, of maintaining minimum levels of 30 per cent free allocation to non-EITE sectors until 2030, is not in line with the conclusions in this chapter and will, at least partially, undermine the benefits brought about by the amendments.

Unless this information is well understood, the overstatement of carbon leakage levels could also occur in other countries that have recently adopted, or are planning to adopt, an ETS and be used to justify the inclusion of measures to assist industries deemed to be at risk in the ETS legislation. The selection of the optimal leakage policies by new ETSs and the gradual review of current practices by existing schemes is central to promoting effective and meaningful global emissions reductions.

5. Free allocation and linking emissions trading schemes: the case for harmonisation

1. INTRODUCTION

A large body of literature has identified problems with the use of free allocation for single jurisdiction emissions trading schemes (ETSs). A smaller volume of studies also suggest that different allocation methods are problematic to trade between sectors liable under independent ETSs.[1] This chapter examines key distinct aspects of the legal framework for the free allocation of permits in two case studies that could potentially have been harmonised when negotiating the linking of the independent ETSs.

The first case study reviews data from the first and second trading periods in the European Union Emissions Trading Scheme (EU ETS) – when the different Members had their separate National Allocation Plans (NAPs) – as a model for independent ETSs under a linking arrangement. In the EU ETS context, different allocation rules generated concerns over the competitiveness of industries subject to different NAPs.

---

[1]   Also see Elena Aydos, 'Levelling the Playing Field or Playing on Unlevel Fields: the Industry Assistance Framework under the European Union ETS, the New Zealand ETS, and Australia's CPM' in Larry Kreiser et al (eds), *Market Based Instruments: National Experiences in Environmental Sustainability*, Critical Issues in Environmental Taxation (Edward Elgar Publishing, 2013) vol XIII, 135; Fitsum G. Tiche, Stefan E. Weishaar and Oscar Couwenberg, 'Carbon Leakage, Free Allocation and Linking Emissions Trading Schemes' (2013) *University of Groningen Faculty of Law Reseach Paper Series* <http://ssrn.com/abstract=2354235>; Alexander Rossnagel, 'Evaluating Links Between Emissions Trading Schemes: An Analytical Framework' (2008) 2(4) *Carbon & Climate Law Review* 394, 401. Rossnagel argued that the differences in the allocation structures impacted on the trading possibilities of participants differently during the introductory phase of the ETS and led to competitive distortions between enterprises from different ETSs which were in direct competition with one another.

The second case study identifies key design principles in the legal framework of the EU ETS and the Australian Carbon Pricing Mechanism (AUS CPM) which could have affected the trade between companies liable under the two schemes. The linking between the EU ETS and the AUS CPM was announced in 2013 to take place in 2015, but was never implemented. Due to the similarities of the benchmarks to determine the free allocation levels in the New Zealand ETS and the AUS CPM, the New Zealand ETS will not be assessed in this chapter.[2]

The study focuses on direct emissions, that is, the greenhouse gas (GHG) emissions directly associated with an emissions-intensive activity. The amount of direct emissions released by an activity is essentially related to the technology adopted by each facility, which allows the comparison of the assistance given to emissions-intensive trade-exposed (EITE) industry sectors between the three schemes.

The allocation of emissions permits associated with indirect emissions is not assessed in this chapter. The differences in the electricity generation technology in place in the EU (mix of nuclear, gas, hydroelectric and fossil fuel) and Australia (mainly fossil fuel-based) would add complexity and is not necessary for the intended comparison.

2. THE EUROPEAN UNION EMISSIONS TRADING SYSTEM PHASES I AND II: PROTOTYPE FOR AN INTERNATIONAL EMISSIONS TRADING SCHEME

In the first two trading periods of the EU ETS (phases I and II) the systems for cap-setting and permit allocation varied significantly across Member States due to the highly decentralised system adopted by the then European Community (EC). In this respect, the first two trading periods of the EU ETS can be seen as a 'study prototype' for the issues that may occur when sectors liable under independent ETSs are in competition with each other.[3]

---

[2] The main difference between the system for determining the assistance levels in the NZ ETS and the AUS CPM is the superior assistance rate adopted by the AUS CPM and the methodology for the calculation of the phase-out rate. For details see Aydos, above n 1.

[3] Denny Ellerman, 'The EU's Emissions Trading Scheme: A Prototype Global System?' (MIT, 2009).

During phases I and II of the EU ETS, the Member States developed individual National Allocation Plans (NAPs)[4] determining the total amount of emissions allowances (or a cap) for the period and a description of how the European Union Allowances (EUAs) would be allocated at the installation level. This decentralised, bottom-up process of national decision-making coexisted with the European Commission's (Commission) role of coordination and, ultimately, approval of each individual NAP.[5]

In terms of the distribution of the EU-wide cap across the Member States, the generic cap-setting criteria and difficulties in obtaining reliable emissions data within the ETS sectors contributed to an overly generous emissions cap in most ETS Member States.[6] The Member States' overall allocation factors at national level varied considerably. For example, the *ex post* analysis of the allocation and emissions data demonstrated that Lithuania received more than twice the number of allowances compared to its actual emissions.[7] Keeping the analogy with the linked schemes, this would be equivalent to two independent ETSs having different stringencies in their cap-setting.[8]

---

[4]   Directive 2003/87/EC of the European Parliament and of the Council of 13 October 2003 Establishing a Scheme for Greenhouse Gas Emission Allowance Trading within the Community and Amending Council Directive 96/61/EC [2003] OJ L 275/32 (ETS Directive), annex III provided general guidelines to be observed by Member States when preparing NAPs. For example, the NAPs should not discriminate between companies or sectors; should provide for the treatment of new entrants and accommodate early action, when possible through the use of benchmarks on the best available technology. Interestingly, annex III suggested that Member States adopt measures to deal with the risk of competitiveness concerns from outside the EU ETS.

[5]   ETS Directive, art 9(1), annex III.

[6]   Denny Ellerman, Frank Convery and Christian De Perthuis, *Pricing Carbon: the European Union Emissions Trading Scheme* (Frank J. Convery, Christian de Perthuis and Emilie Alberola trans, Cambridge University Press, 2010) 36–9.

[7]   Niels Anger and Ulrich Oberndorfer, 'Firm Performance and Employment in the EU Emissions Trading Scheme: An Empirical Assessment for Germany' (2008) 36 *Energy Policy* 12, 15; Claudia Kettner et al, 'Stringency and Distribution in the EU Emissions Trading Scheme: First Evidence' (2008) 8 *Climate Policy* 41.

[8]   For a detailed analysis of how discrepancies in the stringency of the emissions caps can represent a barrier to the linking of ETSs, see Andreas Tuerk et al, 'Linking Carbon Markets: Concepts, Case Studies and Pathways' (2009)

The discrepancies in the overall industry allocations triggered a non-uniform allocation on an installation level. For example, the installations in Ireland and the UK were allocated less allowances vis-à-vis their respective emissions ('net short' position), while companies from most countries in the EU received an excess of allowances compared to their actual emissions ('net long' position).

The main features of the allocation process in the EU ETS second trading period were very similar to the pilot phase, with Member States still developing individual NAPs. However, at this stage the overall cap was tightened and fewer EUAs were made available to participants.[9]

Aircraft operators of flights within the European Economic Area (EEA) entered the ETS in the last year of the second period, and received free allocations of permits based on historical aviation emissions.[10] As the allocation of EUAs to the aircraft operators is separate to the overall allocation to industry, it will not be analysed in this chapter.[11]

The system for the allocation of permits on a sectoral level across Member States is analysed below, and concludes that the decentralised allocation of EUAs incentivised a 'race for rents' in most Member States. Due to the heavy lobbying invested in influencing the allocation rules, some participants in the EU ETS benefitted from windfall profits, particularly electricity generators and a number of emissions-intensive sectors.

Concerns with unfair competition led to a legislative process for the harmonisation of the allocation rules amongst Member States. Competitiveness concerns during phases I and II, and the subsequent harmonisation of the allocation rules, provide invaluable lessons for the future linking of independent ETSs.

2.1 National Allocation Plans in Phases I and II

The process of elaborating the first national plans (NAP1) was demanding for Member States, especially due to the scarcity of data at the installation level to inform the appropriate levels of individual allocations

---

9(4) *Climate Policy* 341; M.J. Mace et al, 'Analysis of the Legal and Organisational Issues Arising in Linking the EU Emissions Trading Scheme to Other Existing and Emerging Emissions Trading Schemes' (FIELD, IEEP, WRI, 2008).

[9]   Ellerman, Convery and Perthuis, above n 6, 60.

[10]   ETS Directive, art 3c(1).

[11]   However, see further details on the inclusion of the aviation sector in the ETS in Chapters 2 and 3.

of EUAs and the tight time schedule.[12] Further challenges included inconsistent definitions for determining the installations covered in the different Member States and issues related to monitoring, reporting and verification.[13]

Annex III to the ETS Directive determines that the NAPs shall specify how Member States propose to allocate EUAs among installations covered by the ETS, and shall not discriminate between companies or sectors. NAPs should provide for the treatment of new entrants and accommodate early action, when possible, through the use of benchmarks on the best available technology. The plan may also contain measures to deal with the risk of competitiveness concerns from outside the EU ETS.[14]

The ETS Directive also provided that allowances shall be valid for emissions during the period for which they were issued.[15] That is, the banking of EUAs from the first period into the second trading period would not be allowed. At the beginning of the second period, any EUAs remaining from the first trading period were meant to be cancelled.[16] Finally, the Community did not accept *ex post* adjustments, as it would 'encourage firms to seek this form of administrative relief [readjustment of allocations at the end of the period] instead of trading allowances and would encourage the incorporation of a carbon price into production decisions'.[17]

Despite the significant disparities, the common elements to most NAPs during phases I and II can be identified, including: the grandfathering of

---

[12]   See Denny Ellerman, Barbara Buchner and Carlo Carraro (eds), *Allocation in the European Emissions Trading Scheme: Rights, Rents and Fairness* (Cambridge University Press, 2007); Ellerman, Convery and Perthuis, above n 6, 38.

[13]   Christian Egenhofer et al, 'The EU Emissions Trading System and Climate Policy towards 2050: Real incentives to reduce emissions and drive innovation?' (CEPS, 2011). On monitoring, reporting and verification issues see Jonathan Verschuuren and Floor Fleurke, 'Entracte: Report on the Legal Implementation of the EU ETS at Member State Level' (Tilburg Sustainability Center, 2012).

[14]   ETS Directive, annex III.

[15]   Ibid., art 13(1).

[16]   Ibid., art 13(2).

[17]   Ellerman, Convery and Perthuis, above n 6, 42. Also see *Federal Republic of Germany v Commission of the European Communities* (T-374/04) [2007] ECR II-4441.

nearly 100 per cent of EUAs with very limited auctioning;[18] the allocation of EUAs based on historical emissions; new entrants' reserves (NER) and closure provisions; and an overall surplus of permits allocated to installations falling within the scope of the system.

2.1.1 Grandfathering

Grandfathering, rather than the auctioning of permits in phases I and II of the EU ETS was a regulatory choice. While the Member States were allowed to trade up to 5 per cent of the cap in the first trading period, most allocated 100 per cent of their EUAs free of cost to installations falling within the scope of the scheme.[19] Only four Member States sold permits in phase I, which accounted for 0.13 per cent of the total allocation.[20]

Of these four, Denmark was the only Member State to sell the whole of the allowed amount and it did so through market intermediaries rather than by auctioning.[21] Ireland sold EUAs in January 2006, just before the price collapsed in April/May 2006.[22] Hungary and Lithuania did not manage to sell any permits prior to the price collapse. Despite its inflated surplus of allowances, Lithuania sold EUAs in September 2007 for only six eurocents.[23]

In phase II, the ETS Directive provided that at least 90 per cent of the allowances should be allocated free of charge to participants in the

---

[18]   European Commission, 'Green Paper on Greenhouse Gas Emissions Trading within the European Union' (2000) 18. Also see Ellerman, Convery and Perthuis, above n 6, 61. During the consultation process leading up to the adoption of the ETS Directive, the Commission expressed its preference towards the auctioning of allowances. However, from the consultation process with stakeholders in 2002 it became clear to the Commission that the free allocation of allowances was a political condition to the implementation of the emissions trading. In the co-decision process that followed, the European Parliament also suffered from the pressure of some Member States to adopt the grandfathering method. As a result, art 10 of the ETS Directive provided that at least 95 per cent of the emissions allowances should be allocated free of charge.

[19]   Ellerman, Buchner and Carraro, above n 12.

[20]   Denny Ellerman, Frank Convery and Christian De Perthuis, 'The European Carbon Market in Action: lessons from the First Trading Period' (2008) 11.

[21]   Ellerman, Convery and Perthuis, above n 6, 62–3.

[22]   Ibid., 63. EUAs were sold for 26.32 Euros/EUA. See Chapter 3 for further details on the issue of surplus allowances in the EU ETS.

[23]   Ibid. The proceeds from Lithuania's auctions were approximately equal to the cost of conducting the auction.

second trading period.[24] Despite the Commission's encouragements for Member States to auction a greater percentage of the permits, the auctioning in the second period was again maintained below the allowed limit. The auction average in all the EU Member States was 3 per cent, with the UK and Germany having the highest number of EUAs auctioned.[25]

It is relevant to mention that the NAPs were only meant to provide for the allocation of permits within a trading period. That is, guarantees of free allocation beyond the second trading period were not allowed by the Commission as it could potentially violate EU State aid rules and limit 'the scope for further harmonisation of the allocation methodology across the internal market in the context of the EU ETS review'.[26]

The remaining unallocated NAP1 allowances were either transferred to replacement facilities (Germany, Italy and Greece), cancelled (Latvia and Lithuania), auctioned (Ireland) or added to the NER (Austria, Belgium, Denmark, Finland, Germany, Hungary, Italy, Luxembourg, Poland, Portugal, UK). As mentioned above, only Denmark, Hungary, Lithuania and Ireland sold or auctioned the excess permits, and this may be attributed to the 2006 price crash which lasted until the end of the first period.[27]

2.1.2 Historical emissions versus benchmarking

Benchmarking consists of determining an emissions rate, for example, based on efficient production, which can then be applied for calculating the number of permits allocated to each installation. During the consultation process preceding the implementation of the EU ETS, the Commission expressed its preference for the use of benchmarks to determine the levels of allocation to individual installations and to reward early action:

> A simple historical emissions approach, e.g., based on emissions in 1990 like the Kyoto Protocol, would reward the largest emitters at that time and penalise those who, before 1990, had already taken early action. A refinement

---

[24]   ETS Directive, art 10.

[25]   European Commission, *Phase 2 Auctions* (08 May 2015) Climate Action <http://ec.europa.eu/clima/policies/ets/pre2013/second/index_en.htm>.

[26]   Communication from the Commission to the Council and to the European Parliament COMM/2006/275, on the Assessment of National Allocation Plans for the Allocation of Greenhouse Gas Emission Allowances in the Second Period of the EU Emissions Trading Scheme Accompanying Commission Decisions of 29 November 2006 on the National Allocation plans of Germany, Greece, Ireland, Latvia, Lithuania, Luxembourg, Malta, Slovakia, Sweden and the United Kingdom in accordance with Directive 2003/87/EC [2006] 11.

[27]   Ellerman, Convery and Perthuis, above n 6, 69.

of the 'grandfathering' option would be free allocation on the basis of performance standards or 'benchmarks' (e.g., tonnes of CO_2-equivalent per tonne of steel produced in a certain year).[28]

Nevertheless, the vast majority of the Member States under NAP1 provided that the allocation of the EUAs would be based on historical emissions, also known as grandfathering of allowances. That is, the number of EUAs issued to each installation was calculated according to the individual average emissions over a certain period of time.[29] Further-more, the Member States selected different base years to calculate the volumes of the free allocations, with variations also in place according to the sector.[30] The few exceptions to the use of historical emissions over benchmarking included specific sectors in the Netherlands, Denmark, Italy, Spain and Poland and in the allocations to new entrants, where historical data on emissions was not available.

In phase II more Member States used benchmarking. However, bench-marking was limited to the electricity sector, where allocation was differentiated by the fuel type or other process parameters.[31]

2.1.3 New entrants' reserves and closure provisions

The original definition of 'new entrant' in the ETS Directive included changes in the nature or functioning and expansion of existing facilities, although it excluded increases in production from an increased use of existing capacity.[32] During the EU ETS first trading period, all the Member States had provisions for the NER, which were predominantly used to support the expansion of existing facilities.[33]

The rules for the NER in NAP1 varied considerably amongst Member States. Betz, Eichhammer and Schleich described political concerns with the trade distortions between Member States due to asymmetric NERs, stating that 'some countries like Austria and Slovenia, which had originally planned to have new entrants buy allowances on the market

---

[28] European Commission, above n 18, 19. Also see Ellerman, Convery and Perthuis, above n 6, 64.

[29] Mikael Skou Andersen and Paul Ekins (eds), *Carbon-energy Taxation: Lessons from Europe* (Oxford University Press, 2009).

[30] Mikael Skou Andersen, 'Environmental and Economic Implications of Taxing and Trading Carbon: Some European Experiences' in *The Reality of Carbon Taxes in the 21st Century* (Vermont Law School 2008).

[31] Ellerman, Convery and Perthuis, above n 6, 66.

[32] ETS Directive, art 3(h) (definition of new entrant).

[33] Ellerman, Convery and Perthuis, above n 6, 67.

(the approach preferred by the Commission), changed their mind for fear of becoming a less attractive location for newcomers'.[34]

The sizes of the NERs ranged significantly, from less than 1 per cent of the total national cap (Germany, Cyprus, Poland, Slovakia and Slovenia) to 26 per cent of the national cap (Malta). Such discrepancies were justified based on the different estimated growth rates in each Member State attributed to expansions and/or new installations.[35]

In some cases, correctly determining the amount of NER was challenging due to transfer provisions, allowing the remaining permits from a closed installation to be transferred to a new 'replacement facility'.[36] Ellerman, Convery and De Perthuis observed that 'when a transfer provision is present, sizing the reserve is no longer just a matter of expected new facilities but also of how many will take advantage of the transfer rule'.[37]

In the case of shortages of the NERs, the Member States generally committed to the purchase of permits in the market, raising concerns with 'the danger of state aid issues with the European Commission'.[38] However, consistent with the overall excessive national caps in the first trading period, most countries ended the first trading period with NER surpluses.

Germany, Italy, Lithuania and Slovenia allocated close to all their NER permits, while Malta, the country with the highest percentage of NERs relative to its national cap (26 per cent), ended the first period with a 100 per cent surplus. Only seven Member States cancelled their end-of-period reserve surplus EUAs in their respective registries.[39]

Closure provisions, in general, determined the removal or cancelling of EUAs allocated upon the closure of installations. While it seems fair that installations should return unused permits in the event of the cessation of operations, closure provisions have the negative effect of incentivising inefficient firms to remain functioning. Unlike new entrants, the definition of closure varied considerably among the Member States. While

---

[34]   Regina Betz, Wolfgang Eichhammer and Joachim Schleich, 'Designing National Allocation Plans for EU Emissions Trading: A First Analysis of the Outcome' (2004) 15(3) *Energy & Environment* 375.

[35]   Alyssa Gilbert et al, 'Comparative Analysis of National Allocation Plans for Phase I of the EU ETS' (ECOFYS, 2006).

[36]   Ellerman, Convery and Perthuis, above n 6, 68. Where transfer is completed within a specified timeframe.

[37]   Ibid.

[38]   Gilbert et al, above n 35, 13.

[39]   Ibid., 14.

some Member States defined closure as a complete cessation of operations, others established thresholds to determine minimum levels of production or emissions.[40]

In Germany, the closure arrangements were described as an 'attempt to avoid shut-down premiums for plant closure'.[41] Indeed, stakeholders believed that the absence of closure provisions would further incentivise production to move elsewhere. The Member States were pressured by businesses to include closure provisions in the NAP1 and most countries adopted NERs, with the only exceptions being Sweden and the Netherlands.[42]

2.1.4 Overall surplus

The power sector was the only sector in an overall demand position during the first trading period. The ratio of allocations versus emissions was smaller compared to the manufacturing sector due to the capacity of the generators to pass on the carbon costs to consumers.[43] However, the power sector was also the greatest beneficiary of windfall profits from the free allocation of EUAs.[44] The sector passed through overestimated carbon costs – particularly before May 2006 – in high electricity prices while simultaneously being compensated through the grandfathering of the EUAs.[45] The wholesale electricity markets in Germany and the Netherlands, for example, benefited from opportunity cost pass-through rates varying between 60 per cent and 100 per cent, earning aggregate profits estimated at billions of Euros for the period 2005–08.[46]

---

[40] Ibid., 21. For example, the German closure threshold was an emissions drop below 10 per cent of the base year period.

[41] Felix Christian Matthes and Franzjosef Schafhausen, 'Germany' in A. Denny Ellerman, Barbara K. Buchner and Carlo Carraro (eds), *Allocation in the European Emissions Trading Scheme* (Cambridge University Press, 2007), 102.

[42] Gilbert et al, above n 35, 21.

[43] Raphael Trotignon and Anais Delbosc, 'Allowance Trading Patterns During the Trial Period: What Does the CITL reveal?' (Mission Climate, 2008), 24; Andersen and Ekins, above n 29.

[44] Egenhofer et al, above n 13, 4. Egenhofer et al explained that 'those industries that could and can pass on the additional carbon costs have in fact a net gain, since potential losses of revenues, through for example lower sales, may be compensated or even overcompensated by receiving allowances free of charge and earning "windfall profits"'.

[45] Ingrid Jegou and Luca Rubini, 'The Allocation of Emissions Allowances Free of Charge: Legal and Economic Considerations' (ICTSD, 2011) 18.

[46] Jos Sijm, Karsten Neuhoff and Yihsu Chen, 'CO2 Cost Pass-Through and Windfall Profits in the Power Sector' (2006) 6(1) *Climate Policy* 49.

In relation to the other participants in the EU ETS, the excessive allocation of EUAs has been an ongoing issue since the commencement of phase I of the EU ETS. Research on the 2006 allocation data across countries in the EU found that, of the 12 countries with available data in English, 11 allocated more permits to their ETS sectors (liable entities under the ETS) than their historical emissions in 2000. Poland, Luxembourg, Lithuania and the Czech Republic went one step further, allocating permits to industries above their business as usual (BAU) estimates.[47]

In the first trading period, the banking of permits was limited to the liability years within the trading period (2005–07), and not extended to the second trading period.[48] Two Member States, France and Poland, had provisions in their NAP1s for the banking of EUAs from the first period into the second period. With regard to such non-recognised arrangements, the Commission decided that any first-period allowances banked for use in phase two would be deducted from the approved Member State's total emissions cap in the second period.[49]

Despite the reduced emissions caps, over-allocation still took place in phase II, with many sectors gaining windfall profits from the grandfathering of permits.[50] The free allocations to the power sector were largely reduced in the second trading period, and in the third trading period most electricity generators will not be entitled to free of charge permits, as explained below.[51] Unlike in phase I, the surplus allowances from phase II were bankable for use in the third trading period and beyond.

---

[47]   Hans H. Kolshus and Asbjorn Torvanger, 'Analysis of EU Member States' National Allocation Plans' (CICERO, 2005). The countries with sufficient available information in English at the time of this research were: Austria, Czech Republic, Denmark, Finland, Germany, Greece, Hungary, Ireland, Italy, Poland, Portugal and United Kingdom. The authors recommend caution when analysing the results from this research due to the lack of information on the remaining 13 Member States.

[48]   Frank Convery and Luke Redmond, 'The European Union Emissions Trading Scheme: Issues in Allowance Price Support and Linkage' (2013) *Annual Review of Resource Economics* 1.

[49]   Commission Decision Concerning the National Allocation Plan for the Allocation of Greenhouse Gas Emission Allowances Notified by Germany in Accordance with Directive 2003/87/EC of the European Parliament and of the Council [2006] 12.

[50]   Egenhofer et al, above n 13.

[51]   Ibid., 5. Egenhofer et al demonstrated that:

Free allocation in the first two phases has generated 'windfall profits' mainly but not only to the power sector. Power generators could pass on the full CO_2 costs while having received allowances for free. Windfall profits have been

2.2 Competitiveness Concerns in the First Phase of the EU ETS

The ETS Directive recommended that NAPs should expressly identify 'the manner in which the existence of competition from countries or entities outside the Union will be taken into account'.[52] The risk of competitiveness distortions between the EU and non-EU industry sectors had been largely dealt with through the grandfathering of most of the EUAs to trade-exposed installations covered by the scheme.

Due to the decentralised allocation methodology and the consequent discrepancies between the NAPs, concerns were also expressed in relation to the competitiveness distortions within the EU. The following statement from the Commission during the consultation process that preceded the implementation of the EU ETS illustrates this point well:

> A company in one Member State that has to buy allowances through auctioning may feel disadvantaged in relation to a competitor in another Member State that has been 'grandfathered' its allowances for free. Depending on how 'grandfathering' is undertaken in different Member States, companies may also feel disadvantaged in relation to their competitors, and hence competition distortions could arise.[53]

To prevent unfair distortions between the installations located in different Member States, the ETS Directive determined that the Member States should observe the EU competition rules.[54] Indeed, under former criterion five in Annex III, the NAPs should 'not discriminate between companies or sectors in such a way as to unduly favour certain undertakings or activities in accordance with the requirements of the Treaty, in particular Articles 87 and 88 thereof'.[55] Annex III also provided that 'the total quantity of allowances to be allocated shall not be more than is likely to be needed for the strict application of the criteria of

---

estimated to amount to as much as €13 billion annually. This in return has heightened interest in the auctioning of allowances (as opposed to free allocation) and finally in the (almost) full auctioning of the allowances to the power sector as of the third phase 2013–20' (citations omitted).

52   ETS Directive, annex III (11).
53   European Commission, above n 8, 19.
54   Treaty on European Union, opened for signature 7 February 1992, [2009] OJ C 115/13 (entered into force 1 November 1993) [cited as amended] arts 87, 88.
55   ETS Directive, annex III (5).

this Annex',[56] including the Member State's obligation to limit its GHG emissions.[57]

Despite the criteria in Annex III, a 'race to the bottom' process took place, with industry sectors pressuring the Member States to receive equivalent amounts of permits as their competitors in different Member States, advantaging most participants in the first trading period at the expense of the functioning of the EU ETS.[58] The trade-exposed sectors were privileged with higher volumes of permits than the non-trade-exposed sectors.[59]

The different national interpretations of the definition of covered installations,[60] and ultimately the different allocation methodologies in NAP1 between the Member States, made it likely that comparable companies received a varying allocation, depending on their location.[61] The competitive advantages provided to some installations were exacerbated by windfall gains, which increased the perception of unfairness and competitive distortions between competitors in the different Member

---

[56]   Ibid., annex III (1).

[57]   Ibid., annex III (2).

[58]   Egenhofer et al, above n 13, iii.

[59]   Kolshus and Torvanger, above n 47. The countries with sufficient available information in English at the time of this research were: Austria, Czech Republic, Denmark, Finland, Germany, Greece, Hungary, Ireland, Italy, Poland, Portugal and United Kingdom. The authors recommend caution when analysing the results from this research due to the lack of information on the remaining 13 Member States. But see Niels Anger and Ulrich Oberndorfer, 'Firm Performance and Employment in the EU Emissions Trading Scheme: An Empirical Assessment for Germany' (2008) 36 *Energy Policy* 12. Anger and Oberndorfer assessed the impacts of the EU ETS first trading period to the competitiveness of industry in Germany. The study did not find empirical evidence to demonstrate a significant impact of the levels of allowances allocated to different firms on firm revenue and employment levels in 2005. Firms with a higher allocation factor could not increase their revenues vis-à-vis firms with a lower allocation factor during the EU ETS first trading period.

[60]   Betz, Eichhammer and Schleich, above n 34.

[61]   Gilbert et al, above n 35, 62. Also see Karsten Neuhoff and et al, 'Emission Projections 2008–2012 versus National Allocation Plans II' (2006) 6(4) *Climate Policy* 395; Karsten Neuhoff and et al, 'Implications of Announced Phase II National Allocation Plans for the EU ETS' (2006) 6(4) *Climate Policy* 411; Sijm, Neuhoff and Chen, above n 46.

States. To illustrate, this was the case with a number of power generators located in different Member States during the first trading period.[62]

In practice, the system for allocation based on historic emissions impacted on the volumes of allowances received by installations vis-à-vis intra-EU competitors. The Member States were free to elect the base year and, as a consequence, early base years, when the technology was less efficient, were applied in the Member States' NAPs to certain specific industry sectors.[63] The lack of consistent definitions and grouping of sectors also made comparisons across sectors difficult.[64]

Distortions were also introduced by the disparities in the NERs and the closure provisions in each Member State.[65] For example, participants in one Member State could be incentivised to expand capacity or to keep facilities open in order to receive permits free of cost.[66]

The elements in the NERs that can influence investors' decisions, when favouring one country over another, include the ready availability of allowances from the NER, the transparency of the allocation process and the amount of units available to new facilities. These elements are particularly relevant for new investments in highly-electricity-intensive sectors.

The new entrants' reserves created incentives for firms to expand capacity often using polluting/non-efficient technology.[67] Such arrangements were deemed to be capable of influencing investment decisions in phases I and II of the EU ETS as the different Member States allocated

---

[62] Angus Johnston, 'Free Allocation of Allowances Under the EU Emissions Trading Scheme: Legal Issues' (2006) 6 *Climate Policy* 115. Johnston observed that:

> it seems clear not only that aid is granted by the free allocation of allowances, but also that it goes far beyond that expected simply from the free allocation of allowances in the first place. The extra element, beyond the value of the allowance itself, is the ability to use the fact of holding that allowance to pass through to customers the opportunity costs associated with holding that allowance.

[63] Andersen, above n 30. Also see Joëlle de Sépibus, 'The European Emission Trading Scheme Put to the Test of State Aid Rules' (WTI, 2007) 14.

[64] Kolshus and Torvanger, above n 47, 30.

[65] Ellerman, Convery and Perthuis, above n 6, 12.

[66] Ibid., 67.

[67] Robert Hahn and Robert Stavins, 'The Effect of Allowance Allocations on Cap-and-Trade System Performance' (2011) 54 *Journal of Law & Economics* S267–286; Ellerman, Convery and Perthuis, above n 6, 19; Julia Reinaud, 'Issues Behind Competitiveness and Carbon Leakage: Focus on Heavy Industry' (IEA; OECD, 2008) 80.

different numbers of allowances to similar installations.[68] To illustrate, Ellerman, Convery and Perthuis calculated that the distinct new entrants' rules applicable to similar coal-fired plants in Germany and the UK would result in a significant difference of 10 per cent of the wholesale electricity price.[69]

The closure provisions can also influence decisions related to plant closures, 'because the firm earns the allocation *if and only if* it continues to operate the installation'.[70] The existence of such provisions, in practice, functions as a subsidy to maintain production levels. It is worth mentioning that the transfer arrangements allowing the transfer of permits from a closed installation to a replacement facility may have the positive impact of accelerating the closure of inefficient plants and improving the environmental efficiency of the remaining capital, without the negative trade-off of impacting on global market shares.[71]

Several issues relating to the new entrants and closure provisions were recognised at the technical level, with the Member States being recommended not to include them in NAP1.[72] Despite this, the decision to provide NER and closure arrangements was essentially political.[73] Ellerman, Convery and De Perthuis concluded that the decentralised NER and closure provisions 'led to some potential contraventions of EU policy with respect to market integration, state aid and, more generally, equal treatment in a single EU market'.[74] The decentralised allocation system

---

[68]   Gilbert et al, above n 35, 16. Gilbert et al reported that 'the size and structure of the reserve can alter the degree of certainty, in relation to the cost of the NER, for prospective investors, potentially causing them to favour one country over another'.

[69]   Ellerman, Convery and Perthuis, above n 6, 68.

[70]   Reinaud, above n 67, 80.

[71]   Ibid., 81.

[72]   Ellerman, Convery and Perthuis, above n 6, 68.

[73]   Ibid., 12.

[74]   Ibid., 68; Ellerman, Buchner and Carraro, above n 12, 17. The authors explain that:

the endowment of a quantity of allowances to new entrants reduces the cost of entry and thereby lowers the long-term price effect of the carbon constraint from what it would be without these provisions. Similarly, the adoption of rules that take allowances away from closed facilities will keep those facilities operating longer than would otherwise be the case to the extent that the loss incurred in operating the plant is less than the value of the allowances retained. The result is more capacity than is needed to meet demand and some resulting inefficiency in the allocation of capital and labor.

adopted in phases I and II of the EU ETS affected the transparency of the NAPs, while increasing their complexity and the transaction costs.[75]

The European Commission became aware of these issues and engaged in a more thorough examination of the NAPs in the second trading period. To illustrate, the Commission decision on the second German NAP identified that the allocation guarantees from NAP1, which would be applicable in phase II, were providing preferential treatment to more recent installations based on the assumption that 'they have no or only a lower reduction potential'.[76] The Commission assessed that the guarantees were unduly favouring the mentioned installations against otherwise comparable existing installations, which would receive free allowances under the less favourable general allocation methodologies of the German NAP.[77]

The Commission stated that 'the starting date of operation cannot be used as the primary justification for discrimination between existing installations'[78] and determined the amendment of the German NAP2. Germany was warned to notify the Commission in case it maintained or introduced such allocation guarantees as they 'would be likely to become subject of a separate State aid investigation procedure to be opened by the Commission pursuant to Article 88 of the Treaty'.[79]

The issue of the compatibility of the Member States' first and second series of NAPs with the EU State aid rules was highly contentious in legal literature.[80] De Sépibus has described the Commission's assessments of the National Allocation Plans as 'poorly reasoned and stressing

---

[75] Commission Decision, above n 49, para 19. During the assessment of the second series of NAPs the Community once again concluded that 'the allocation of allowances free of charge to certain activities confers a selective economic advantage to undertakings which has the potential to distort competition and affect intra Community trade'.

[76] Ibid., para 21.

[77] Ibid., para 20.

[78] Ibid., para 23.

[79] Ibid., para 26.

[80] Since the EU ETS allocation system has been harmonised from phase III onwards, a detailed examination of the provisions on State aid rules and the jurisprudence of the European Courts against NAP 1 and 2, at this point, would be futile. Nevertheless, the Commission's analysis of specific NAPs in phases I and II are noteworthy. A helpful summary of the legal debate on the compatibility of NAP 1 and 2 with the EU State aid provisions can be found in De Sépibus, above n 63.

the provisional character of its decisions', which was not taken positively by stakeholders.[81]

A harmonisation process commenced during the NAP2 and was fully implemented in the EU ETS third trading period, raising the question of whether common rules for the allocation of permits might be negotiated under linking agreements between independent ETSs in order to prevent distortions to industry competitiveness. The case study that follows attempts to answer this question based on the proposed link between the EU ETS and the former AUS CPM.

3. LESSONS FROM A HYPOTHETICAL LINKING BETWEEN THE EU ETS AND THE AUS CPM[82]

A direct linking of the EU ETS and the former AUS CPM was negotiated to be the first ever inter-continental linking of ETSs.[83] The linking was scheduled to commence with a transition period starting from 1 July 2015, during which a unilateral link would be put in place and permits from the EU ETS could be used for compliance under the AUS CPM. A full bilateral link would take effect in 2018. However, after a tortuous political process,[84] culminating in a change of government in Australia, the Carbon Pricing Mechanism was repealed and the already approved projects for linking never took place.[85]

A number of changes to the AUS CPM were provided for in order to facilitate the linking of the EU ETS and the AUS CPM. Reviews to the

---

[81]   Ibid., 26.

[82]   Also see Aydos, above n 1.

[83]   The European Commission and the Hon Greg Combet, Minister for Climate Change and Energy Efficiency, Australian Government, 'Australia and European Commission agree on pathway towards fully linking emissions trading systems' (Media release, 28 August 2012).

[84]   For a more detailed analysis of the process that led to the repeal of the AUS CPM see Chapter 3. Also see Elena Aydos, 'What Went Wrong? Lessons from a Short-Lived Carbon Price in Australia' in Leonardo de Andrade Costa, Ana Alice De Carli and Ricardo Lodi Ribeiro (eds), *Tributacao e Sustentabilidade Ambiental* (FGV Editora, 2015) 75.

[85]   A legislative package, also known as the 'carbon tax repeal legislation', passed through the House of Representatives and received Royal Assent on 17 July 2014. The legislation entered into effect from 1 July 2014. Australia is now the first country to discard a domestic carbon price, generating uncertainty regarding its capacity to meet domestic emissions reduction goals by 2020 and beyond.

AUS CPM included a removal of the price floor, new limits to the quantity of eligible Kyoto units under the scheme and changes to the original auctioning framework.[86]

Nevertheless, no adjustment was made with respect to the system for free allocation of permits to the EITE sectors. Indeed, the Australian Government declared that the 'Jobs and Competitiveness Program will remain an important mechanism to support the competitiveness of industries whose prices are set by international markets and drive further efficiencies in our manufacturing industries which are currently emissions-intensive'.[87]

That is, the EU and Australia did not take the opportunity to discuss and agree on a more coordinated approach to their free allocation methods when the linking agreement took place. The following analysis demonstrates that the disparities between the free allocation systems of the two independent ETSs could, in reality, have created trade distortions between similar participants liable under the two schemes.

3.1 The European Union Emissions Trading System Third Trading Period

A 2008 review of the ETS Directive, undertaken partially due to concerns with unfairness and competitive distortions between the Member States, provided for the adoption of 'communitywide and fully-harmonised implementing measures' applicable to the free of cost allocation of emissions permits, including the allocation of permits to the EITE sectors.[88] That is, individual NAPs will no longer exist and the method-ology for the distribution of permits will be harmonised at the EU level.[89]

The harmonisation of the allocation method, despite limiting ETS countries' discretion, was considered a necessary step to eliminate the competitiveness distortions caused by the different NAPs and to increase transparency in the allocation process.[90] The process for the harmon-isation of the allocation system commenced during the NAP2 but was

---

[86]   Australian Government, 'Fact Sheet: Linking and Australian Liable Entities' (2012) <http://www.cleanenergyfuture.gov.au/linking-and-australian-liable-entities>.

[87]   Ibid., 3.

[88]   ETS Directive, art 10a(1). No free-of-cost allocation will be given to electricity generators, as per art 10a(3).

[89]   Ibid., art 10a.

[90]   Gilbert et al, above n 35, 6. Ellerman, Convery and Perthuis, above n 6, 84 also suggest that there was also 'a sense of fatigue on the part of the member

fully implemented in the EU ETS third trading period. The harmonised rules for allocation were negotiated at the EU level.[91]

Most participants would still receive a percentage of allowances free of charge in phase III as a transitional assistance measure. The amount of free of charge allocations to incumbents[92] in 2013 was set at 80 per cent, decreasing annually by equal amounts and reaching 30 per cent in 2020, with a view to a phase out by 2027.[93]

A formula was created to determine the distribution of the auction rights between the ETS countries, according to which 88 per cent of the estimated amount of the allowances to be auctioned would be distributed to ETS countries according to their basic entitlement, which is based on the Member State's share of 2005 verified emissions;[94] 10 per cent would be distributed among 19 ETS countries, in different percentages, for the 'purpose of solidarity and growth within the Community'.[95] Finally, 2 per cent of the allowances to be auctioned were distributed between nine eastern European ETS countries as an early-action bonus.[96]

3.1.1 Use of benchmarks

In terms of the individual allocation per installation, the EU adopted harmonised *ex ante* benchmarks to be used from the third trading period onwards. These *ex-ante* product-specific benchmarks were calculated based on the arithmetic average of the GHG performances of the 10 per cent most GHG efficient installations in 2007 and 2008.[97] Product

---

states with the unrewarding process of getting national totals accepted by the Commission and then allocating the allowed total among affected facilities'.

[91]   Ellerman, Convery and Perthuis, above n 6, 83.

[92]   Commission Decision 278/2011/EU of 27 April 2011 Determining Transitional Union-wide Rules for Harmonised Free Allocation of Emission Allowances Pursuant to Article 10a of Directive 2003/87/EC of the European Parliament and of the Council [2011] OJ L 130/1. Incumbent installations are installations covered by the scheme by 30 June 2011, which excludes new entrants from this definition.

[93]   ETS Directive, art 10a(11).

[94]   Ibid., art 10(2)(a).

[95]   Ibid., art 10(2)(b). Member States' shares are specified in annex IIa.

[96]   Ibid., art 10(2)(c), annex IIb.

[97]   Ibid., art 10a(1)(2); European Commission (2011), Draft Commission decision on free allocation rules for the emissions trading scheme: Explanatory paper prepared by DG Climate Action for MEPs. Where product benchmarks (based on the 10 per cent most efficient installations) are not feasible, at least one of the following methodologies may be used: heat benchmarking (t CO_2/TJ of heat consumed); fuel benchmarking (t CO_2/TJ of fuel used) or a process

benchmarks were then multiplied by the installation's historical activity during the period from 1 January 2005 to 31 December 2008 (historical baseline), or, where it was higher, by the median production during the period from 1 January 2009 to 31 December 2010.[98] Benchmarks were adopted in early 2011 and will remain in place until 2020.[99]

For the non-EITE participants, the numbers of free permits issued in 2013 were calculated at 80 per cent of the quantity determined in accordance with the product benchmarks and historical baselines, with the percentage gradually decreasing each year and reaching 30 per cent in 2020.[100] The EITE sectors, in contrast, will continue to receive permits free of cost corresponding to 100 per cent of the quantity determined in accordance with the product benchmarks and historical baselines at least until 2020.[101] Finally, a uniform cross-sectoral correction factor may also apply to the formula if necessary to ensure that the maximum amount of free allocations is not exceeded.[102]

The harmonised allocation rules and thresholds for determining sectors as carbon leakage exposed are provided by the ETS Directive, which meant that a review would require a formal process of amendment to the Directive. The Commission was left with the prerogative, for example, of determining the assumed carbon price that will be applied when calculating carbon leakage exposure based on the Directive's thresholds.

The list of installations and the quantity of EUAs to be allocated, according to the harmonised rules, is published and submitted to the Commission every year.[103] According to Sandbag, 'these developments signal the beginning of the end for some of the EU's carbon Fatcats who gorged themselves on excessive free allocation in the previous phase'.[104]

---

emissions approach (in this case allocation is 97.00 per cent of historical emissions).

[98] Commission Decision 278/2011/EU, above n 92, 92. The median of the years 2005–08 implies excluding the highest and the lowest year, and calculating the mean of the remaining two middle years. The median of the years 2009–10 is equivalent to the mean of 2009–10

[99] Ibid., annex I.

[100] ETS Directive, art 10a(11).

[101] Ibid., art 10a(12). On the eligibility thresholds to be considered emissions-intensive trade-exposed see Chapter 4.

[102] Ibid., art 10a(5).

[103] Ibid., art 11.

[104] Sandbag, 'Slaying the Dragon: Vanquish the Surplus and Rescue the ETS' (Sandbag, 2014) 45–6.

3.1.2   New entrants and closure provisions

The reviewed ETS Directive provided for a harmonised definition of new entrants.[105] The definition of new entrants according to the reviewed Directive encompasses new installations receiving a permit after 30 June 2011 – installations which may be entering the ETS scope for the first time or re-entering the ETS after a cessation of operations – as well as significant capacity extensions at existing installations after 30 June 2011.[106] The NER is administered at the EU level, being set at an equivalent of 5 per cent of the annual EU-wide free allocation for the industrial sectors.[107]

The definitions of cessation and partial cessation (closure) of installations were also harmonised at the EU level. Installations no longer operating as an ETS installation, and not able to start operating again within six months, are considered to have ceased operation. Allowances will no longer be allocated to these installations as of the year following the closure.[108]

3.1.3   Allocations to the electricity sector

Due to the experience with windfall profits in phases I and II of the EU ETS, the power sector will no longer receive free allowances, with the exception of heat delivered to district heating and for industrial uses.[109] Certain ETS countries will have the option of allocating free EUAs as a transitional measure to support the modernisation of electricity generators in those states.[110]

The Member States that qualify for this exemption[111] must submit a national plan to the Commission and an annual report on investments made in upgrading infrastructure and clean technologies. The national plans consist of the last remnants of the individual NAPs from phases I and II, and may be rejected by the Commission within six months from the application.[112]

---

[105]   ETS Directive, art 3(h) (definition of new entrant).
[106]   European Commission, 'Guidance Document n°7 on the Harmonized Free Allocation Methodology for the EU-ETS Post 2012' (2011) 7.
[107]   ETS Directive, art 10a(7).
[108]   European Commission, above n 106, 35.
[109]   ETS Directive, art 10c.
[110]   Ibid. Also see Ellerman, Convery and Perthuis, above n 6, 76.
[111]   Mainly new Member States, according to the ETS Directive, art 10c(1)(a), (b), (c).
[112]   Ibid., art 10c(6).

The transitional free allowances allocated to electricity generators will be deducted from the Member State's auction rights and are limited to a maximum of 70 per cent of the average 2005–07 verified emissions from such electricity generators.[113] New entrants in the electricity production sector are not entitled to receive any free allocation of permits and the transitional assistance to eligible electricity generators should be phased out by 2020.[114]

In practice, most electricity generators were obliged to purchase all of their allowances at auction in 2013. A compromise was agreed with a few electricity generators in key Eastern European Member States which have joined the European Union since 2004. In order to assist these countries to modernise their electricity sectors and diversify their energy mix, the Directive provides for transitional assistance in the form of free permits that will diminish to zero by 2020.[115]

In general, the power sector went from receiving around 92 per cent of permits necessary for their compliance free of charge between 2008 and 2012, to around 24 per cent for free in 2013. To illustrate, Sandbag reported the massive drop in surplus registered by Duferco, which went down 91 per cent in 2013.[116] Sandbag also estimates that Duferco's and Termoelectrica's surplus should be exhausted before the end of the third trading period.[117]

3.2 Industry Assistance in the Former AUS CPM: The Jobs and Competitiveness Program

In Australia, the AUS CPM was implemented by the Clean Energy Act.[118] The Clean Energy Act provided that Regulations would formulate

---

[113] Ibid., art 10c(2).

[114] See Proposal 2015/148 (COD) for a Directive of the European Parliament and of the Council Amending Directive 2003/87/EC to enhance cost-effective emission reductions and low-carbon investments [2015]. The proposal for amendment of the ETS Directive provides for guaranteed assistance for the modernising of electricity sectors at least until 2030.

[115] ETS Directive, art 10c.

[116] Sandbag, above n 104, 46. Sandbag reports that:

Due to massive changes to its activity levels visible already in 2009, Duferco amassed surpluses completely out of proportion to its needs, yet in phase 2 the Scheme was not equipped to address this problem. The new rules make a vigorous contribution to solving this aspect of chronic over-allocation.

[117] Ibid.

[118] Clean Energy Act 2011 (Cth).

a programme, known as the Jobs and Competitiveness Program, in order to assist industry by allocating free of cost Australian Carbon Units (ACUs).[119] To be eligible for assistance under the Jobs and Competitiveness Program, activities must pass both the emissions-intensity and trade-exposure thresholds, as discussed in Chapter 4.

The amount of ACUs allocated free of cost to each eligible activity under the Jobs and Competitiveness Programme was calculated based on two set assistance rates, conditional on the emissions-intensity of the activity,[120] product benchmarks,[121] and the volume of production for a given financial year (output-based).[122]

In the 2012–13 financial year, the assistance rate to moderately emissions-intensive activities was set at 66 per cent of the benchmark, while assistance for highly emissions-intensive activities was set at 94.5 per cent of the benchmark.[123] These rates would decline by a linear factor of 1.3 per cent a year, also known as the 'carbon productivity contribution'.[124] Clearly the different levels of assistance across sectors within schemes and across the independent ETSs in themselves have an impact, as further discussed below.

Unlike the harmonised allocation system in the third trading period of the EU ETS, where benchmarks were based on the most efficient technology, in Australia the benchmarks were calculated according to an industry's average efficiency during the financial years of 2006–07 and 2007–08.[125] The final amount of carbon units to be allocated varied according to the volume of production for a given financial year (output-based). The allocation to new facilities would follow similar criteria, although the maximum amount available to be allocated to new entrants was capped.[126]

---

[119]   Ibid., Pt 7.
[120]   See Chapter 4.
[121]   Also referred to as 'allocative baselines'.
[122]   Clean Energy Regulations 2012 (Cth) s 906.
[123]   Ibid., s 907(4). Also see Elena Aydos, 'Australia's Carbon Pricing Mechanism' in Larry Kreiser et al (eds), *Carbon Pricing, Growth and the Environment*, Critical Issues in Environmental Taxation (Edward Elgar Publishing, 2012) 261, 266. The former CPRS Green Paper originally set the assistance rates at 60 per cent (moderately emissions-intensive) and 90 per cent (highly emissions-intensive). Rates were then adjusted to 66 per cent and 94.5 per cent due to the global financial crisis and never returned to their original amounts.
[124]   Clean Energy Regulations 2012, s 907(4)(b).
[125]   Ibid., s 401.
[126]   Ibid., ss 205, 707, 911.

Once the linking with the EU ETS was announced a number of amendments to the legislation were put in place. The Federal Government predicted that the amendments would benefit the EITE industries in Australia with higher effective assistance rates:

> However, provided Kyoto units trade at a lower price than Australian and European allowances, these entities should receive higher effective assistance rates. This is because they will receive assistance in the form of higher value Australian carbon units, but will be able to meet 12.5 per cent of their liabilities through lower cost Kyoto units.[127]

Australian entities would be able to meet their liabilities – initially up to 12.5 per cent – with emissions permits from the EU ETS (EUAs). With the predicted increase in the limit of EUAs eligible to meet compliance responsibilities in the AUS CPM, it could be expected that the price for ACUs would eventually be set by the European market. That is, it would become cheaper for liable entities in the AUS CPM to meet compliance. Despite the reduced compliance costs, the levels of assistance were not adjusted.[128]

Units allocated free of charge during the fixed price period were not bankable. However, entities were able to return the ACUs allocated free of cost to the Regulator through a buy-back mechanism.[129] Carbon units would be sold back to the Government for the market value of the permit from September 1 of the compliance year in which they were issued until February 1 of the following compliance year.

3.2.1 Review of the Jobs and Competitiveness Program

In terms of the governance of the assistance measures, the Australian system was one step ahead of the EU ETS. The Clean Energy Act provided that a detailed framework for the Jobs and Competitiveness Program would be set by Regulations, allowing for greater flexibility in the program.[130] The legislation also provided for regular reviews of the program by an independent research and advisory body, the Productivity Commission.[131]

---

[127] Australian Government, 'Establishing the Eligibility of Activities under the Jobs and Competitiveness Program' (2011) 3.

[128] Tiche, Weishaar and Couwenberg, above n 1.

[129] Explanatory Memorandum, Clean Energy Bill 2011 (Cth) 5.19.

[130] Clean Energy Act 2011.

[131] The Productivity Commission is the Australian Government's independent research and advisory body on a range of economic, social and environmental issues affecting the welfare of Australians.

While the first review was scheduled for the third year of the mechanism (financial year 2014–15), the Government was authorised to request an early review in case there was strong evidence of windfall gains as a result of the assistance granted to a specific sector.[132] The Productivity Commission's review of the Jobs and Competitiveness Program would cover operational aspects, the impacts on the EITE industries and the economic and environmental efficiency of the program, for example, whether the program was effectively avoiding carbon leakage or otherwise.[133]

In its first review, the Productivity Commission would consider whether the method of issuing the free units should be reviewed based on Garnaut's 'principled approach'.[134] According to this approach, the assistance to EITE sectors will be limited to the equivalent of the gap between the world's expected product prices with a global carbon price and without global carbon pricing.[135]

Criticisms of the structure of the review process included its heavy focus on competitiveness issues rather than on the assessment of real carbon leakage which may lead to policies that are not environmentally effective, as well as resulting in a lack of transparency in industry data.[136] Finally, industry was given a five-year period of guaranteed assistance[137] followed by a three years' notice guarantee prior to any changes that could negatively affect the levels of assistance under the program.[138]

3.3 Issues Arising from the Different Assistance Levels

A first observation to be drawn is that the disparate data availability, sector definitions and groupings of sectors makes the comparison of the

---

[132]   Clean Energy Act 2011, s 155(1); Explanatory Memorandum, Clean Energy Bill 2011, 5.27.

[133]   Ibid., 5.28.

[134]   Ibid., s 156. Also see Ross Garnaut, *The Garnaut Climate Change Review: Final Report* (Cambridge University Press, 2008), 345. Garnaut suggested a crediting system, in the form of cash or cash-equivalent reduction to obligation, in which the eligible participants would 'receive a credit against their permit obligations equivalent to the expected uplift in world product prices that would eventuate if our trading competitors had policies similar to our own'.

[135]   Ross Garnaut, 'Garnaut Climate Change Review Update: Carbon Pricing and Reducing Australia's Emissions' (Commonwealth of Australia, 2011) 36.

[136]   Tony Wood and Tristan Edis, 'New Protectionism under Carbon Pricing: Case Studies of LNG, Coal Mining and Steel Sectors' (Grattan Institute, 2011) 3.

[137]   Clean Energy Act 2011, s 157(3).

[138]   Explanatory Memorandum, Clean Energy Bill 2011, 5.29.

industry assistance under each ETS challenging and adds extra costs to businesses.[139] Given this, it is surprising that the EU Commission and the Australian Government failed to negotiate even basic provisions in relation to free allocation under the linking agreement.

Similarly to the competitiveness concerns among Member States during the first two trading periods of the EU ETS, the discrepancies between the assistance frameworks in the EU ETS and the AUS CPM would likely raise competitiveness concerns for certain liable sectors, even in the absence of a linking agreement.[140] The comparative analysis above demonstrates that, in terms of calculating the levels of support, the EU ETS multiplies the best technology benchmarks by the historical activity levels, while the AUS CPM calculated the average baselines and multiplied those by the industry output.

The product benchmarks under the EU ETS are more stringent than the AUS CPM baselines, since the former are based on the best available technologies and the latter on industry averages. While the less efficient industries under the EU ETS have an incentive to innovate up to the efficiency levels of the current best available technology, the entities in Australia would not have similar incentives. Indeed, Tiche, Weishaar and Couwenberg demonstrated that under the AUS CPM, any innovation would negatively impact on the number of permits distributed to the entire sector in the future.[141]

The use of historical levels of emissions to calculate the number of EUAs that individual entities would receive under the EU ETS benefited inefficient installations that had emitted large volumes of GHGs over the years.[142] Furthermore, unless the output of a facility dropped drastically, triggering closure provisions, the volumes of the free allowances received by the participants remained unchanged, even where an installation reduces production, allowing surpluses to readily accumulate when output is reduced.[143] For example, Sandbag identified a clear relationship between the surpluses in 2013 and drops in production relative to the

---

[139]   See, e.g. Kolshus and Torvanger, above n 47, 32.

[140]   OECD, *The Economics of Climate Change Mitigation: Policies and Options for Global Action Beyond 2012* (2009) 57, 123. The OECD points out that 'different rules for a given sector could raise competitiveness concerns; firms covered by a more stringent scheme might compete with firms that are exempt from binding commitments in the other'.

[141]   Tiche, Weishaar and Couwenberg, above n 1, 10.

[142]   Sandbag, above n 104, 37. Sandbag explains that, in practice, the selection of 2005–07 as base years benefited most industries.

[143]   Ibid., 37.

baselines in key industries, arguing that 'the new rules for awarding free allowances primarily serve to reward failure and punish success rather than encouraging cleaner industries to thrive'.[144]

An output-based system, such as adopted by the AUS CPM, might be preferable over the EU ETS criteria of historical activity, in order to incentivise the maintenance of, or increase in, production levels. In practice, an output-based allocation system works as a production subsidy, providing an incentive for industry to maintain production levels and, in the case of the former AUS CPM, guaranteeing the free allocation of ACUs for expanded production or new installations.

The downside of this system is that inefficient installations would tend to maintain production in order to uphold the levels of assistance, particularly where average benchmarks are in place, rather than benchmarks based on the most efficient technologies. That is, the combination of best technology benchmarks (EU) and an output-based allocation (AUS) would be likely to lead to preferable outcomes. Furthermore, the volume of the permits allocated under the former AUS CPM was calculated to compensate for the carbon price based on direct and indirect emissions, resulting in a generous assistance system.[145]

It is important to keep in mind that the European emissions-intensive sectors had the advantage of having accumulated a surplus of free of cost permits from the EU ETS's second trading period. As noted by the EC, 'this accumulation of free allowances is likely to continue until the end of 2012. By then the surplus is estimated to amount to 500–800 million allowances with an economic value of around €7–12 billion'.[146] As surpluses from the second trading period were bankable into the third trading period, these permits remained in the hands of the ETS participants.

The increased auctioning levels and new harmonised free-allocation rules applicable to the third trading period resulted in a fall in the free allocations to the power sector from 92 per cent of emissions (phase II) to 24 per cent in 2013, and to the manufacturing sector from 123 per cent of emissions (phase II) to 96 per cent in 2013.[147] However, Sandbag demonstrated that installations had been decreasing production since 2013 in order to accumulate surplus EUAs under the harmonised rules, estimating that the surpluses will remain beyond 2020 for all EITE

---

[144]   Ibid., 38.
[145]   Tiche, Weishaar and Couwenberg, above n 1, 12.
[146]   European Commission (2011), above n 97, 2.
[147]   Sandbag, above n 104, 29.

sectors, particularly the cement and lime sector, which is likely to remain oversupplied beyond 2040.[148]

Indeed, the impacts on trade caused by the discrepancies in the assistance measures, particularly in the cases of windfall profits and over-allocation, have the potential to severely impact the competitiveness of competitors liable under different ETSs. The levels of free allocation to competing industry sectors under different schemes may become a factor to be taken into account when deciding where to locate new investment. The competitiveness issues may be further exacerbated where only a few countries have sufficiently strong economies to provide such assistance to energy-intensive sectors.

Finally, the analysis of phases I and II of the EU ETS demonstrated that the ready availability of allowances from NERs, the amounts of units available to new facilities, and the transparency of the allocation process are elements that provide certainty for new investment. These elements are particularly relevant for new investments in highly-electricity-intensive sectors, such as the aluminium refining and steel sectors.

The treatment of new entrants should be comparable to that of other installations already present in the sector in order to avoid competitive distortions between the new entrants and the other participants. The Australian system was consistent with this framework.

4. CONCLUSION

The analysis of phases I and II of the EU ETS exposes the issues raised by adopting distinct allocation frameworks across ETSs. In practice, the decentralised system affected the transparency of the allocation plans, while increasing the complexity and transaction costs. The existence of different national allocation plans also encouraged a 'race to the bottom' process where installations pressured the Member States to allocate larger volumes of permits.[149]

In the case of the announced linking of the AUS CPM and the EU ETS, the free allocation of permits to EITE sectors remained significantly different, even after the EU and Australia decided to link their independent ETSs. It is possible that minimum levels of harmonisation across the

---

[148]   Ibid., 42.
[149]   Egenhofer et al, above n 13, 15.

allocation systems would have been necessary over time, similar to the harmonisation process adopted by the EU ETS in its third trading period.[150]

The uneven benchmarks and output-based allocations versus the historical emissions data are particularly problematic, and can result in a significant variation of the allocation levels, with the potential to impact on trade and distort the competition between the liable installations which are in competition with each other. Countries negotiating the future linking of independent ETSs should attempt to achieve a greater compatibility of the allocation systems in order to reduce the negative impacts on competiveness. Harmonised product descriptions could also be applied to specific sectors across different linked ETSs.

As a best practice principle, benchmarks based on the best available technology should be coupled with an output-based allocation rather than the historical emissions to determine the level of assistance. The treatment of new entrants must be comparable to that of other installations already present in the sector in order to avoid competitive distortions between the new entrants and the other participants.[151]

Objective, consistent and predictable rules should be adopted to prevent over-compensation (allocation in excess of the extra carbon costs) and windfall profits (entities receiving free carbon units and still passing through the opportunity costs). These rules may be monitored and reviewed by the administrator of the ETS or a different entity.

---

[150] Intergovernmental Panel on Climate Change, 'Work Group III Assessment Report 5: Mitigation of Climate Change' (2014) ch 13, 71. The IPCC AR5 states:

In principle, a wide variety of national climate policies can be harmonised across countries. This holds for cap-and-trade systems (e.g., a global emissions permit trading system), as we discuss in the context of linkage below, as well as for national carbon or other GHG taxes. (citations omitted).

See also Tobias Hausotter, Sibyl Steuwer and Dennis Tänzler, 'Competitiveness and Linking of Emission Trading Systems' (Federal Environmental Agency (Germany), 2011) 47. The authors argue that:

Hence, the harmonisation of allocation methods may be one topic to be addressed during a linking process. In addition, if different compensation measures exist (e.g. free allocation vs. BAMs) harmonisation has to be achieved, e.g., by agreeing on a uniform free allocation approach throughout the linked system.

[151] Ellerman, Buchner and Carraro, above n 12, 21.

Industry over-compensation and windfall profits are not consistent with the aims of an emissions trading scheme, thus crossing the boundaries of environmental policy and entering the arena of subsidisation.

6. The free allocation of permits and the WTO discipline of subsidies

1. INTRODUCTION

This chapter creates the necessary bridge between the in-depth analyses of the implications of the methodology for free allocation of permits to emissions-intensive trade-exposed (EITE) sectors presented in previous chapters and the application of the Agreement on Subsidies and Counter-vailing Measures (SCM Agreement),[1] as interpreted by the World Trade Organization (WTO)[2] judiciary.

Free allocation of permits is, indeed, a subsidy in accordance with the definition in the SCM Agreement. Furthermore, the free allocation system may be a prohibited or actionable subsidy, according to the different thresholds for allocation and levels of assistance set by each scheme.

Respectable voices in the literature have expressed concerns over the treatment of free allocation of permits as an actionable or prohibited subsidy.[3] However, the SCM Agreement has an important role in protecting the WTO Members affected by abusive free allocation systems or inappropriate countervailing measures. The SCM Agreement also

---

[1] Marrakesh Agreement Establishing the World Trade Organization, opened for signature 15 April 1994, 1867 UNTS 3 (entered into force 1 January 1995) Annex 1A ('Agreement on Subsidies and Countervailing Measures') (SCM Agreement).

[2] Ibid.

[3] See, e.g., James Windon, 'The Allocation of Free Emissions Units and The WTO Subsidies Agreement' (2009) 41 *Georgetown Journal of International Law* 1893; Denny Ellerman, '*Ex-post* Evaluation of Tradable Permits: The U.S. SO2 Cap-and-Trade Program' (CEEPR, 2003); Felicity Deane, *Emissions Trading and WTO Law: A Global Analysis* (Edward Elgar Publishing, 2015) 3; Lauren Henschke, 'Going it Alone on Climate Change. A New Challenge to WTO Subsidies Disciplines: Are Subsidies in Support of Emissions Reductions Schemes Permissible Under the WTO' (2012) 11(1) *World Trade Review* 273.

provides the guidelines and parameters which support the final recommendations in this book, that is, the adoption of best practice principles in the free allocation frameworks.

2. THE WTO LAW ON SUBSIDIES AND COUNTERVAILING MEASURES

In general terms, subsidies[4] are a form of public intervention in the economy by which a Government provides an economic advantage to some targeted groups,[5] often endangering the welfare of unsubsidised firms located in other States.[6] Domestically, the beneficiary groups will advocate policies that protect their interests, which is often endorsed by public opinion, adding to the political pressure upon local governments.[7]

From an international trade perspective, industrial subsidies can lead to a 'prisoner's dilemma' situation, where different countries acting in their own private interests subsidise domestic industries, with the final result being that every country is made worse off.[8] As such, subsidies can

---

[4] This chapter focuses on subsidies from a WTO law perspective. For an economics perspective on subsidies, see, e.g., Luca Rubini, *The Definition of Subsidy and State Aid: WTO and EC Law in Comparative Perspective* (Oxford University Press, 2010); Nikolaos Zahariadis, *State Subsidies in the Global Economy* (Palgrave Macmillan, 2008); Neil Bruce, 'Measuring Industrial Subsidies: Some Conceptual Issues' (OECD, 1990).

[5] See, e.g., Panagiotis Delimatsis, *International Trade in Services and Domestic Regulations: Necessity, Transparency, and Regulatory Diversity* (Oxford University Press, 2007) 49, 50.

[6] Robert Ford and Wim Suyker, 'Industrial Subsidies in the OECD Economies' (OECD, 1990). The Organisation for Economic Co-operation and Development (OECD) report concluded that 'the degree to which industrial subsidies, and their control, is a serious policy problem depends on how large they actually are and the size of the associated welfare effects'.

[7] Delimatsis, above n 5, 50. Delimatsis discusses how the pressure from interest groups concerned with protecting domestic production influences policymakers.

[8] WTO, 'World Trade Report: Exploring the Links Between Subsidies, Trade and the WTO' (World Trade Organization, 2006); Bruce, above n 4, 3. On environmentally harmful subsidies and the space for reform, see OECD, 'Environmentally Harmful Subsidies: Challenges for Reform' (OECD, 2005); OECD, 'Subsidy Reform and Sustainable Development: Political Economy Aspects' (OECD, 2007).

create barriers to trade and make markets less open, which is contrary to the aims of the WTO.[9]

From as early as the second half of the nineteenth century, international efforts have been made to limit the use of harmful subsidies.[10] While the General Agreement on Tariffs and Trade (GATT)[11] originally did not contain a provision on subsidies, in 1955 Article XVI was added to it providing, among other things, that the subsidising country must notify of any subsidy operating to increase exports of any product from, or to reduce imports of any product into, its territory. Subsidies were addressed through non-violation complaints according to Article XXIII(1)(b) of the GATT.[12]

However, Article XVI of the GATT did not provide for a definition of a subsidy. In 1961, a GATT Panel, established to work on subsidies, reached the conclusion that 'it was neither necessary nor feasible to seek an agreed interpretation of what constituted a subsidy', expressing the difficulties of reaching an internationally agreed definition for subsidies.[13]

Over 30 years later, a comprehensive multilateral treaty disciplining the use of subsidies and countervailing measures, the SCM Agreement, was negotiated under the auspices of the WTO, adopting for the first time an international legal definition of a subsidy. This definition not only defines the scope of the SCM Agreement but it also applies across other WTO agreements, such as the Agreement on Agriculture[14] and the GATT.[15]

---

[9]   WTO, above n 1.

[10]   Harald B. Malmgren, *International Order for Public Subsidies* (Trade Policy Research Centre, 1977) 4. Malmgren states that 'the earliest known efforts to limit subsidies were contained in national pledges not to grant export bounties, which had become common, in commercial treaties between European countries, during the second half of the ninetieth century'.

[11]   General Agreement on Tariffs and Trade, opened for signature 30 October 1947 [1947] 55 UNTS 194 (entered into force 1 January 1948).

[12]   On the history of the regulation of subsidies under the GATT see Douglas A. Irwin, Petros C. Mavroidis and Alan O. Sykes, *The Genesis of the GATT* (Cambridge University Press, 2008) 156–9; Rubini, above n 4.

[13]   WTO, above n 8; WTO, 'Basic Instruments and Selected Documents' (GATT Secretariat, 1962); Rubini, above n 4, 107.

[14]   World Trade Organization, above n 1, annex 1A (Agreement on Agriculture). Although arts 9 and 10 of the Agreement on Agriculture regulate export subsidies in the agriculture sector, they do not provide a definition of a subsidy. See Rubini, above n 4, 127. Rubini explains that, 'when reading the AG, and in particular when defining the notion of subsidy, it seems appropriate to look at the SCM Agreement for contextual guidance'.

[15]   The SCM Agreement applies to all sectors of the economy except for services.

The WTO Panel has proposed that the object and purpose of the SCM Agreement is 'the establishment of multilateral disciplines "on the premise that some forms of government intervention distort international trade, [or] have the potential to distort [international trade]"'.[16] Mavroidis suggested that the main purpose of the SCM Agreement is more specific. It was aimed at discouraging subsidies that might harm producers in importing countries.[17] For example, the use of countervailing measures is only authorised in the event of injury to a domestic industry in an importing country,[18] while the impacts on other members are open to challenge pursuant to Dispute Settlement Understanding (DSU) provisions.

In this chapter, the role of the SCM Agreement is seen as twofold. First, it guides and informs WTO Members pursuant to their rights and obligations relating to subsidies and countervailing measures. Secondly, it provides a corrective mechanism for WTO Members affected by subsidies or countervailing measures.[19]

The two functions are relevant to the issue of the free allocation of emissions permits.[20] As demonstrated in previous chapters, an increasing number of countries are adopting new Emissions Trading Schemes (ETSs) and these schemes provide for the free allocation of permits as a measure to protect industry. Free allocation systems can provide economic benefits precisely to those industry sectors that should instead be paying a carbon price and have the potential to distort trade. Therefore, the guidance role of the SCM Agreement provided the parameters to support the final recommendations in this book for the adoption of best practice principles in free allocation frameworks, while the corrective role protects the WTO Members affected by abusive free allocation systems or inappropriate countervailing measures.

---

[16] Panel Report, *Canada – Measures Affecting the Export of Civilian Aircraft*, WTO Doc WT/DS70/R (14 April 1999) [9.119] (*Canada – Civilian Aircraft*); WTO, *WTO Analytical Index: Guide to WTO Law and Practice: Agreement on Subsidies and Countervailing Measures* (Cambridge University Press, 3rd edn, 2011).

[17] Petros Mavroidis, *Trade In Goods: The GATT and the Other WTO Agreements Regulating Trade in Goods* (Oxford University Press, 2012) 525; Rubini, above n 8.

[18] Mavroidis, ibid., 524.

[19] Windon, above n 2.

[20] In this chapter I use the terminology 'permits'.

2.1 Is the Free Allocation of Permits a Subsidy?

The legal definition of a subsidy in the SCM Agreement encompasses a range of transactions by which a Government may transfer something of economic value to the advantage of a recipient,[21] from a direct transfer of funds by a Government or public body, to any form of income or price support. It differs from the broader, economics-based definitions[22] in the sense that not all Government measures that confer a benefit to recipients are considered to be a subsidy.[23]

The legal analysis of whether the free allocation of permits to the EITE sectors amounts to a subsidy involves a filtering process of four cumulative inquiries. The first inquiry is whether there is a financial contribution, income or price support by a Government. The SCM Agreement provides an extensive list of actions that amount to a financial contribution.[24]

The second inquiry is whether a 'benefit is thereby conferred' (Article 1.1(b)). At this point, if the first two questions are answered in the affirmative, a subsidy is deemed to be in place. As demonstrated below, the free allocation of permits is arguably a subsidy for the purpose of the SCM Agreement.

Not all subsidies are prohibited under the SCM Agreement.[25] A subsidy will only be subject to the provisions of the SCM Agreement if it is 'specific', that is, limited to specific enterprises or industries. Specificity is the third inquiry.

---

[21] Appellate Body Report, *United States – Final Countervailing Duty Determination with Respect to Certain Softwood Lumber from Canada*, WTO Doc WT/DS257/AB/R, AB-2003-6 (19 January 2004) [51] (*US – Softwood Lumber IV*).

[22] OECD, *Glossary of Statistical Terms* (OECD, 2007) Definition of subsidy. The OECD adopted an economics-based definition of a subsidy, as 'a result of a government action that confers an advantage on consumers or producers, in order to supplement their income or lower their costs'.

[23] Panel Report, *United States – Measures Treating Exports Restraints as Subsidies*, WTO Doc WT/DS194/R (29 June 2001) (*US – Exports Restraints*) [8.65]: Appellte Body, *US – Softwood Lumber IV*, [52].

[24] SCM Agreement art 1.1(a)(1).

[25] Appellate Body Report, *Canada – Measures Affecting the Export of Civilian Aircraft*, WTO Doc WT/DS70/AB/RW, AB-1999-2 (2 August 1999) [47] (*Canada – Civilian Aircraft*); Mavroidis, above n 17, 523. Mavroidis explains that 'the agreement was meant, through the various disciplines imposed, to remove the incentive to purposefully confer an artificial advantage on a specific class of producers through subsidization'.

The SCM Agreement provides for two types of prohibited subsidies (local content and export). These are deemed to be specific and are prohibited *per se*. Even where a subsidy is not prohibited, a fourth inquiry determines whether a specific subsidy is actionable, that is, whether it causes injury to other Members.

3. FIRST INQUIRY: FINANCIAL CONTRIBUTION

The SCM Agreement provides an exhaustive[26] not mutually-exclusive[27] list of what constitutes a financial contribution.[28] The list covers: a direct transfer of funds or potential direct transfers of funds or liabilities: (i) Government revenue that is otherwise due and is foregone (ii) and a provision of goods or services other than general infrastructure (iii).

The free allocation of permits to participants of an ETS is a multi-faceted transaction. Through the introduction of an ETS the polluting businesses – in theory – bear a new production cost, aimed at internalising a negative externality. At the same time, in order to achieve emissions mitigation in the most economically efficient way, the trading of emissions permits ('rights' to pollute) is allowed, so that the abatement will occur where it is more efficient.

Consequently, the emissions permits have economic value in two ways. First, emissions permits operate as a licence to pollute. From this perspective, the purchase of emissions permits is a condition for firms to carry out economic activities, that is, it is a cost of business. Secondly,

---

[26] Panel Report, *United States – Measures Affecting Trade in Large Civil Aircraft (Second Complaint)*, WTO Doc WT/DS353/R (31 March 2011) (*US – Large Civil Aircraft (Second Complaint)*); Panel Report, *US – Exports Restraints*. Also see Rubini, above n 4, 110–11.

[27] That is, the same transaction may be covered by more than one subparagraph. See Appellate Body Report, *United States – Measures Affecting Trade in Large Civil Aircraft (Second Complaint)*, WTO Doc WT/DS353/AB/R, AB-2011-3 (12 March 2012) [613] FN 1287 (*US – Large Civil Aircraft (Second Complaint)*); World Trade Organization, above n 16, 101–5; Appellate Body Report, *Canada – Certain Measures Affecting The Renewable Energy Generation Sector, Canada – Measures Relating To The Feed-In Tariff Program*, WTO Doc WT/DS412/AB/R WT/DS426/AB/R, AB-2013-1 (6 May 2013) [5.120] (*Canada – Renewable Energy*).

[28] SCM Agreement art 1.1(a)(1). Panel Report, *US – Large Civil Aircraft (Second Complaint)*, WTO Doc WT/DS353/R [7.955].

the emissions permits are assets held by firms which may be traded in secondary markets.[29]

The dual nature of the emissions permits is evident and they have impacted on, for example, the accounting policies of liable companies, as well as the tax treatment of emissions permits in different jurisdictions. Black identified a lack of uniformity in the financial accounting treatment of transactions involving emissions permits across jurisdictions with an ETS in place and the companies operating therein.[30] The most common approach is to recognise the emissions permits in financial statements, either as intangible assets carried by the company[31] (tradable asset character), a government grant[32] (transfer of resources) or a liability[33] (licencing character). As pointed out by Black, 'accounting profits are

---

[29] Robert Howse and Antonia L. Eliason, 'Domestic and International Strategies to Address Climate Change: An Overview of the WTO Legal Issues' in Thomas Cottier, Olga Nartova and Sadeq Z Bigdeli (eds), *International Trade Regulation and the Mitigation of Climate Change* (Cambridge University Press, 2009) 48, 53. Howse and Eliason concluded that even where carbon permits or credits resemble financial services, they have elements similar to those seen in commodities trading, and commodities are unquestionably goods. Also see Henschke, above n 2, 30.

[30] Celeste Black, 'Accounting for Carbon Emission Allowances in the European Union: In Search of Consistency' (2014) 10(2) *Accounting in Europe* 223.

[31] According to the definition in the International Financial Reporting Standards (IFRS), 'an intangible asset is an identifiable non-monetary asset without physical substance' controlled by a firm and where future economic benefits are expected (International Accounting Standard (IAS) 38 – Intangible Assets [8], [10]).

[32] According to the IFRS definition:

Government grants are assistance by government in the form of transfers of resources to an entity in return for past or future compliance with certain conditions relating to the operating activities of the entity. They exclude those forms of government assistance which cannot reasonably have a value placed upon them and transactions with government which cannot be distinguished from the normal trading transactions of the entity. (International Accounting Standard (IAS) 20 – Accounting for Government Grants and Disclosure of Government Assistance [3]).

[33] International Accounting Standard (IAS) 37 – Provisions, Contingent Liabilities and Contingent Assets [14], [36]. Black, above n 30, 225–6. Black explains:

Finally, the emission obligation under the EU ETS should be recognised as a provision consistent with IAS 37 Provisions, Contingent Liabilities and Contingent Assets, given that it is a present obligation as emissions are

increasingly relied upon as the starting point for determining taxation obligations, thereby impacting government revenue'.[34]

The accounting treatments and their impacts on the taxation regime applied to emissions permits reveals the assumption – common to the private sector and governments – that, where emissions permits are allocated free of cost or for a reduced value, the participants receive something of economic value. This aspect will be further analysed in the relevant sections below.

The following sections demonstrate that the free allocation of emissions permits may be interpreted under Article 1.1(a)(1) of the SCM Agreement as a foregoing of revenue that is otherwise due (ii) and/or as a provision of goods other than general infrastructure (iii), depending on which element in the transaction is considered predominant, the licensing aspect and/or the asset aspect of the emissions permits.

In contrast, this type of transaction is less likely to be regarded as a direct or potentially direct transfer of funds (i). A direct transfer of funds or potential direct transfers of funds or liabilities includes not only grants, loans, loan guarantees and equity infusions, which are the specific examples listed in Article 1.1(a)(1)(i), but also other similar transactions such as debt forgiveness, extension of loan maturity, debt-to-equity swaps, among others.[35] The allocation of emissions permits would not easily fit into any of these transactions. The normal fluctuations in the price of an emissions permit – its market value might change considerably after the allocation date – is incompatible with the description of a direct or potentially direct transfer of funds.[36]

Finally, Article 1.1(a)(1)(iv) refers to situations in which a private body is being used as a 'proxy' by the government in order to carry out one or more of the functions specified in Article 1.1(a)(1)(i)–(iii).[37] Paragraph (iv) is not applicable to the current ETSs, where the permits are allocated by governments. Nevertheless, paragraph (iv) may be relevant in future

---

produced, where the issue of determining the best estimate of the expenditure required to meet the obligation becomes relevant.

[34]   Ibid., 224.

[35]   Panel Report, *Korea – Measures Affecting Trade in Commercial Vessels*, WTO Doc WT/DS273/R (7 March 2005) [7.411] – [7.413]; Appellate Body Report, *US – Large Civil Aircraft (Second Complaint)*, WTO Doc WT/DS353/AB/R [615].

[36]   Henschke, above n 2.

[37]   Appellate Body Report, *United States – Countervailing Duty Investigation on Dynamic Random Access Memory Semiconductors (DRAMS) from Korea*, WTO Doc WT/DS296/AB/R, AB-2005-4 (27 June 2005) [108] (*US – DRAMS*).

ETSs, in the case where a private body is entrusted by the government to allocate emissions permits to firms.

3.1 Revenue Foregone that is Otherwise Due

The WTO Agreement is a negative integration contract with respect to taxation.[38] That is, the WTO Members are sovereign to design and make adjustments to their national taxation systems.[39] Therefore, the inclusion of the foregoing of revenue otherwise due, as a measure that constitutes financial contributions, aims at preventing tax regimes that, in practice, achieve 'outcomes equivalent to the results that are achieved where a government provides a direct payment'.[40]

A financial contribution is deemed to exist where the 'government revenue that is otherwise due is foregone or not collected'.[41] The foregoing of revenue occurs when the 'government has given up an entitlement to raise revenue that it could "otherwise" have raised'.[42] This definition clearly covers exemptions as well as reductions to the amount of tax or 'other form of revenue' that is not collected compared to what would otherwise be applicable.[43]

Since the WTO Members are, in principle, free to charge – or not to charge – any particular category of revenue,[44] for a financial contribution to be in place the revenue foregone must be 'otherwise due'. The SCM Agreement does not provide one theoretical benchmark on how to determine whether a tax or other revenue is 'otherwise due', leaving the WTO adjudicating bodies with the task of interpreting it.[45] In *US – FSC* the Panel applied a 'but for' test, in order to determine whether the

---

[38]   Mavroidis, above n 17, 534.

[39]   Appellate Body Report, *US- Large Civilian Aircraft (Second Complaint)*, WTO Doc WT/DS353/AB/R [811].

[40]   Ibid.

[41]   SCM Agreement, art 1.1(a)(1)(ii).

[42]   Appellate Body Report, *United States – Tax Treatment for 'Foreign Sales Corporations'* WTO Doc WT/DS108/AB/R, AB-1999-9 (24 February 2000) [90] (*US-FSC*); Appellate Body Report, *US – Large Civilian Aircraft (Second Complaint)*, WTO Doc WT/DS353/AB/R [806].

[43]   Appellate Body Report, *US – Large Civilian Aircraft (Second Complaint)*, WTO Doc WT/DS353/AB/R. The Appellate Body found that a reduced rate in the Washington State business and occupation tax (B&O) advantaging commercial aircraft and component manufacturers was deemed to be a subsidy.

[44]   Appellate Body Report, *US – FSC*, WTO Doc WT/DS108/AB/R [90].

[45]   Ibid., [7.43].

Government revenue was 'otherwise due'. The test involved investigating whether revenue would be raised in the absence of the exemption rule.[46]

The Appellate Body upheld the Panel's approach and clarified that the basis of comparison must be the tax rules applied by the Member in question.[47] That is, the definition of revenue that is 'otherwise due' depends on the rules of taxation or revenue adopted by each Member.[48] A similar approach was adopted by the Appellate Body in *Canada – Certain Measures Affecting the Automotive Industry* (*Canada – Automotive Industry*), which found that the exemption of import duties granted to certain motor vehicles consisted of a foregoing of revenue otherwise due.[49] Nevertheless, the Appellate Body in *US – Large Civilian Aircraft (Second Complaint)* and *US – FSC*, emphasised that although the 'but for' test may be appropriate to assess whether revenue is otherwise due, it is not an exclusive methodology that must be applied to all cases.[50]

In applying the 'but for' test, the first step is to identify the tax treatment applicable to the income of the alleged recipients. The second step is to determine a legal benchmark based on the tax treatment of the comparable income of comparably situated taxpayers.[51] The base of comparison is the tax system or other form of government revenue which would be applicable at the time when the exception rule is taking place. That is, the definition of the general rule of taxation must not be based solely on a historical comparison.[52] The third step consists of examining the reasons for the differential treatment compared to the benchmark identified.[53]

An investigation into the reasons for the differential treatment is relevant for the purposes of identifying situations in which revenue foregone does not confer a benefit – i.e. a subsidy is not deemed to exist – in accordance to Footnote 1 and Annexes I–III of the SCM Agreement.

---

[46] Panel Report, *United States – Tax Treatment for 'Foreign Sales Corporations'*, WTO Doc WT/DS108/R (8 October 1999) [7.45] (*'US-FSC'*).

[47] Appellate Body Report, *US – FSC*, WTO Doc WT/DS108/AB/R [90].

[48] Panel Report, *US-FSC*, WTO Doc WT/DS108/R [7.42].

[49] Appellate Body Report, *Canada – Certain Measures Affecting the Automotive Industry*, WTO Doc WT/DS139/AB/R (31 May 2000) footnote V [90] (*Canada – Automotive Industry*).

[50] Appellate Body Report, *US – Large Civilian Aircraft (Second Complaint)*, WTO Doc WT/DS353/AB/R [818]; Appellate Body Report, *US – FSC*, WTO Doc WT/DS108/AB/R [91].

[51] Ibid. [812]–[814].

[52] Ibid. [823]; World Trade Organization, above n 16, 105.

[53] Appellate Body Report, *US – Large Civilian Aircraft (Second Complaint)*, WTO Doc WT/DS353/AB/R, [812]–[814].

For example, Footnote 59 (Annex I) excludes from the definition of subsidy exemption measures aimed at avoiding the double taxation of foreign-source income earned by its enterprises, or the enterprises of another Member.[54] Similarly, the exemption from domestic consumption duties or taxes on exported domestic products shall not be deemed to be a subsidy according to Footnote 1.

3.2 The Free Allocation of Emissions Permits as a Foregoing of Revenue Otherwise Due

In order to analyse whether the free allocation of permits is a subsidy, it is crucial to demonstrate that an emissions permit price would have normally been paid to the Treasury 'but for' the adoption of an assistance measure.[55] The independent ETSs vary in structure and there is not a common international practice determining whether permits are allocated free of cost or sold at a price. Hence, the enquiry will vary according to the framework of each scheme.

Taking the EU ETS, the NZ ETS and the former AUS CPM as case studies, it is more or less clear that revenue is otherwise due, depending on the legal frameworks of these systems. Therefore, in a dispute resolution, the WTO Panels would take into consideration the structure of the ETS in order to assess whether comparably situated liable entities would have to pay for the right to pollute while others did not. In *US – Large Civil Aircraft (Second Complaint)* the Appellate Body observed that:

> In some cases, the principles will be ones well recognized in the tax regimes of Members; in other cases, they will be unique to the particular domestic regime. It may be that disparate tax measures, implemented over time, do not easily offer up coherent principles serving as a benchmark. In any event, the task of the panel is to develop an understanding of the tax structure and principles that best explains that Member's tax regime, and to provide a

---

[54]   SCM Agreement. Also see Appellate Body Report, *US – FSC*, WTO Doc WT/DS108/AB/R.

[55]   See Javier De Cendra, 'Can Emissions Trading Schemes be Coupled with Border Tax Adjustments? An Analysis vis-à-vis WTO Law' (2006) 15(2) *RECIEL* 131, 136. De Cendra argued that 'if it was considered that a government can auction allowances and generate revenues, the decision to allocate them for free would be considered to forego revenues, and that would constitute a subsidy'.

reasoned basis for identifying what constitutes comparable income of comparably situated taxpayers.[56]

3.2.1 The foregoing of revenue under the EU's Emissions trading system

Analysing the first two phases of the EU ETS, the normative benchmark was the free of cost allocation of permits known as European Emissions Allowances (EEAs).[57] The participants under the EU ETS were covered by a 'blanket exemption',[58] in which the exemption is 'sufficiently broad so as not to be considered a financial contribution' under Article 1.1(a)(1)(ii).[59]

From the third trading period onwards (2013–20), individual NAPs are no longer in place and the methodology for the allocation of the EEAs is harmonised at EU level.[60] The new methodology is based on the benchmarks of emissions performance.[61] The participants who attained the benchmark performance level received 80 per cent of the allowances free of cost in 2013. Less efficient firms would receive a proportionately lower allocation of EEAs and may have to reduce emissions and/or purchase the required permits to meet compliance.

An increasing percentage of the EEAs will be issued via auction, with the free allocations reducing annually and reaching 30 per cent in 2020. Nevertheless, the sectors deemed at risk of carbon leakage (EITE sectors) would still receive, for free, most of the permits required for compliance.

Therefore, a differential treatment among the liable entities is already in place and is expected to become more salient after 2027, when the free allocation of permits ceases to benefit all liable entities under the EU ETS.[62] With the majority of the EUAs being issued in the market by auctioning, it is likely that a financial contribution will be in place

---

[56] Appellate Body Report, *US – Large Civil Aircraft (Second Complaint)*, WTO Doc WT/DS353/AB/R [813].

[57] The allocation system in phase I and II of the EU ETS is analysed in detail in Chapter 4.

[58] Windon, above n 2, 205.

[59] Panel Report, *US-FSC*, WTO Doc WT/DS108/R, 10 [7.119]. See Henschke, above n 2, 35.

[60] Directive 2003/87/EC of the European Parliament and of the Council of 13 October 2003 Establishing a Scheme for Greenhouse Gas Emission Allowance Trading within the Community and Amending Council Directive 96/61/EC [2003] OJ L 275/32 (ETS Directive) art 10a. Further details are available in Chapter 4.

[61] Ibid., art 10a(2).

[62] Ibid., art 10a(11).

favouring those EITE sectors which will still receive free of cost EUAs after 2027. These transactions are likely to be deemed to be a foregoing of revenue otherwise due in the terms of Article 1.1(a)(1)(ii).

3.2.2 The foregoing of revenue under the Australian carbon pricing mechanism

The nature of free permits as revenue that is foregone is even clearer under the AUS CPM. The Australian scheme was innovative in its methodology for the allocation of emissions permits, known as Australian Carbon Units (ACUs), inasmuch as the sale of ACUs was the general rule from the launching of the ETS.[63] The emissions permits were sold for a fixed charge (fixed charge years) with legislation providing for the introduction of auctioning from July 2015 (flexible charge years).[64]

From the commencement of the scheme, certain sectors were favoured by an allocation of free of cost ACUs. Indeed, the ACUs were allocated free of charge to the EITE sectors under the Jobs and Competitiveness Program and to electricity generators under the Energy Security Fund.[65] Furthermore, a Steel Transformation Plan Package provided for an additional allocation of permits exclusively to the steel sector.[66]

A useful example of how the assistance to the EITE sectors worked in practice was provided by Deane:

> Company A, a liable entity under the CPM, is carrying on an eligible activity under the JCP and is categorised as a highly emissions intensive company. During an eligible year of the CPM Company A has emitted 500,000 tonnes of carbon dioxide equivalent (CO_2-e). The consequence of assistance measures of the JCP is that where Company A would have been required to purchase 500 carbon units, they need only purchase 27 units. The other 473 have been provided free by the regulator in accordance with the JCP. The regulator has foregone revenue from 473 units.
>
> The alternative may be demonstrated by considering Company B. Company B does not carry on an EITE activity and is therefore ineligible for assistance. If Company B emits 500,000 tonnes of CO_2-e it must purchase all 500 carbon units. If the first fixed price period is used in this example, Company A would be liable to pay $621 while Company B's expense would amount to $11,500.

---

[63] The methodology for the issue and/or allocation of the ACUs is explained in detail in Chapters 4 and 5.

[64] Clean Energy Act 2011 (Cth) s 100 (CE Act).

[65] Ibid., Pts 7 and 8.

[66] Steel Transformation Plan Act 2011 (Cth).

Therefore, when the circumstances of the market within Australia are examined, it can be demonstrated that the JCP enables revenue that is otherwise due, to be foregone. It follows that the JCP satisfies the first requirement of a subsidy.[67]

In the case of a re-introduction of an ETS in Australia in the future, with the likelihood of the EITE companies lobbying for at least the same – if not superior – standards of assistance in the form of a total or partial waiving of the cost of carbon units, there will be space for debating the nature of this assistance as a subsidy. Likewise, other ETSs that may be implemented in the future which have methodologies that resemble the former AUS CPM are also likely to be considered as providing a subsidy in the form of a government revenue foregone that is otherwise due.[68]

3.2.3 The foregoing of revenue under the New Zealand emissions trading scheme

The third case to consider is the NZ ETS. A transition phase has been in effect since 1 July 2010, in which the transport, energy and industry sectors are required to surrender only one eligible emission unit for every two tonnes of carbon dioxide equivalent (CO_2-e) produced.[69] The practical effect of this is that the cost of the New Zealand Units (NZUs) has reduced to 50 per cent of its original amount.[70] Furthermore, the industrial activities identified as EITE are eligible to receive free of cost NZUs.[71]

As the sale of NZUs for less than the full price is currently a broad concession to all industry sectors, it may not be characterised as revenue that is 'otherwise due'. Nevertheless, the free allocation to the EITE sectors may be deemed to be a subsidy, following the same argument applied to the former AUS CPM.

3.3 Provision of Goods

Article 1.1(a)(1)(iii) provides for three actions by a Government which are deemed to be a financial contribution: (a) the provision of goods

---

[67] Felicity Deane, 'Subsidies of the Australian Clean Energy Package' (2013) 12(2) *The Journal of Law and Financial Management* 3, 25.

[68] Cf Henschke, above n 2, 38.

[69] Climate Change Act 2002 (NZ) s 222A(2). This policy feature is commonly referred to as 'one-for-two surrender obligation' or '50 per cent progressive obligation'.

[70] Further details are available in Chapter 4.

[71] Climate Change Act 2002 (NZ) s 222A(2).

other than general infrastructure; (b) the provision of services other than general infrastructure; and (c) the purchase of goods. Purchases of services are excluded from the definitions of subsidies.[72]

The provision of goods and services other than general infrastructure is regarded as a financial contribution because it has the 'potential to lower artificially the cost of producing a product by providing, to an enterprise, inputs having a financial value'.[73] In a presumed dispute before the WTO adjudicating bodies, the issue of whether the 'emissions permits' are defined as 'goods' under the SCM Agreement would be crucial.[74]

As with other treaties under the WTO, in order to reach a consensus in the negotiation stages of the SCM Agreement, the members opted for the use of open-ended terms. The Vienna Convention on the Law of Treaties[75] provides general rules for the interpretation of treaties.

Article 31(1) of the Vienna Convention provides that 'a treaty shall be interpreted in good faith in accordance with the ordinary meaning to be given to the terms of the treaty in their context and in the light of its object and purpose'. It also provides that 'when a treaty has been authenticated in two or more languages, the text is equally authoritative

---

[72]   Panel Report, *US – Large Civil Aircraft (Second Complaint)*, WTO Doc WT/DS353/R [7.968]–[7.969]. In *US – Large Civil Aircraft (Second Complaint)* the Panel analysed the history of the negotiations of the SCM Agreement and concluded that the provision of services was deliberately excluded from the definition of a financial contribution. Cf, Appellate Body Report, *US – Large Civil Aircraft (Second Complaint)*, WTO Doc WT/DS353/AB/R [620]. The Appellate Body Report declared the Panel's interpretation to be moot and of no legal effect based on judicial economy, as it understood that:

> this interpretative issue does not need to be resolved by us because it is not relevant for purposes of resolving the dispute before us, that is, whether the NASA procurement contracts and USDOD assistance instruments, which we have found to resemble joint ventures, constitute financial contributions within the meaning of Article 1.1(a)(1) of the SCM Agreement.

[73]   Appellate Body Report, *US – Softwood Lumber IV*, WTO Doc WT/DS257/AB/R [53].

[74]   Ibid. [69]. The definition of the term 'provides' is less ambiguous. In *US – Softwood Lumber IV* the Appellate Body held that the term 'provides' means, inter alia, 'to put at the disposal of' or 'supply or furnish for use; make available'. This definition is compatible with the act of allocating, via electronic transfer or other means, emissions permits to participants in an ETS.

[75]   Vienna Convention on the Law of Treaties, 23 May 1969, 1155 U.N.T.S. 331; 8 International Legal Materials 679 (Vienna Convention) art 31(1).

in each language, unless the treaty provides or the parties agree that, in case of divergence, a particular text shall prevail'.[76]

In *US – Softwood Lumber IV*[77] the US Department of Commerce (USDOC) concluded that the harvesting of softwood lumber was subsidised by provincial Governments in Canada through the 'provision' of permissions (stumpage) to harvest softwood. The USDOC imposed import duties as a countervailing measure on softwood lumber from Canada. Canada contested the existence of a subsidy, questioning 'whether the term "goods" in Article 1.1(a)(1)(iii) captures trees before they are harvested, that is, standing timber attached to the land (but severable from it) and incapable of being traded across borders as such'.[78]

In this case, the Appellate Body Report parted from a general definition of the term 'goods', drawn from the *Shorter Oxford English Dictionary*, which includes '"property or possessions" especially – but not exclusively – "movable property"'.[79] The Appellate Body Report also agreed with the Panel that the ordinary meaning of the term 'goods' includes – but it did not limit the meaning to – 'items that are tangible and capable of being possessed'.[80]

The Appellate Body noted that the extraction of definitions from the dictionary – so often found in the submissions of the WTO Members as well as in the Reports of the Panels and the Appellate Body – offer a 'useful starting point' for extracting the ordinary meaning of the terms of an Agreement, but their usefulness is limited.[81] This is the case, particularly, where 'the meanings of terms used in the different authentic texts of the WTO Agreement are susceptible to differences in scope'.[82] The ordinary meaning of the term 'goods' in the French version of the SCM

---

[76]   Ibid., art 33(1).

[77]   Appellate Body Report, *US – Softwood Lumber IV*, WTO Doc WT/DS257/AB/R [51].

[78]   Ibid., [57]. It is remarkable that the 'right to harvest timber', conferred by certain provincial governments to entities through stumpage programs, was compared in this case to the actual provision of softwood lumber to harvesters. In other words, the adjudicator understood that the provision of an intangible right to harvest standing timber was equivalent to providing tangible goods in the form of standing timber. The focus was, therefore, on whether the tangible timber that would be harvested could be defined as 'goods' under the SCM Agreement, rather than whether the intangible 'right to harvest' was a 'good'.

[79]   Ibid., [58].

[80]   Ibid., [59].

[81]   Ibid.

[82]   Ibid.

Agreement (*biens*) and in the Spanish version of the SCM Agreement (*bienes*) includes a wide range of property rights, suggesting that a broader definition to the term 'goods' in the English version must be adopted.[83]

The Appellate Body Report also interpreted the object and purpose of the SCM Agreement and the context of Article 1.1(a)(1) and concluded that 'Article 1.1(a)(1)(iii) recognizes that subsidies may be conferred, not only through monetary transfers, but also through *in-kind* transfers.'[84] That is, Article 1.1(a)(1) makes a distinction between the transfer of monetary inputs (i) and other forms of non-monetary (*in-kind*) inputs or goods (iii). Furthermore, under the terms of the latter, the only exception to categorising the provision of 'goods' as a financial contribution is when those goods are provided in the form of 'general infrastructure'.[85]

3.3.1 Are intangible assets 'goods'?

The adoption of a broad definition of the term 'goods' was confirmed in *Canada – Renewable Energy*, where the Panel and the Appellate Body Reports held that the purchase of electricity produced from renewable sources by the Ontario Power Authority (OPA) amounts to a purchase of 'goods' within the meaning of Article 1.1(a)(1)(iii) of the SCM Agreement.[86]

The definition of the intangible asset of electricity as a 'good' – in particular where the transaction is viewed as a transfer of an 'entitlement' to electricity, rather than the taking of physical possession of the electricity – has been accepted by the Panel and not discussed at the appellate level. This decision is in line with European Court of Justice case law, where the court has consistently found that electricity constitutes a good.[87]

The acceptance of this definition had clear repercussions for the Appellate Body's conclusion that the purchase of electricity at a guaranteed rate provided a financial contribution to producers of wind-power and solar photovoltaic (PV) energy. Had the Appellate Body concluded

---

[83]   Ibid.

[84]   Ibid., [64].

[85]   Ibid., [60].

[86]   Appellate Body Report, *Canada – Renewable Energy*, WTO Doc WT/DS412/AB/R [5.110]–[5.111].

[87]   See, e.g., *Commission of the European Communities v Italian Republic* (C-158/94) [1997] ECR I-05789; Janusz Bielecki and Melaku Geboye Desta, *Electricity Trade in Europe: Review of the Economic and Regulatory Changes* (Kluwer Law International, 2004).

that the provision of electricity is a 'service', the transaction would fall outside the very scope of the SCM Agreement.[88]

It appears that the interpretation of the term 'goods' has been sufficiently broad as to encompass intangible assets. For the purposes of this chapter, emissions permits, as intangible assets, may well be included in the broader meaning of the French concept of *'biens'* and the Spanish definition for *'bienes'*.

Similar approaches have long been adopted by the Members of the European Union in the context of Renewable Energy policy. For example, the Flemish Decree on the organisation of the electricity market of 17 July 2000 (Electricity Decree) instituted a scheme to support electricity produced from renewable energy sources. The Electricity Decree defined green certificates as 'a transferable intangible good which indicates that a producer, in a year declared therein, has generated a quantity of green energy as declared therein, expressed in kWh'.[89]

The recent interpretation by the Appellate Body in *Canada – Renewable Energy*, accepting the parties' definition of the intangible asset of electricity as a 'good' under Article 1.1(a)(1)(iii), indicates that an expansive interpretation of the definition, in order to include emissions permits, is not out of the question. Therefore, it is very likely that emissions permits would fall within the definition of a 'good' for the purpose of the SCM Agreement.

---

[88]   See Aaron Cosbey and Luca Rubini, 'Does it FIT? An Assessment of the Effectiveness of Renewable Energy Measures and of the Implications of the Canada – Renewable Energy/FIT Disputes' (TheE15Initiative, 2013) 7.

[89]   Vlaams decreet houdende de organisatie van de elektriciteitmarkt [Flemish decree on the organization of the electricity market] (Belgium) 17 July 2000, Belgisch Staatsblad [Belgian Official Gazette] 2000, 32166 [author's trans]. See also *Essent Belgium NV v Vlaamse Reguleringsinstantie voor de Elektriciteits- en Gasmarkt* (C-204/12) [2014] 2192. See Panagiotis Delimatsis, 'Financial Innovation and Climate Change: the Case of Renewable Energy Certificates and the Role of the GATS' (2009) 8(3) *World Trade Review* 439. Delimatsis discussed the nature of these certificates and argued that the trading of renewable energy certificates involves 'a series of financial services that financial institutions may supply until a deal for transfer of RECs is concluded, such as brokerage, trust, clearing, and settlement'.

3.4 Emissions Permits are Goods for the Purpose of the SCM Agreement

Emissions permits are intangible assets, comparable to the Canadian stumpage,[90] even though they do not transfer to industries a tangible good, such as standing timber.[91] The Appellate Body Report in *US – Softwood Lumber IV* recognised that the provision of goods and services falls into the definition of a subsidy because such 'transactions have the potential to lower artificially the cost of producing a product by providing, to an enterprise, inputs having a financial value'.[92]

Emissions permits are inputs with a financial value. By allocating permits free of cost to a number of selected industries, the Government provides a financial contribution *in kind* that lowers the production cost of the benefited sectors.

It is increasingly the case that companies have been registering emissions permits as assets in their financial statements.[93] The acceptance – and often regulation – of the accounting treatment of emissions permits as intangible goods clearly indicates a Government practice that recognises the nature of permits as tradable assets.[94]

---

[90] Cf Gary Clyde Hufbauer, Steve Charnovitz and Jisun Kim, *Global Warming and the World Trading System* (Peterson Institute for International Economics, 2009) 62. *Contra* Cendra, above n 55, 137. De Cendra suggests that 'one ton of carbon dioxide equivalent cannot reasonably be considered as a good, as it is a by-product without market value *per se*'. De Cendra claimed that emissions permits 'can be defined as a licence for this purpose, which is to be severed from the concept of good'.

[91] Ingrid Jegou and Luca Rubini, 'The Allocation of Emissions Allowances Free of Charge: Legal and Economic Considerations' (ICTSD, 2011) 31.

[92] Appellate Body Report, *US – Softwood Lumber IV*, WTO Doc WT/DS257/AB/R [53].

[93] For further details on the taxation of permits in Australia and New Zealand, see Celeste Black and Michael Dirkis, 'Farming Carbon: Taxation Implications of the Carbon Farming Initiative' (2012) 21(1) *Revenue Law Journal* art 3; Celeste Black, 'Tax Accounting for Transactions under an Emissions Trading Scheme: An Australasian Perspective' (2011) 1 *Carbon & Climate Law Review* 91; Celeste Black And Alex Evans, 'A Critical Analysis Of The Tax Treatment Of Dealings Under Australian Domestic Emissions Reduction and Abatement Frameworks' (2011) 26(2) *Australian Tax Forum* 287; Celeste Black, 'Climate Change and Tax Law: Tax Policy and Emissions Trading' (Sydney Law School, 2009).

[94] Ibid.

The nature of the emissions permits as tradable goods was very clear under the AUS CPM, where the ACUs were granted the legal status of personal property.[95] Furthermore, the ACUs issued for free and held in excess by entities during the fixed charge years could be cancelled in exchange for a payment of a 'buy-back' amount by Government.[96]

Nevertheless, even schemes such as the EU ETS and the NZ ETS, where emissions allowances are not formally declared as property rights,[97] allow permits to be transferable to third parties, including third countries, to be traded in the secondary market and also to feature in a variety of derivative contracts. Furthermore, the tradable character of this asset demonstrates the predominant character of permits as being a 'good'.[98]

It is worth mentioning, that the allocation of permits may be defined as a transfer of goods even where permits are allocated for a reduced price rather than 100 per cent free of cost. In a case involving subsidies under the Agreement on Agriculture, the Appellate Body stated:

> If goods or services are supplied to an enterprise, or a group of enterprises, at reduced rates (that is, at below market-rates), 'payments' are, in effect, made to the recipient of the portion of the price that is not charged. Instead of receiving a monetary payment equal to the revenue foregone, the recipient is paid in the form of goods or services. But, as far as the recipient is concerned, the economic value of the transfer is precisely the same.[99]

3.5 Income Support in the Sense of Article XVI of the General Agreement on Tariffs and Trade

The granting of emissions permits to entities may be analysed from the perspective of an 'income support in the sense of Article XVI of

---

[95]   CE Act 2011, s 103: 'A carbon unit is personal property and, subject to sections 105 and 106, is transmissible by assignment, by will and by devolution by operation of law'. Also see Rosemary Lyster, 'Australia's Clean Energy Future Package: Are We There Yet?' (2011) 28 *Environmental and Planning Law Journal* 446.

[96]   See details of the buy-back mechanism in Chapter 4.

[97]   The resistance to legally confer emissions permits property rights appears to be aimed at preventing Government liability in the event that the ETS is reviewed and emissions permits are cancelled.

[98]   Robert Howse, 'Climate Mitigation Subsidies and the WTO Legal Framework: A Policy Analysis' (iisd, 2010) 11.

[99]   Appellate Body Report, *Canada – Measures Affecting the Importation Of Milk And The Exportation Of Dairy Products*, WTO Doc WT/DS103/AB/R WT/DS113/AB/R, AB-1999-4 (13 October 1999) [113].

GATT' (Article 1.1(a)(2)).[100] Article XVI of GATT refers to export subsidies.[101] Rubini explains that the phrase 'in the sense of Article XVI of GATT 1994 in Article 1.1(a)(2)':

> means that the measure must operate to increase exports of the product benefiting from the subsidy or decrease the imports of competing products. This refers to the *effect* of the subsidy, that is to the strengthening of the beneficiary of the subsidy and, ultimately, to the consequent increase of its exports or decrease of its competitors' imports.[102]

The existing methodologies for the allocation of free permits are targeted to assist the EITE sectors to remain competitive. In some jurisdictions, the level of assistance varies according to the production levels, encouraging an increase in product output and, consequently, exports.[103]

As explained in Chapter 5, the closure provisions also interfere in decisions concerning inefficient firms continuing production. These provisions determine the removal or cancelling of permits allocated upon the closure of installations, which may incentivise inefficient firms to remain functioning.

---

[100]   Rubini, above n 4, 124. Rubini demonstrated that 'income and price supports are forms of government intervention aimed at sustaining the income of a certain category or at maintaining the price of a certain commodity at a given, usually minimum, desired level'.

[101]   Section A of Article XVI provides that:

> If any contracting party grants or maintains any subsidy, including any form of income or price support, which operates directly or indirectly to increase exports of any product from, or to reduce imports of any product into, its territory, it shall notify the CONTRACTING PARTIES in writing of the extent and nature of the subsidization, of the estimated effect of the subsidization on the quantity of the affected product or products imported into or exported from its territory and of the circumstances making the subsidization necessary. In any case in which it is determined that serious prejudice to the interests of any other contracting party is caused or threatened by any such subsidization, the contracting party granting the subsidy shall, upon request, discuss with the other contracting party or parties concerned, or with the CONTRACTING PARTIES, the possibility of limiting the subsidization.

[102]   Rubini, above n 4, 124 (emphasis in original).

[103]   See Chapter 4 for further details.

However, the income support approach is less certain due to the limited case law. While there are a small number of cases analysing price support, the same is not true in regard to the definition of income support.[104]

In a dispute settlement around the free allocation of permits, it is likely that the adjudicator would analyse the issue from the perspective of a financial contribution and exercise judicial economy with regard to the definition of income support, exactly as it did in *Canada – Renewable Energy*.[105] In this case, the Appellate Body observed that a 'panel need only address those claims which must be addressed in order to resolve the matter in issue in the dispute', rejecting Japan's claim that the Panel exercised false judicial economy, and declining to make a finding on whether the FIT Programme and Contracts may be characterised as 'income or price support'.[106]

By exercising judicial economy, the adjudicator limits the scope of the decision or the precedent created.[107] The WTO judiciary has also been known to use judicial economy when it chooses to avoid certain issues.[108] Bush and Pelc account that 'in 41 per cent of all [WTO] cases, panels exercise *judicial economy*, a practice by which they rule not to rule on

---

[104]   An interesting, but risky, interpretation is given by Rubini, above n 4, 125. Rubini suggests that a more expansive reading of art 1.1(a)(2) is likely to be seen in future case law, encompassing complex regulatory measures such as trading schemes or border measures that would not constitute a financial contribution. The issue would then be that most government grants would arguably be deemed to be a subsidy.

[105]   Appellate Body Report, *Canada – Renewable Energy*, WTO Doc WT/DS412/AB/R WT/DS426/AB/R [5.133]–[5.139].

[106]   Ibid.

[107]   See Marc L. Bush and Krzysztof J. Pelc, 'The Politics of Judicial Economy at the World Trade Organization' (2010) 64 *International Organization* 257 on the exercise of judicial economy by the WTO Panels as a response to the concerns of the wider membership. See also Alberto Alvarez-Jiménez, 'The WTO Appellate Body's Exercise of Judicial Economy' (2009) 12(2) *Journal of International Economic Law* 393 drawing a distinction between procedural and substantive judicial economy at the Appellate Body level. On judicial economy in international adjudication more generally, see Fulvio Maria Palombino, 'Judicial Economy and Limitation of the Scope of the Decision in International Adjudication' (2010) 23 *Leiden Journal of International Law* 909. On judicial activism, see Fuad Zarbiyev, 'Judicial Activism in International Law – A Conceptual Framework for Analysis' (2012) *Journal of International Dispute Settlement* 1.

[108]   Bush and Pelc, ibid., 260.

certain of the litigants' legal arguments, deeming these unnecessary to solving the dispute at hand'.[109]

The scarcity of case law and the likelihood that transactions involving the free allocation of permits may be defined as a financial contribution are indicative that the adjudicators might exercise judicial economy on deciding whether the free allocation of permits may be defined as income support under Article 1.1(a)(2).

4. SECOND INQUIRY: BENEFIT ANALYSIS

Assuming that the free allocation of emissions permits is a financial contribution or an income support this transaction will only be deemed to be a subsidy where the financial contribution or income support confers a 'benefit' to the recipient.[110] The Appellate Body has, on several occasions, clarified that the existence of a financial contribution and the conferral of a benefit are two distinct requirements.[111]

Unlike a 'financial contribution', the SCM Agreement did not define the term 'benefit'.[112] That is, the adjudicator is called upon to clarify the rule and apply this provision.[113] Case law has established that, while the question of whether a financial contribution is in place is addressed from the perspective of the donor, the conferral of a benefit analysis must be taken from the perspective of the recipient.[114]

---

[109]   Ibid., 257.

[110]   SCM Agreement art 1.1(b).

[111]   Appellate Body Report, *Brazil – Export Financing Programme For Aircraft*, WTO Doc WT/DS46/AB/R AB-1999-1 (2 August 1999) [157] ('*Brazil – Aircraft*'); Appellate Body Report, *US – Softwood Lumber IV*, WTO Doc WT/DS257/AB/R [51].

[112]   Rubini, above n 4, 218 citing Patrick Low, 'The Treatment of Subsidies in the WTO Framework' in Claus-Dieter Ehlermann and Michelle Everson (ed), *European Competition Law Annual 1999: Selected Issues in the Field of State Aids* (Hart Publishing, 2001) 103. Rubini explained that:

> the concept of 'benefit' is not developed at all in the SCM agreement, seemingly as a result of disagreement between the negotiating parties, some seeking to refer to commercial benchmarks, others to the cost to the subsidizing government, others to the recipients of the subsidy. This can be contrasted with the 'financial contribution'.

[113]   Rubini, ibid., 219.

[114]   Mavroidis, above n 17, 542 commenting the Panel Report, *European Communities – Countervailing Measures On Dynamic Random Access Memory*

In other words, the focus of the enquiry under Article 1.1(b) is not on the Government's cost but on the advantageous position that the recipient is placed in due to the financial contribution.[115] In *Canada – Civilian Aircraft* the Appellate Body clearly stated that 'there can be no "benefit" to the recipient unless the "financial contribution" makes the recipient "better off" than it would otherwise have been, absent that contribution'.[116]

Despite the distinctions between the two concepts, a financial contribution and a benefit are interconnected by a sequential structure. Where a financial contribution is not deemed to be in place, no benefit is conferred.[117] Consequently, the methodology that supports the analysis of a benefit may vary according to the type of financial contribution, as demonstrated below.[118]

4.1 Analysis of Benefit and the Provision of Goods and Services

Article 14 of the SCM Agreement provides guidelines to calculate the amount of the subsidy when an importing member imposes countervailing measures. It applies to transactions characterised as a provision of equity investments, loans and loan guarantees (Article 14(a)–(c)). Further, and of greater importance for the analysis herein, is the provision in Article 14(d), which applies to the provision of goods and services and the purchase of goods.

Article 14(d) of the SCM Agreement states:

> The provision of goods or services or purchase of goods by a government shall not be considered as conferring a benefit unless the provision is made for less than adequate remuneration, or the purchase is made for more than adequate remuneration. The adequacy of remuneration shall be determined in

---

Chips From Korea, WTO Doc WT/DS299/R (17 June 2005) [7.212], [7.175] (*EC – DRAM*).

[115] Panel Report, *Canada – Civilian Aircraft*, WTO Doc WT/DS70/R [9.112]. The Panel Report stated that 'in our opinion the ordinary meaning of "benefit" clearly encompasses some form of advantage. We do not consider that the ordinary meaning of "benefit" per se includes any notion of net cost to the government'.

[116] Appellate Body Report, *Canada – Civilian Aircraft*, WTO Doc WT/DS70/AB/R [157].

[117] Mavroidis, above n 17, 542 analysing Appellate Body Report, *US – DRAMS*, WTO Doc WT/DS296/AB/R [205].

[118] Appellate Body Report, *Canada – Renewable Energy*, WTO Doc WT/DS412/AB/R WT/DS426/AB/R [5.130].

relation to prevailing market conditions for the good or service in question in the country of provision or purchase (including price, quality, availability, marketability, transportation and other conditions of purchase or sale).

The comparison based on the prevailing market conditions, set in Article 14(d), has been repeatedly adopted by DSB reports (Dispute Settlement Body reports) as a guide to the analysis of 'benefit' under Article 1.1(b).[119] The adjudicator has consistently held that a 'benefit' is in place if the goods or services are 'provided on terms that are more advantageous than those that would have been available to the recipient on the market'.[120]

However, the choice of the right marketplace to be adopted in the comparison is a more complex matter.[121] Despite the text of Article 14(d), case law has determined that the private prices in the subsidising country are not the exclusive benchmark in the assessment of a benefit.[122]

In *US – Softwood Lumber IV* the Panel applied Article 14(d) in the context of calculating the benefit.[123] The Panel Report stated that 'the

---

[119]   Panel Report, *US – Large Civil Aircraft (Second complaint)*, WTO Doc WT/DS353/R [7.475]. Also see Panel Report, *Canada – Civilian Aircraft*, WTO Doc WT/DS70/R [9.112]. The Panel Report in *US – Large Civil Aircraft (Second Complaint)* held that 'it is well established that a financial contribution confers a benefit within the meaning of Article 1.1(b) of the SCM Agreement if the terms of the financial contribution are more favourable than the terms available to the recipient in the market'. See also Appellate Body Report, *European Communities And Certain Member States – Measures Affecting Trade In Large Civil Aircraft*, WTO Doc WT/DS316/AB/R, AB-2010-1 (18 May 2011) [705]; Panel Report, *Brazil – Export Financing Programme For Aircraft*, WTO Doc WT/DS46/R (14 April 1999) [7.24].

[120]   Panel Report, *Canada – Civilian Aircraft*, WTO Doc WT/DS70/R [9.112]. Also see Appellate Body Report, *Canada – Civilian Aircraft*, WTO Doc WT/DS70/AB/R [157] (the Appellate Body Report upheld the Panel's understanding); Panel Report, *EC – DRAMs*, WTO Doc WT/DS299/R [7.175] (The Panel in *EC – DRAM* also adopted the prevailing market conditions as a benchmark to the analysis of benefit).

[121]   On the complexity in defining market benchmarks see Rubini, above n 4, 218–39.

[122]   Mavroidis, above n 17, 553. Mavroidis pointed out that 'the wording of art 14 SCM provides unambiguous support for the view that benchmarks for calculating a benefit are exhaustively provided in this provision. Yet, case law followed the opposite route'.

[123]   Ibid., 552. The calculation of a benefit in the context of a countervailing measure is distinct from the assessment of a benefit in the terms of Article 1.1(b). However, Mavroidis explains that 'art. 14 SCM on its face, seems to be as much about the existence of a benefit as it is about the calculation of the amount of the benefit'.

determination of the adequacy of remuneration has to be made "in comparison with" prevailing market conditions for the goods in the country of provision, and thus no other comparison will do when private market prices exist'.[124]

The Appellate Body overturned the Panel's finding, interpreting that the term 'in relation to' in Article 14(d) implies a 'broader sense of relation, connection, reference', rather than exclusivity.[125] The prevailing market conditions can be sought outside the country or consist of a created benchmark where the prevailing market conditions in the subsidising country are replicated.[126]

The controversial Appellate Body report in *Canada – Renewable Energy*[127] held that the marketplace in the subsidising country may not be the appropriate benchmark for comparison where the Government intervenes to 'create' a market that would otherwise not exist. The Appellate Body understood that the market for renewable energy was established by the Canadian Province of Ontario[128] and distinguished between the concepts of market creation, where there would not be a market if the Government had not created it, and market intervention.[129]

While this approach provides the adjudicator with more leverage to interpret the SCM Agreement with a view to environmental concerns – granting the State more policy space[130] – it certainly creates judicial

---

[124] Appellate Body Report, *US – Softwood Lumber IV*, WTO Doc WT/DS257/AB/R [88].

[125] Ibid., [89].

[126] Ibid., [90].

[127] The Appellate Body Report in this case received mixed reactions. See, e.g., European Commission, 'EU welcomes WTO ruling in support of clean energy' (2013) <http://trade.ec.europa.eu/doclib/press/index.cfm?id=895>, welcoming the ruling. See also Aaron Cosbey and Petros C. Mavroidis, 'A Turquoise Mess: Green Subsidies, Blue Industrial Policy and Renewable Energy: The Case for Redrafting the Subsidies Agreement of the WTO' (2014) *Journal of International Economic Law* 1 … on a less enthusiastic assessment of the methodology adopted by the Appellate Body, particularly in relation to the benefit analysis; Luca Rubini, 'What Does the Recent WTO Litigation on Renewables Energy Subsidies tell us about Methodology in Legal Analysis? The Good, the Bad, and the Ugly' (2014) *EUI Working Papers* 1.

[128] Appellate Body Report, *Canada – Renewable Energy*, WTO Doc WT/DS412/AB/R, WT/DS426/AB/R [5.185]. The Appellate Body report proposes that 'in the absence of such government intervention, there could not be a market with a constant and reliable supply of electricity'.

[129] Ibid., [5.188].

[130] A similar approach has been adopted by the European Court of Justice in a number of cases. See, e.g., *Essent Belgium NV v Vlaamse Reguleringsinstantie*

uncertainty. It is unclear at this point whether the 'market creation *versus* market intervention' has formalised a distinction between like products based on its environmental objective and whether the approach would be followed in a dispute involving the free allocation of permits.

4.1.1 Benefit analysis under the EU emissions trading system

In Case T-387/04, the court stated that the European Commission argued that 'an emission allowance was equivalent to an intangible asset the value of which was determined by the market and that, therefore, the fact that the State gave it to undertakings free of charge gave them an advantage'.[131] Similarly to feed-in-tariff programmes, the market for emissions trading is often created by Government regulation.[132] However, in the case of emissions trading, parallel to the distribution of permits by the Government – by auctioning or free of cost – there is the formation of a secondary market for the trading of these permits.

Howse describes that, as long as there is market liquidity, the carbon market may be used as the benchmark for comparison:

> In cases where there is a liquid emissions trading market in the country to whose exports countervailing duties are applied, the price of carbon *in that market* might be used to determine the 'benefit' – within the meaning of Article 14(d) of the SCM Agreement – that is conferred on firms by a given allowance or permission to emit carbon (...) And to the extent that the market price for carbon is not being charged by the government for this allowance or entitlement, there is, again, a "benefit" conferred within the meaning of the SCM Agreement.[133]

Where such market conditions are not available, 'a market price might need to be constructed based on the observed price in functioning markets such as the EC [*sic*], with due adjustment for differences in

---

voor de Elektriciteits- en Gasmarkt (C-204/12) [2014] 2192; *PreussenElektra AG v Schhleswag AG* (C-379/98) [2001] ECR I-02099.

[131]   *EnBW Energie Baden-Württemberg AG v Commission of the European Communities* (T-387/04) [2007] ECR II-1201, II-1209.

[132]   For further details on the functioning of the Ontario feed-in-tariff program see Cosbey and Mavroidis, above n 127; Luca Rubini, 'Ain't Wastin' Time no More: Subsidies for Renewable Energy, The SCM Agreement, Policy Space, and Law Reform' (2012) 15(2) *Journal of International Economic Law* 525. On other policies to foster renewable energy, see Rosemary Lyster and Adrian Bradbrook, *Energy Law and the Environment* (Cambridge University Press, 2006); Delimatsis, above n 89.

[133]   Howse, above n 98, 9.

market and regulatory condition affecting prices'.[134] The study concluded that 'to the extent that the market price for carbon is not being charged by the government for this allowance or entitlement, there is, again, a 'benefit' conferred within the meaning of the SCM'.[135]

A similar approach was taken by the European Commission in a State aid decision in relation to the free allocation of permits under the UK Emission Trading Scheme (UK ETS).[136] The UK Government claimed that recipients of free of cost permits did not receive an advantage as these companies would incur expenses in reducing their emissions to their target levels. However, the EC concluded that the free allocation constituted State aid under Article 107 of the Treaty on the Functioning of the European Union (TFEU),[137] as these permits could be sold on a market:

> The state allocates a limited number of transferable emission permits free of charge to the direct participants. The state thus provides these companies with an intangible asset for free, which can be sold on a market to be created. The fact that there will be a market is a sign of the value of the asset being allocated. This has to be considered to be an advantage to the recipient companies.
>
> The fact that companies will have to make expenses in order to realise the value of the allowances does not change the existence of an advantage, but can be considered a positive element in the assessment of the compatibility of the measure.
>
> This advantage distorts competition between companies. Companies able to make a profit from the allowances can use the profit for their business competing with other companies not having access to such a scheme. This can affect trade between Member States.[138]

---

[134]　Howse and Eliason, above n 29.

[135]　Ibid.

[136]　European Commission, State Aid n 416/2001: United Kingdom Emission Trading Scheme. Brussels, 28.11.2001 C(2001)3739fin.

[137]　*Treaty on the Functioning of the European Union*, opened for signature 7 February 1992, [2009] OJ C 115/199 (entered into force 1 November 1993): 'Save as otherwise provided in this Treaty, any aid granted by a Member State or through State resources in any form whatsoever which distorts or threatens to distort competition by favouring certain undertakings or the production of certain goods shall, insofar as it affects trade between Member States, be incompatible with the common market'.

[138]　European Commission, State Aid n 416/2001: United Kingdom Emission Trading Scheme. Brussels, 28.11.2001 C(2001)3739fin 9.

As mentioned above, there are instances in which companies benefit from the windfall profits associated with the free allocation of permits, as the practical experience with the EU ETS has demonstrated.[139] De Sépibus demonstrates that the assessment of economic benefit – in the context of State Aid – should take into account benefits gained from windfall profits.[140] Windfall profits 'are directly linked to the gratuitous character of the allocation process and disappear in the case of auctioning',[141] and should also be taken into consideration when analysing whether a 'benefit' is conferred under Article 1.1(b) of the SCM Agreement.[142]

4.2   Analysis of Benefit and Revenue Foregone that is Otherwise Due

Differently to the complex analysis of the prevailing market conditions applicable where a financial contribution, in the form of a provision of goods, is deemed to be in place, in the case of a waiver of Government revenue, it is more straightforward to establish the existence of a 'benefit'. Indeed, the applicability of Article 14 and assessment of 'benefit' through the use of a market benchmark would not be logical in the context of revenue foregone by government.[143]

Mavroidis proposed that 'where the financial contribution consists of revenue foregone or not collected, there is an obvious benefit to the recipient'.[144] The WTO jurisprudence confirms this approach. In *US – FSC* the Panel Report held that 'in our view, the financial contribution

---

[139]   Edwin Woerdman, Oscar Couwenberg and Andries Nentjes, 'Energy Prices and Emissions Trading: Windfall Profits from Grandfathering?' (2009) 28 *European Journal of Law and Economics* 185, 190. See *Iberdrola SA and Gas Natural SDG SA* (C-566/11, C-567/11, C-580/11, C-591/11, C-620/11 and C-640/11) [2013] ECR I-660. The European Court of Justice held that the combination of the free allocation system with the pricing system on the electricity generation market in Spain resulted in windfall profits for electricity producers.

[140]   Joëlle de Sépibus, 'The European Emission Trading Scheme Put to the Test of State Aid Rules' (WTI, 2007) 13.

[141]   Ibid. Also see Angus Johnston, 'Free Allocation of Allowances Under the EU Emissions Trading Scheme: Legal Issues' (2006) 6 *Climate Policy* 115, 119.

[142]   See, e.g., Johnston, ibid., 118–19.

[143]   Ibid.

[144]   Mavroidis, above n 18, 543.

clearly confers a benefit, in as much as both FSCs and their parents need not pay certain taxes that would otherwise be due'.[145]

From the perspective of a Government revenue that is foregone, the free allocation of permits confers an obvious 'benefit' to its recipients, regardless of the eventual sale of these permits in the future.[146] The waiver of the total or partial costs of emissions permits to entities, resulting in less revenue collected by the Treasury and reduced costs to companies than would be the case if the permits were auctioned, benefits the liable entities as it is clearly intended by the nature of the policy.

Finally, overcompensation may occur where firms are allocated more permits than the amount necessary for compliance under the scheme. Even where overcompensation does not occur, firms may still pass through the opportunity costs of the grandfathered emissions allowances.[147] In both cases, the emissions permits generate profits to those who are receiving them for free.[148]

---

[145] Panel Report, *US-FSC*, WTO Doc WT/DS108/R [7.103].

[146] See, e.g., Hufbauer, Charnovitz and Kim, above n 91, 61.

[147] Jegou and Rubini, above n 92, 18. Also see Woerdman, Couwenberg and Nentjes, above n 140, 189. Woerdman, Couwenberg and Nentjes explained the distinction between windfall profits and over allocation:

> Windfall profits should not be confused with profits arising from 'over-allocation', meaning that companies get more (in this case free) allowances than they need, which they can sell for cash on the market (provided that there is still sufficient demand). Over-allocation arises solely from leniency in the setting of the emission target; windfall profits arise solely from the allocation method of grandfathering. With stringent targets, electricity producers will still realize windfall profits, because the grandfathered allowances entail opportunity costs for them. However, with a smaller number of free allowances, the price of those rights will be higher. Therefore, a more stringent emission cap does not necessarily reduce the size of the windfall profits, but might even increase those profits.

[148] Johnston, above n 41; Christian Egenhofer et al, 'The EU Emissions Trading System and Climate Policy towards 2050: Real Incentives to Reduce Emissions and Drive Innovation?' (CEPS, 2011) 4. Egenhofer et al explain that 'those industries that could and can pass on the additional carbon costs have in fact a net gain, since potential losses of revenues, through for example lower sales, may be compensated or even overcompensated by receiving allowances free of charge and earning "windfall profits"'. Also see *Iberdrola SA and Gas Natural SDG SA* (C-566/11, C-567/11, C-580/11, C-591/11, C-620/11 and C-640/11) [2013] ECR I-00000. For further information on the issue of windfall profits from the free allocation of permits see Chapter 5.

5. WHAT TYPE OF SUBSIDY? THIRD AND FOURTH INQUIRIES

Up to this point, the analysis has focused on whether the free allocation of permits in the studied jurisdictions is likely to be a subsidy for the purpose of the SCM Agreement, according to the criteria set out in Article 1.1. Even where the answer to this inquiry is positive, the remaining provisions in the SCM Agreement will only be relevant if this subsidy is also 'specific' in the terms of Article 2.[149]

Subsidies contingent upon export performance and subsidies contingent upon the use of domestic over imported goods are deemed to be specific,[150] and are prohibited *per se* according to Article 3. Other 'specific' subsidies not falling within the category of prohibited subsidies may be actionable where it is proved that they cause adverse effects to another Member.[151]

Apart from the provisions in the SCM Agreement for actionable and prohibited subsidies, no other action can be taken against a subsidy of another member except in accordance with the provisions of GATT 1994.[152] Article XVI of the GATT requires the members to notify any subsidy operating to increase exports of any product from, or to reduce imports of any product into, its territory. This provision may be relevant and applicable to most of the current systems of free allocation of permits.

Due to the international relevance of the EU ETS and the volume of international trade to and from the EU, the analysis that follows will look at the case study of the allocation of permits to the EITE sectors under the EU ETS. The overall assistance to participants started to be phased-out from the third trading period onwards. Only industries deemed to be exposed to carbon leakage are eligible to receive 100 per cent assistance.[153]

---

[149]   SCM Agreement, art 1.2. WTO, 'World Trade Report: Exploring the Links Between Subsidies, Trade and the WTO' (WTO, 2006) 54.

[150]   SCM Agreement, art 2.3.

[151]   Ibid., art 5.

[152]   Ibid., art 32.1.

[153]   For further details see Chapter 4.

The ETS Directive[154] provides three alternative quantitative thresholds to determine whether a sector or subsector is deemed to be exposed to a 'significant risk of carbon leakage':[155]

(i)   emissions-intensive and trade-exposed: where there is an additional production cost of at least 5 per cent of the gross value added; *and* a trade-intensity above 10 per cent;[156] *or*
(ii)   highly emissions-intensive: where the additional production costs are of at least 30 per cent gross value added;[157] *or*
(iii) highly trade-exposed: activities with a trade-intensity above 30 per cent.[158]

5.1 The Trade-Exposure Threshold and the Treatment of Prohibited Subsidies

Article 3 of the SCM Agreement prohibits subsidies contingent upon export performance and subsidies contingent upon the use of domestic over imported goods.[159] These subsidies are deemed to be 'specific' in accordance to Article 2.3 and are prohibited *per se*, that is, a member shall neither grant nor maintain this category of subsidies.[160]

The use of prohibited subsidies by a member would warrant a request for consultations.[161] Where no mutually agreed solution is reached, the matter would be referred to the WTO Dispute Settlement Body (DSB),[162] where a Panel may recommend the withdrawal of the subsidy within a time-period determined by the DSB.[163]

The first type of subsidies in the prohibited category involve subsidies contingent, in law or in fact, whether solely or as one of several other

---

[154] ETS Directive, art 10a(15)(16).

[155] Ibid., art 10a(17). The ETS Directive also provides for a qualitative analysis to be taken in order to determine whether a sector or subsector not covered by the thresholds is at risk of carbon leakage, for example when trade exposure or direct and indirect cost increase rates are close to one of the qualitative thresholds; when profit margins are a potential indicator of long-run investment or relocation decisions and so on.

[156] Ibid., art 10a(15).

[157] Ibid., art 10a(16)(a).

[158] Ibid., art 10a(16)(b).

[159] SCM Agreement, art 3.1(a)(b).

[160] Ibid., art 3.2.

[161] Ibid., art 4.1.

[162] Ibid., art 4.4.

[163] Ibid., art 4.7.

conditions, upon export performance.[164] The EU ETS's third qualitative threshold, the sole trade-exposure threshold, may at first glance be indicative of the existence of a prohibited subsidy. Arguably, a closer analysis of the definition of trade-exposure challenges such a conclusion.

The ETS Directive determines the intensity of trade with third countries by calculating the 'ratio between the total value of exports to third countries plus the value of imports from third countries and the total market size for the Community (annual turnover plus total imports from third countries)'.[165] Where the intensity of trade is above 30 per cent a sector or subsector is eligible for assistance.[166] As discussed in Chapter 4, the application of the single trade-exposure threshold has been supporting the subsidisation of nearly 120 sectors in the EU ETS.[167]

One interpretation of the sole trade-exposure threshold against Article 3.1 of the SCM Agreement in the literature has been to consider that the protectionist nature of the assistance measure classifies it as an export subsidy.[168] Authors have expressed concerns over the consequences of such an outcome due to the perceived need to protect certain sectors from the risk of carbon leakage.[169] These concerns were not confirmed in the analysis in Chapter 4, which demonstrates that the risks of carbon leakage have been widely overestimated, and that the sole trade-exposure thresholds should ultimately be removed from the EU ETS. However, it is unlikely that the WTO judiciary would engage in a broad interpretation of the term 'export performance'.

While the sole trade-exposure criterion clearly benefits sectors with a high export performance, it also protects sectors facing high levels of competition in the EU market from third countries. Sectors trading primarily in the internal market and facing strong competition from imported products – for example, where producers from outside the EU have more than 30 per cent of the total market size for the Community – would be eligible for a subsidy, in the form of free permits, even though the subsidy is clearly disconnected from the producer's export performance.

This study concludes that the sole trade-exposure, as legislated in the ETS Directive, does not give rise to a prohibited subsidy. However, it would appear very clear that subsidies granted based on a trade-exposure

---

[164]   Ibid., art 3.1(a)(b).
[165]   ETS Directive, art 10a(16)(b).
[166]   Ibid.
[167]   See Chapter 4 for further details.
[168]   Deane, above n 3, 156.
[169]   Ibid.; Henschke, above n 3.

threshold would be subject to the notification rule provided by Article XVI, A(1) of the GATT, which states that:

> If any contracting party grants or maintains any subsidy, including any form of income or price support, which operates directly or indirectly to increase exports of any product from, or to reduce imports of any product into, its territory, it shall notify the CONTRACTING PARTIES in writing of the extent and nature of the subsidization, of the estimated effect of the subsidization on the quantity of the affected product or products imported into or exported from its territory and of the circumstances making the subsidization necessary. In any case in which it is determined that serious prejudice to the interests of any other contracting party is caused or threatened by any such subsidization, the contracting party granting the subsidy shall, upon request, discuss with the other contracting party or parties concerned, or with the CONTRACTING PARTIES, the possibility of limiting the subsidization.[170]

The EU has been failing to comply with its notification requirements pursuant to Article XVI(1) of the GATT in relation to subsidies provided to industry sectors that fall under the sole trade-exposure threshold.[171] A similar conclusion can be extended to other thresholds that combine EITE criteria. In that case, the EU and Australia would have also failed to comply with notification of their subsidies provided to sectors deemed to be emissions-intensive and trade-exposed.[172] The notification requirement is still applicable in case the proposed amendment to the EU ETS is adopted, providing for two levels of assistance based on a combined emissions-intensity and trade-exposure criterion.[173]

Due to the NZ ETS design, which assumes trade-exposure for all activities, unless otherwise determined, it is less likely that it would be under an obligation to comply with the notification requirements in

---

[170]　General Agreement on Tariffs and Trade 1994.

[171]　See New and Full Notification Pursuant to Article XVI:1 Of The GATT 1994 and Article 25 Of The Agreement on Subsidies and Countervailing Measures: European Union, WTO Doc G/SCM/N/284/EU (7 August 2015). In its 2015 notification of subsidies granted during the period 2013 and 2014 and subsidy programmes which are currently in force, the EU has omitted to include the expenditure with permits allocated free of cost to its domestic industry.

[172]　See ibid.; New and Full Notification Pursuant to Article XVI:1 Of The GATT 1994 and Article 25 Of The Agreement on Subsidies and Countervailing Measures: Australia, WTO Doc G/SCM/N/253/AUS (11 September 2013). Australia omitted any subsidies provided in relation to the AUS CPM.

[173]　Proposal 2015/148 (COD) for a Directive of the European Parliament and of the Council Amending Directive 2003/87/EC to enhance cost-effective emission reductions and low-carbon investments [2015].

Article XVI(1) of the GATT. Despite the importance of the notification requirements to increase the transparency in the use of subsidies by WTO Members, there are no sanctions or further consequences for the members who fail to notify a subsidy.

It is also worth noting that when a country adopts subsidies in certain areas or sectors, it is often the case that other jurisdictions will follow their example and subsidise their own domestic producers. New schemes must not make the free allocation of permits conditional upon criteria such as export performance and/or upon the use of domestic over imported goods.[174]

5.2   The Emissions-Intensity Threshold and the Treatment of Actionable Subsidies

Specific subsidies not falling within the category of prohibited subsidies may be actionable where it is proven that they cause adverse effects to another member.[175] Using the EU ETS case study, there is scope to assert that the free allocation of permits may be a specific subsidy for the purpose of the SCM Agreement.

Subparagraphs (a)–(c) of Article 2.1 provide the criteria to determine whether a subsidy, as defined in Article 1.1, is specific to an enterprise or industry, or group of enterprises or industries within the jurisdiction of the granting authority. As demonstrated below, a subsidy may be *de jure* specific or *de facto* specific.

5.2.1   *De jure* specificity
Subparagraph (a) relates to specificity *de jure*, that is, where explicit rules limit access to a subsidy to certain enterprises. Limiting a subsidy to 'certain enterprises' means making it available to an 'industry' or 'group of industries' only, generally referred to by the type of products they produce.[176]

Contrarily, where the eligibility requirements imposed by 'the granting authority' or by 'legislation pursuant to which the granting authority

---

[174]   See, e.g., Appellate Body Report, *Canada – Renewable Energy*, WTO Doc WT/DS412/AB/R WT/DS426/AB/R. Although feed-in-tariffs were a widespread practice, the matter was not brought to the DSB until 'the use of domestic over imported goods' condition was adopted by Ontario's program.

[175]   SCM Agreement, art 5.

[176]   SCM Agreement, art 2.1(a). See also Panel Report, *United States – Subsidies on Upland Cotton*, WTO Doc WT/DS267/R (8 September 2004) (*US – Upland Cotton*) [7.1139]–[7.1143].

operates' are objective, a subsidy will not be deemed specific.[177] As explained in the Footnote to Article 2, objective criteria or conditions 'mean criteria or conditions which are neutral, which do not favour certain enterprises over others, and which are economic in nature and horizontal in application, such as number of employees or size of enterprise'.[178]

The enquiry that must be made, therefore, is whether the legislative criteria to determine the eligibility for the free allocation of permits are 'sufficiently broadly available throughout an economy as not to benefit a particular limited group of producers of certain products'.[179]

Looking at the thresholds for assistance in the three case studies, the emissions-intensity and trade-exposure criteria are economic in nature and horizontal in application. In other words, most activities meeting the economic thresholds are eligible for assistance.[180]

In the EU ETS, for example, the latest carbon leakage list provides for assistance to around 60 per cent of the ETS sectors and nearly 99.55 per cent of all ETS activities in the EU ETS,[181] making a strong case, at least formally, for the conclusion that the subsidy is not specific for the purpose of Article 2.1(a) and (b). If anything, the three thresholds combined seem to be excessively broad, benefiting most sectors covered by the EU ETS.

5.2.2 Sole energy-intensity threshold: a 'de facto' specific subsidy

Subparagraph (c) provides for *de facto* specificity, that is, instances in which a subsidy is specific despite not clearly satisfying the eligibility

---

[177]   SCM Agreement, art 2.1(b). That is, provided that the eligibility is automatic and that such criteria and conditions are strictly adhered to. The criteria or conditions must be clearly spelled out in law, regulation, or other official document, so as to be capable of verification. See Appellate Body Report, *United States – Definitive Anti-Dumping and Countervailing Duties on Certain Products from China*, WTO Doc WT/DS379/AB/R, AB-2010-3 (11 March 2011) (*US – China*) [366]–[371].

[178]   SCM Agreement, art 2 n 2.

[179]   Panel Report, *US – Upland Cotton*, WTO Doc WT/DS267/R [7.1139]–[7.1143].

[180]   Most activities meeting the economic thresholds are eligible for assistance, with some exceptions particular to each scheme. For example, in the EU ETS, the exclusion of the power sector.

[181]   Sandbag, 'Slaying the Dragon: Vanquish the Surplus and Rescue the ETS' (Sandbag, 2014) 36.

requirements of Article 2.1(a) or (b).[182] Where there are reasons to believe that a subsidy may be *de facto* specific, an authority may analyse other indicators, such as the use of the subsidy limited to certain enterprises, the predominant use by certain enterprises, the granting of disproportionately large amounts of subsidy to certain enterprises, and the manner in which discretion has been exercised by the granting authority in the decision to grant a subsidy. Furthermore, account shall be taken of the extent of the diversification of economic activities within the jurisdiction of the granting authority and the length of time during which the subsidy programme has been in operation.[183]

Despite the existence of objective thresholds to determine carbon leakage exposure under the EU ETS, making the subsidy formally available throughout the economy, there are strong indicia to support the argument that the sole emissions-intensity threshold was included in the Directive in order to perpetuate a targeted subsidisation of a small number of enterprises from the cement sector, which were already being favoured by the decentralised National Allocation Plans during the first and second trading periods. Indeed, in the first carbon leakage list,[184] only two sectors received assistance based on the sole emissions-intensity threshold,[185] that is, the manufacture of cement and the manufacture of lime.

Due to the inclusion of other GHGs in the coverage of the EU ETS, the production of Hydrogen, Nitrogen and Oxygen also fell within the second carbon leakage list, applicable for the period 2015–19. However, there is strong evidence to support the view that the sole emissions-intensity threshold was adopted specifically in order to include the cement and lime manufacturing sectors.[186]

---

[182] See Appellate Body Report, *United States – China*, WTO Doc WT/DS379/AB/R, AB-2010-3 (11 March 2011) [366]–[371] on the interpretation and application of the principles set in subparagraphs (a)–(c).

[183] SCM Agreement, art 2.1(c).

[184] Commission Decision 2010/2/EU of 24 December 2014 Determining, Pursuant to Directive 2003/87/EC of the European Parliament and of the Council, a List of Sectors and Subsectors which are Deemed to be Exposed to a Significant Risk of Carbon Leakage, OJ L 1/236.

[185] ETS Directive, art 10a(16)(a).

[186] See Commission Decision 2014/746/EU of 27 October 2014 Determining, Pursuant to Directive 2003/87/EC of the European Parliament and of the Council, a List of Sectors and Subsectors which are Deemed to be Exposed to a Significant Risk of Carbon Leakage, for the Period 2015 to 2019 [2014] OJ L 308/114.

Five large companies belonging to the cement sector have been consistently accumulating disproportionately large amounts of surplus allowances compared to other participants in the scheme, granting them a position within the group of companies that Sandbag has nicknamed Europe's 'Carbon Fatcats'.[187] According to Sandbag, around ten companies have received a disproportionately large amount of subsidies in the past six years.[188] These 'Carbon Fatcats' have accumulated nearly 22 per cent of the surplus of EUAs (over 483 Mt from a total of 2.2 billion tonnes) despite being responsible for only 10 per cent of emissions covered by the scheme (1.1 billion tonnes from a total of 11.6 billion tonnes).[189]

Among the top ten companies, in terms of cumulative EUA surpluses over 2008–13, five belong to the Cement sector. These are Lafarge, Holcim, Heidelberg Cement, Cemex and Italcementi.[190] The five cement companies hold the fastest growing surpluses, which are expected to remain long beyond 2030.[191]

In other words, not only is the cement industry the predominant user of free EUAs under the sole emissions-intensity threshold, but these companies are actually benefiting from disproportionately large amounts of surplus allocation,[192] large enough to support a claim of *de facto* specificity. As mentioned above, the subsidy may be actionable if found to have adverse effects on the interest of other members.

Felicity Deane has also identified the assistance package to the steel sector under the former AUS CPM as a *de facto* specific subsidy.[193] The sector was eligible to receive cumulative benefits under the Jobs and Competitiveness Program as well as a sector-specific assistance program

---

[187]   Sandbag, above n 181.

[188]   Ibid., 45.

[189]   Ibid.

[190]   Ibid.

[191]   Ibid., 41, 42. The remaining five 'Carbon Fatcats' in the list are from the steel and power sectors. These sectors have consistently received surplus EUAs in the past, with the power sector benefiting from large amounts of windfall profits, as discussed in Chapter 3. With the harmonised allocation rules implemented from the third trading period onwards, the disproportionate level of free allocation received by the steel sector is now being reduced while most electricity generators are no longer eligible to receive free EUAs, which will result in a gradual exhaustion of the surplus EUAs accumulated in the past few years in the sector.

[192]   Ibid., 47.

[193]   See Deane, above n 3, 30.

known as the Steel Transformation Plan.[194] The Grattan Institute assessed that the levels of assistance made available to the steel industry were excessive and that they would generate windfall gains to steel producers, protecting the sector beyond the scope of the Jobs and Competitive Program and preventing structural adjustments which would otherwise occur due to shifts in global steel prices and exchange rates.[195]

Regardless of any adverse effects, members have the responsibility of yearly notifying specific subsidies maintained within their territory, addressing all the specific points set out in Article 25.3.[196] Arguably, the EU, as well as Australia between 2012 and 2014, have failed to comply with this requirement in relation to subsidies granted under the EU ETS and the AUS CPM.[197] Other countries with ETSs in place may also be failing to notify similar specific subsidies, due to the lack of an understanding of the nature of free allocation as a specific subsidy, as demonstrated below.

Finally, it is worth mentioning that a proposal for the amendment of the EU ETS has been presented by the European Commission in July 2015.[198] The amendment would eliminate the sole emissions-intensity threshold, providing for two alternative levels of assistance based on a combined emissions-intensity and trade-exposure criteria. At the time of writing, it is not clear whether the amendment will be adopted by the Member States.

---

[194]   Steel Transformation Plan Act 2011 (Cth). The Steel Transformation Plan provided a significant subsidy to industry. Entities were able to claim up to AU$100 million assistance in addition to the free allocation of ACUs.

[195]   Tony Wood and Tristan Edis, 'New Protectionism under Carbon Pricing: Case Studies of LNG, Coal Mining and Steel Sectors' (Grattan Institute, 2011) 3, 27.

[196]   SCM Agreement, art 25.

[197]   See New and Full Notification Pursuant to Article XVI:1, above n 171; In its 2015 notification of the subsidies granted during the period 2013 and 2014 and the subsidy programmes which are currently in force, the EU has omitted the subsidisation of the cement sector under the EU ETS. Australia has also omitted any subsidies provided between 2012 and 2014 to the steel sector under the Clear Energy Package.

[198]   Proposal 2015/148 (COD) above n 173.

5.3 Is the Specific Subsidy Causing Adverse Effects on the Interests of Other Members?

Where certain liable industries receive free permits at a level that allows them to engage in price cutting and/or market share expansion (or retention) beyond that which would occur without the free allocation, the conduct may injure the domestic industry of another WTO Member or cause serious prejudice to its interest.[199]

Injury to a domestic industry, as provided by Article 5(a), must be substantiated on the basis of positive evidence and harmonised with the specific provisions on injury elements in Article 15.[200] The economic factors that may guide the assessment include actual and potential decline in output, sales, market share, profits, productivity, return on investments, or utilization of capacity, as well as actual and potential negative effects on cash flow, inventories, employment, wages, growth, ability to raise capital or investments, amongst others.[201]

Serious prejudice is a different concept to that of injury, and it involves the circumstances listed in Article 6.[202] For example, the key test is whether the subsidy has the effect of displacing or impeding the imports of a like product of another member into the market of the subsidising member, or the effect of displacing or impeding the exports of a like product of another member from a third-country market.[203] Serious

---

[199] OECD, *Recommendation of the Council on Guiding Principles Concerning International Economic Aspects of Environmental Policies* (1972) <http://acts.oecd.org/Instruments/PrintInstrumentView.aspx?Instrument>, 3.

[200] Panel Report, *European Communities and Certain Member States – Measures Affecting Trade in Large Civil Aircraft*, WTO Doc WT/DS316/R (30 June 2010) [7.2068] [7.2080]; SCM Agreement, art 2.4, 5, 15. To illustrate, art 15.4 provides that the examination of the impact of the subsidised imports on the domestic industry shall include an evaluation of 'all relevant economic factors' and indices having a bearing on the state of the industry, including actual and potential decline in output, sales, market share, profits, productivity, return on investments, or utilization of capacity; factors affecting domestic prices; actual and potential negative effects on cash flow, inventories, employment, wages, growth, ability to raise capital or investments and, in the case of agriculture, whether there has been an increased burden on government support programmes. This list is not exhaustive, nor can one or several of these factors necessarily give decisive guidance.

[201] SCM Agreement, art 15.4.

[202] Panel Report, *Korea – Measures Affecting Trade in Commercial Vessels*, WTO Doc WT/DS273/R (7 March 2005) [7.578].

[203] SCM Agreement, art 6.3.

prejudice may be identified, even where the market share of the subsidised product declines, as long as the declining rate is slower than it would have been in the absence of the subsidy.[204] It would be likely to occur where the allocation system is output-based, incentivising the increase in, or maintenance of, production levels beyond output levels which would prevail in the absence of the free allocation mechanism.[205]

It is outside the scope of this chapter to assess the adverse effects from the free allocation methods currently in place. Such analysis would require detailed industry data from the potentially impacted jurisdictions and would start with the identification of 'like products' on the ETS market and on the hypothetically impacted member's market. Members suffering from the adverse effects of the free allocation of permits (subsidy) may seek redress or, in certain cases, impose a countervailing duty to offset the effects of the subsidy.[206]

Finally, Article 8 of the SCM Agreement contained a list of non-actionable subsidies which were applicable during a period of five years.[207] In the absence of an agreement to extend the application of Article 8 or other form of review of the SCM Agreement, the analysis into the rationale of the measure is, in principle, limited to the inquiry of Footnote 1 and Annexes I–III of the SCM Agreement.[208]

---

[204]   SCM Agreement, art 6.4(c).

[205]   Windon, above n 3, 220.

[206]   SCM Agreement, art 15(1). Appellate Body Report, *Japan – Countervailing Duties on Dynamic Random Access Memories from Korea*, WT/DS336/AB/R AB-2007-3 (28 November 2007) [264]. Also see ibid. 217.

[207]   SCM Agreement, art 31 provides for the provisional application of art 8 for a period of five years from the date of entry into force of the WTO Agreement. It also provides that the Committee would review the operation of art 8 with a view to determining whether to extend its application. Such an agreement to extend the application of art 8 was never concluded.

[208]   Mavroidis, above n 7, 534. Also see Cosbey and Mavroidis, above n 127, 35, 36. Cosbey and Mavroidis advocate that a redrafting of the SCM Agreement should take place in order to ensure that the rationale of a subsidy plays a more important role in determining how subsidies are treated under WTO law. The SCM Agreement should distinguish between subsidies that are aimed at promoting public goods, such as public health and environmental protection and those that 'merely transfer income from taxpayers to protect domestic firms'.

6. CONCLUSION

The systems for the free allocation of permits in the three case studies examined in this chapter are subsidies under Article 1.1(a)(1)(ii) and (iii) of the SCM Agreement, although they are not prohibited subsidies under Article 3 of the SCM Agreement.

The EU ETS sole emissions-intensity threshold is narrow and *de facto* specific. The industry assistance to the cement sector under the EU ETS is, therefore, likely to be a *de facto* specific subsidy and must be notified in accordance with Article 25 of the SCM Agreement. Furthermore, the subsidy to the cement sector is actionable and may be challenged if a member can demonstrate that the subsidy is injuring its domestic industry.

The EU, New Zealand and Australia (between 2012 and 2014) are failing, and have failed, to comply with their notification requirements in relation to the free allocation of permits granted under the EU ETS, the NZ ETS and the AUS CPM. Other countries with ETSs in place are likely to be also failing to notify similar subsidies.

The free allocation of permits is a transitional measure that protects polluters, not the environment. Chapters 3, 4 and 5 demonstrated in detail that these subsidies, in most cases, represent an unnecessary cost to society, do not incentivise innovation, may contribute to issues such as surplus permits (e.g., in the EU ETS) and can be problematic to the linking of future independent schemes.

In those sectors where assistance is financially justifiable, the SCM Agreement would not prevent or challenge the free allocation of permits, unless the subsidy is prohibited or, being specific, causes adverse effects on the other Members. The idea that subsidies provided to heavy polluters under an ETS should be free from the guidance and corrective roles of the SCM Agreement is not supported and, indeed, is contradicted by the assessment of real-life ETSs in Chapters 4, 5 and 6 of this book.[209]

---

[209] *Contra* Ellerman, above n 3, 30. Ellerman argued that the SCM Agreement affects the continuing viability of national emissions trading schemes and presents a further challenge to the environmental credentials of the WTO.

7. Summary of the main findings

1. INTRODUCTION

Emissions Trading Schemes (ETSs) are a key policy instrument to achieve cost efficient emissions reductions and the linking of ETSs is a strategic step towards an international carbon price. However, in the absence of a coordinated global effort to price carbon, the free of cost allocation of permits has been a political condition to the acceptance of ETSs in many jurisdictions.

The experience of ETSs in the European Union, Australia and New Zealand is one of heavy subsidisation of emissions-intensive industries.[1] Yet, the legal consequences of this regulatory model have, in general, escaped the scrutiny of legal scholars.

The literature on the possible violations of the SCM Agreement have been generally premised upon the assumption that the free allocation of permits, as currently legislated by domestic schemes, is a necessary and justifiable instrument to prevent carbon leakage. However, these subsidies mostly represent an unnecessary cost to society, do not incentivise innovation, may contribute to issues such as surplus permits and can negatively impact on the trade between liable companies under linked independent schemes.[2]

In order to fully comprehend this issue, the research for this book adopted an interdisciplinary approach, providing a bridge between the economics data, the legal interpretation of the SCM Agreement and a deeper level of understanding of the framework of the ETSs in the case studies. A number of conclusions and recommendations can be drawn from the previous chapters. They are summarised below.

---

[1] Chapters 4 and 5.
[2] Ibid.

2. CLIMATE POLICY REGIMES AND THE ROLE OF LINKED ETS IN THE NEW FRAMEWORK FOR INTERNATIONAL COOPERATION ON CLIMATE CHANGE MITIGATION

The urgency in achieving global greenhouse gas (GHG) emissions reductions has been expressed with near unanimity by the international scientific community and has been accepted by a near universality of countries under the United Nations Framework Convention on Climate Change (UNFCCC). Paradoxically, the same nations have failed for over a decade to achieve a comprehensive legally binding agreement to effectively reduce global GHG emissions.

A new model of international cooperation was initiated with the adoption of the Paris Agreement, based on the complementarity of regional agreements (bottom-up approach) and multilateral agreements (top-down approach). Within this structure, the linking of ETSs can facilitate integration between both the developed and developing countries and promote trust and legitimacy to further deepen commitments to a multilateral platform. For example, the Chinese Government has publicly expressed a desire to investigate the future linking of its national domestic scheme, due to be launched in 2018, and the EU ETS.

As new ETSs are implemented worldwide, more creative frameworks are being developed, including hybrid schemes which combine features of carbon taxes – such as price stability – and the ETSs. In fact, the perceived distinctions between carbon taxes and ETSs are becoming less noticeable, and the political polarity less acute. However, ETSs are complex instruments and whether or not they will achieve their intended outcomes depends on how these schemes are designed.

Concerns over competitiveness distortions and carbon leakage have justified a widespread adoption of the free allocation of permits. Even in the absence of distortions to the efficiency property of ETSs, the free allocation indeed promotes an unfair distribution of resources that often benefits heavy polluters, which does not comply with the equity dimension of the Polluter Pays Principle.

Interestingly, the most promising alternative to the free allocation method, Border Carbon Adjustments (BCAs), has been largely rejected due to the possible WTO impacts, while the free allocation of permits has been generally assumed to be WTO compliant. However, the free allocation measures provide a subsidy to heavy polluters and create disparities between the businesses located in different countries with ETSs in place.

Some countries adopting a free of cost allocation have been failing to comply with their obligations under the SCM Agreement and the GATT, specifically the notification requirements pursuant to Article XVI(1) of the GATT in relation to the subsidies provided to industry sectors that fall under the sole trade-exposure threshold.

3. REAL-LIFE ETSs: LESSONS FROM THE CASE STUDIES

The EU ETS has been described in Chapter 3 as a roller coaster. The serious issue of surplus permits has been ongoing and led to structural reforms to the EU ETS in 2014 and 2015. The initially decentralised National Allocation Plans (NAPs) for the first and second trading periods resulted in an excessive free allocation of permits to liable installations compared to their actual emissions.

In 2009, an amendment to the ETS Directive, effective from the third trading period onwards, was put in place, replacing the decentralised NAPs with a Community-wide emissions cap and objective community-wide criteria for the free allocation of permits. However, the third trading period commenced with a large surplus of allowances, including the European Union Allowances (EUAs) banked from the second trading period. The Commission predicted an overall surplus of around 2 billion allowances to be carried forward into most of phase three, most likely undermining the economic efficiency and environmental effectiveness of the EU ETS, and possibly compromising its future viability.

Several measures to save the EU ETS have since been discussed. As a temporary measure, the Commission back-loaded the supply of phase three EUAs, postponing auctions of 900 million EUAs scheduled for 2013, 2014 and 2015 until 2019–20, creating a temporary boost to allowance prices and allowing time for the restructuring of the scheme. A 'market stability reserve' will be implemented to operate from 2019, allowing for the adjustment of the annual volumes of permits auctioned in situations where the total number of allowances in circulation is outside a certain predefined range. On top of that, a more comprehensive proposal for a Directive to amend the ETS Directive has also been presented by the European Commission. If approved, it will considerably change the provisions for the free allocation of permits in the EU ETS.

In Australia, the lack of political leadership and consistent long-term strategic goals in relation to climate action combined with the power of a group of emissions-intensive sectors sealed the destiny of the AUS CPM, which became the first – and to this date the only – mandatory CO_2 ETS discarded in the world.[3] The AUS CPM was designed as a 'hybrid model', aiming at providing both price certainty and stability to the stakeholders. The first three years of the scheme were known as the fixed charge years, during which permits were either allocated for free or issued for a fixed price, having the practical effect of a carbon tax. Despite the initial effect of a carbon tax, the AUS CPM was unequivocally designed to create a new market which would eventually link to other independent carbon markets. The permits issued by the Federal Government, Australian Carbon Units (ACUs), were given the legal status of personal property and would be tradable from July 2015 onwards. Once the scheme transitioned into the flexible charge years, the carbon market would gradually work like any other ETS.

Despite the potential to achieve sound emissions reductions, a fierce political debate around the nature of the scheme took place. The debate was characterised by a lack of clear understanding of the nature of the AUS CPM, and was dominated by a small group of emissions-intensive sectors interested in postponing the economic transition towards a low carbon future and by the political leader of the opposition party to the Federal Government. Ironically, the emissions-intensive sectors at the front of the opposition to the AUS CPM had already secured generous assistance packages under the scheme. During 2012–13, 104,203,895 ACUs (worth AUD\$23.00 per unit) were allocated free of cost under the Jobs and Competitiveness Program and in the 2013–14 financial year 97,834,540 free ACUs (worth AUD\$23.15 per unit) were allocated to these sectors.[4] No efforts were spared by these key sectors to postpone the transition to a low emissions economy.

The NZ ETS was the first national ETS to be implemented in the Australasian region and remains, to date, the key policy instrument to achieve the country's domestic emissions reduction targets, despite New Zealand's opt-out from the second phase of the Kyoto Protocol. New

---

[3] Also see Wendy Bacon, 'Sceptical Climate Part 2: Climate Science in Australian Newspapers' (Australian Centre for Independent Journalism, 2013) <http://sceptical-climate.investigate.org.au/part-2/>; Wendy Bacon, 'A Sceptical Climate: Media coverage of climate change in Australia' (Australian Centre for Independent Journalism, 2011); Wendy Bacon and Chris Nash, 'Playing the Media Game: The Relative (in)visibility of Coal Industry Interests in Media Reporting of Coal as a Climate Change Issue in Australia' (2012) 13 *Journalism Studies* 243. Bacon argues that the way in which media portrayed climate change in Australia also played a role in the process of decline of the AUS CPM.

[4] For further information on the assistance to the EITE sectors, see Chapters 3, 4 and 5.

Zealand's economy is predominantly agricultural-based, with the presence of small-scale industrial activity and a predominance of hydropower energy generation.

Naturally, the framework of the NZ ETS also presents distinctive features compared to the other two schemes analysed. These include the lack of a carbon cap in the first years of the ETS, the linking with a global carbon market from commencement and the coverage of the forestry and transport sectors, with possible coverage of the agriculture sector in the future.

The NZ ETS was unilaterally linked to the Kyoto ETS, which in turn created an indirect link between the EU ETS and the NZ ETS through the common use of Kyoto credits. During the first commitment period of the Kyoto Protocol, in order to keep within its reduction targets, the NZ Government 'backed' the NZUs issued with an equivalent amount of approved international units, for instance through the retirement of NZ Assigned Amount Units (AAUs) from the first Kyoto commitment period or other international units.

A review of the NZ ETS in 2012 altered this feature of the scheme and introduced a new power for the Government to sell New Zealand units by auction. It also allowed the Government to set an overall cap and finally excluded the eligibility of Kyoto units into the scheme, ending the unilateral linking with the Kyoto mechanism and the indirect linking with the EU ETS.

The review process became necessary as the influx of international units into the NZ ETS became excessive, creating an unnecessary flow of funds offshore. The decision to disconnect from the international carbon trading at this moment will further strengthen the effectiveness of the NZ ETS, with NZUs becoming the predominant unit for compliance under the scheme. Overall, the NZ ETS has proven to be a resilient scheme, with potential to become an even more interesting case study once agriculture becomes a liable sector under the scheme.

4. THE LEGAL CLASSIFICATION OF FREE ALLOCATION OF PERMITS AS SUBSIDIES

Independent domestic ETSs are adopting distinct methods for the allocation of permits free of cost. Where relevant discrepancies are observed, the further question is then whether these discrepancies can impact on the competitiveness of the liable industries under the independent ETSs.

Carbon leakage rates have been historically overestimated,[5] giving way to a race for exemptions and compromises which have ultimately reduced the effectiveness of carbon mitigation policies. There is a considerable incongruity between the risks of carbon leakage projected by the policymakers and the real impacts found by *ex-post* studies. As a result, Governments have historically been providing free permits to a number of sectors which are not significantly exposed to carbon leakage.

Chapter 4 concluded that transitional assistance must be provided exclusively to the most carbon leakage-exposed sectors. These sectors will vary according to the domestic and regional disparities, and can be objectively identified based on two cumulative criteria, the emissions-intensity and trade-exposure thresholds. Therefore, a first recommendation is for countries who are allocating free of cost permits not to adopt – and for amendments to take place where this has been the case – sole trade-exposure thresholds and/or sole emissions-intensity thresholds.

In relation to the discrepancies in the designs of the free allocation methods, the eligibility thresholds adopted in the three case studies vary significantly. For example, each ETS adopts a diverse metric unit or value to measure an industry's emissions-intensity, which makes international comparison difficult.

The discrepancies between the compared ETSs confirms that inconsistent eligibility criteria for the free allocation of permits can distort trade between competitors located in two or more countries with emissions trading in place.[6] Jurisdictions linking their independent ETSs could use the linking agreement to negotiate the harmonisation of their free allocation methodologies in order to minimise the trade distortions to sectors covered under the schemes.

The harmonisation process must follow a best practice approach and avoid having an excessive number of sectors eligible for allocations on the basis that they are exposed to carbon leakage. As mentioned above, the cumulative criteria of high emission-intensity and high trade-exposure thresholds are recommended, with the removal of any sole trade-exposure thresholds and sole emissions-intensity thresholds.

Chapter 5 further contributed to the analysis of whether the differences in the free allocation methods adopted by different ETSs can be problematic, by reviewing the data from the first and second trading periods in the EU ETS, when the Members had their separate NAPs. The

---

5   See Chapter 4.
6   See Chapter 5.

different allocation rules during the first and second trading periods of the EU ETS raised concerns over competitiveness distortions across the Member States.

The legal frameworks of the EU ETS and the AUS CPM were compared, and some key discrepancies were identified. In particular, the product benchmarks under the EU ETS, which were calculated based on the best technology, were more stringent than the AUS CPM baselines, which were calculated based on an industry's average emissions. While the less efficient industries under the EU ETS have an incentive to innovate up to the efficiency levels of the current best available technology, entities in Australia would not have had similar incentives.

The uneven benchmarks described above were multiplied by an output-based allocation level (AUS CPM), or by historical emissions data (EU ETS), once again resulting in significant variations of the allocation levels, with the potential to impact on trade and distort the competition between the liable installations under the linked schemes. Discrepancies in the levels of assistance, particularly in the case of excessive allocation leading to windfall profits, impacts on business liquidity and can distort competitiveness once independent ETSs are linked. These circumstances may become more problematic where not all countries participating in a linked system have sufficiently strong economies to provide such assistance to their energy-intensive sectors. The study concluded that the EU Commission and the Australian Government could have further negotiated the linking agreement in order to include basic provisions in relation to the free allocation of permits.

The in-depth understanding of carbon leakage and the free allocation methodologies provided in the earlier chapters of this book finally allowed for a thorough analysis of the compatibility of the free allocation methods with the WTO regime on subsidies. The specific focus of the analysis was on whether the free allocation of permits is a subsidy under the definition provided by Article 1.1(a)(1) of the SCM Agreement.

Chapter 6 answered this question in the affirmative in relation to the three case studies. Furthermore, it concluded that the subsidies granted based on a trade-exposure threshold are subject to the notification rule provided by Article XVI, A(1) of the GATT. The EU has been failing to comply with this notification requirement in relation to subsidies provided to industry sectors that fall under both the sole trade-exposure threshold and the combined emissions-intensity and trade-exposure criteria. The EU and Australia would have also failed to comply with the notification requirement in relation to their subsidies provided to sectors deemed to be emissions-intensive and trade-exposed. Due to the assumption of trade-exposure in the NZ ETS free allocation method, it is less likely that New Zealand would be obliged to comply with the notification requirements in Article XVI(1) of the GATT. The notification requirement will still apply if the proposed amendment to the EU ETS is adopted, providing for two levels of assistance based on a combined emissions-intensity and trade-exposure criteria.

Not all subsidies are subject to the provisions of the SCM Agreement. Chapter 6 concluded that the free allocation method in the case studies did not give rise to a prohibited subsidy. The answer remains negative for prohibited subsidies, even in relation to the EU ETS sole trade-exposure.

However, in relation to the EU ETS sole emissions-intensity threshold, it appears to have been included in the Directive in order to perpetuate the targeted subsidisation of a small number of enterprises from the cement sector, which were already being favoured by the decentralised National Allocation Plans during the first and second trading periods. Chapter 6 concluded that the cement industry is the predominant user of free EUAs under the sole emissions-intensity threshold and has benefited from disproportionately large amounts of surplus allocation, large enough to support a claim of *de facto* specificity. Accordingly, the subsidy may be actionable if it is found to have adverse effects on the interests of other Members. These subsidies generally represent an unnecessary cost to society, compromise the fairness of a scheme due to excessive allocation and can be problematic to trade.

In those few sectors where assistance is still justifiable, based on competitiveness concerns, the SCM Agreement would not challenge the free allocation of permits, unless the subsidy is prohibited or, being specific, causes adverse effects to other members. In this way, the provisions of the SCM Agreement provide a very much needed measure for restraint in the use of this instrument. The three final chapters in this book challenge the view that subsidies provided to heavy polluters under an ETS should be free from the guidance and corrective roles of the SCM Agreement.

5. FINAL REMARKS

Finally, let me return to the intuition that prompted this investigation into the free allocation of permits in the first place. It is broadly accepted that climate change is a market failure and that polluters should internalise the social costs of their economic activity. However, the practical experience of the ETSs demonstrates that many heavy polluters participating in these schemes are not paying their fair share of the bill.

Carbon leakage exposure rates have historically been overestimated by both industry and Governments, and there are sound economic reasons to support the adoption of very stringent eligibility thresholds when it comes to the free allocation of permits. A best practice approach would ensure greater transparency and facilitate the linking of independent ETSs.

Policies adopted to prevent carbon leakage and unfair competitive distortions vis-à-vis countries with less stringent carbon constraints must uphold incentives for emissions abatement, rather than offer expensive and environmentally ineffective industry support.[7] The eligibility thresholds must combine two criteria, emission-intensity and trade-exposure, and avoid the use of sole trade-exposure thresholds and sole emissions-intensity thresholds. When determining the levels of assistance, benchmarks based on the best available technology are preferable, and should be coupled with an output-based allocation rather than using historical emissions.

Finally, the EU ETS is currently providing an actionable subsidy to its cement sector in the form of free of cost EUAs. The removal of the sole emissions-intensity and sole trade-exposure thresholds in the proposal for a Directive to amend the EU ETS[8] is highly recommended. However, this recommendation comes with a caveat. The compromise offered by the European Commission, of maintaining minimum levels of 30 per cent free allocation to the non-EITE sectors until 2030 contradicts the findings in Chapter 4, and will partially undermine the benefits brought by the amendments. In any case, the EU must still comply with the notification requirements in Article XVI(1) of the GATT in relation to the free allocation of permits.

There are a number of limitations to the reach of this book. Free allocation methodologies are only one issue that may be dealt with through linking agreements. Other issues include negotiating a common time limit to the guarantees of free allocation, the uniformity of data to facilitate comparison (e.g., in terms of sector definitions and groupings of sectors), a uniformity of language and data should be available to the public to increase transparency. It is possible to agree on a central body to control the availability of permits in case of oversupply, following the

---

[7] Julia Reinaud, 'Issues Behind Competitiveness and Carbon Leakage: Focus on Heavy Industry' (IEA; OECD, 2008) 10, 2.

[8] Proposal 2015/148 (COD) for a Directive of the European Parliament and of the Council Amending Directive 2003/87/EC to enhance cost-effective emission reductions and low-carbon investments [2015].

example of the EU ETS market stability reserve. These issues are areas requiring further research.

The recommendations in this book have obvious relevance beyond the case studies. The analysis and recommendations provided in this study are relevant to any Government implementing and/or reviewing ETSs which include the free allocation of permits as an industry assistance measure. However, it remains to be asked whether the findings can be extended to the exemptions under carbon taxes. This enquiry would seem to warrant further exploration.

Bibliography

Alexy, Robert, *A Theory of Constitutional Rights* (Oxford University Press, 2009).

Alvarez-Jiménez, Alberto, 'The WTO Appellate Body's Exercise of Judicial Economy' (2009) 12(2) *Journal of International Economic Law* 393.

Andersen, Mikael Skou, 'Environmental and Economic Implications of Taxing and Trading Carbon: Some European Experiences' in *The Reality of Carbon Taxes in the 21st Century* (Vermont Law School 2008).

Andersen, Mikael Skou and Paul Ekins (eds), *Carbon-energy Taxation: Lessons from Europe* (Oxford University Press, 2009).

Anger, Niels and Ulrich Oberndorfer, 'Firm Performance and Employment in the EU Emissions Trading Scheme: An Empirical Assessment for Germany' (2008) 36 *Energy Policy* 12.

Anger, Niels, Christoph Böhringer and Ulrich Oberndorfer, 'Public Interest vs. Interest Groups: Allowance Allocation in the EU Emissions Trading Scheme' (2008) <ftp://ftp.zew.de/pub/zew-docs/dp/dp08023.pdf>.

Arlinghaus, Johanna, 'Impacts of Carbon Prices on Indicators of Competitiveness: A Review of Empirical Findings' (OECD, 2015).

Asselt, Harro Van and Thomas Brewer, 'Addressing Competitiveness and Leakage Concerns in Climate Policy: An Analysis of Border Adjustment Measures in the US and the EU' (2010) 38 *Energy Policy* 42.

Asselt, Harro van, Thomas Brewer and Michael Mehling, 'Addressing Leakage and Competitiveness in US Climate Policy: Issues Concerning Border Adjustment Measures' (Climate Strategies, 2009).

Australian Government, *The Emissions Reduction Fund: The Safeguard Mechanism* Department of Environment <https://www.environment.gov.au/climate-change/emissions-reduction-fund/publications/factsheet-erf-safeguard-mechanism>.

Australian Government, 'Australia and Europe strengthen collaboration on carbon markets' (2011) <http://www.climatechange.gov.au/ministers/hon-greg-combet-am-mp/media-release/australia-and-europe-strengthen-collaboration-carbon>.

Australian Government, 'Australia and New Zealand advance linking of their emissions trading schemes' (2011) <http://www.climatechange. gov.au/ministers/hon-greg-combet-am-mp/media-release/australia-and-new-zealand-advance-linking-their>.

Australian Government, 'Establishing the Eligibility of Activities under the Jobs and Competitiveness Program' (2011).

Australian Government, 'Australia and European Commission agree on pathway towards fully linking Emissions Trading Systems' (2012) <http://www.climatechange.gov.au/en/media/whats-new/linking-ets.aspx>.

Australian Government, 'Securing a Clean Energy Future: The Australian Government's Climate Change Plan' (2011).

Australian Government, 'Fact Sheet: Linking and Australian Liable Entities' (2012) <http://www.cleanenergyfuture.gov.au/linking-and-australian-liable-entities>.

Aydos, Elena, 'Tributação Ambiental no Brasil: Fundamentos e Perspectivas' (2010) <http://www.egov.ufsc.br/portal/sites/default/files/anexos/33953-44734-1-PB.pdf>.

Aydos, Elena, 'Australia's Carbon Pricing Mechanism' in Larry Kreiser et al (eds), *Carbon Pricing, Growth and the Environment*, Critical Issues in Environmental Taxation (Edward Elgar Publishing, 2012) 261.

Aydos, Elena, 'Levelling the Playing Field or Playing on Unlevel Fields: the Industry Assistance Framework under the European Union ETS, the New Zealand ETS, and Australia's CPM' in Larry Kreiser et al (eds), *Market Based Instruments: National Experiences in Environmental Sustainability*, Critical Issues in Environmental Taxation (Edward Elgar Publishing, 2013) vol XIII, 135.

Aydos, Elena, 'What Went Wrong? Lessons from a Short-Lived Carbon Price in Australia' in Leonardo de Andrade Costa, Ana Alice De Carli and Ricardo Lodi Ribeiro (eds), *Tributacao e Sustentabilidade Ambiental* (FGV Editora, 2015) 75.

Babiker, Mustafa H., 'Climate Change Policy, Market Structure, and Carbon Leakage' (2005) 65 *Journal of International Economics* 421.

Bacon, Wendy, 'A Sceptical Climate: Media coverage of climate change in Australia' (Australian Centre for Independent Journalism, 2011).

Bacon, Wendy, 'Sceptical Climate Part 2: Climate Science in Australian Newspapers' (Australian Centre for Independent Journalism, 2013) <http://sceptical-climate.investigate.org.au/part-2/>.

Bacon, Wendy and Chris Nash, 'Playing the Media Game: The Relative (In)Visibility of Coal Industry Interests in Media Reporting of Coal as a Climate Change Issue in Australia' (2012) 13 *Journalism Studies* 243.

Barde, Jean-Philippe and Olivier Godard, 'Economic Principles of Environmental Fiscal Reform' in Janet E. Milne and Mikael S. Andersen (eds), *Handbook of Research on Environmental Taxation* (Edward Elgar, 2012) 33.

Barker, Terry et al, 'Carbon Leakage from Unilateral Environmental Tax Reforms in Europe, 1995–2005' (2007) 35 *Energy Policy* 6281.

Barret, Scott, 'Self-enforcing International Environmental Agreements' (1994) 46 *Oxford Economic Papers* 878.

Bartels, Lorand, 'The WTO Legality of the Application of the EU's Emission Trading System to Aviation' (2012) 23(2) *The European Journal of International Law* 429.

Bartels, Lorand, 'The Chapeau of the General Exceptions in the WTO GATT and GATS Agreements' (2015) 109(1) *The American Journal of International Law* 95.

Bartleet, Matthew et al, 'Impact of Emissions Pricing on New Zealand Manufacturing: A Short-Run Analysis' (2010).

Baumol, William J. and Wallace E. Oates, 'The Use of Standards and Prices for Protection of the Environment' (1971) 73(1) *The Swedish Journal of Economics* 42.

Berghmans, Nicolas, Oliver Sartor and Nicolas Stephan, 'Reforming the EU ETS: give it some work!' (2013) (28) *Climate Brief: Focus on the Economics of Climate Change* 1.

Bernstein, Paul M., W. David Montgomery and Thomas F. Rutherford, 'Global Impacts of the Kyoto Agreement: Results from the MS-MRT Model' (1999) 21 *Resource and Energy Economics* 375.

Betz, Regina and Misato Sato, 'Emissions Trading: Lessons Learnt from the 1st Phase of the EU ETS and Prospects for the 2nd Phase' (2006) 6 *Climate Policy* 351.

Betz, Regina, Wolfgang Eichhammer and Joachim Schleich, 'Designing National Allocation Plans for EU Emissions Trading: A First Analysis of the Outcome' (2004) 15(3) *Energy & Environment* 375.

Bielecki, Janusz and Melaku Geboye Desta, *Electricity Trade in Europe: Review of the Economic and Regulatory Changes* (Kluwer Law International, 2004).

Black, Celeste, 'Climate Change and Tax Law: Tax Policy and Emissions Trading' (Sydney Law School, 2009)

Black, Celeste, 'Tax Accounting for Transactions under an Emissions Trading Scheme: An Australasian Perspective' (2011) 1 *Carbon & Climate Law Review* 91.

Black, Celeste, 'Linking Land Sector Activities to Emissions Trading: Australia's Carbon Farming Initiative' in Larry Kreiser et al (eds), *Carbon Pricing, Growth and the Environment*, Critical Issues in Environmental Taxation (Edward Elgar, 2012) vol XI, 184.

Black, Celeste, 'Accounting for Carbon Emission Allowances in the European Union: In Search of Consistency' (2014) 10(2) *Accounting in Europe* 223.

Black, Celeste and Michael Dirkis, 'Farming Carbon: Taxation Implications of the Carbon Farming Initiative' (2012) 21(1) *Revenue Law Journal* art 3.

Black, Celeste and Alex Evans, 'A Critical Analysis of the Tax Treatment of Dealings under Australian Domestic Emissions Reduction and Abatement Frameworks' (2011) 26(2) *Australian Tax Forum* 287.

Blyth, William and Martina Bosi, 'Linking Non-EU Domestic Emissions Trading Schemes with the EU Emissions Trading Scheme' (OECD, International Energy Agency, 2004).

Bogojevic, Sanja, 'Ending the Honeymoon: Deconstructing Emissions Trading Discourses' (2009) 21(3) *Journal of Environmental Law* 443

Bolscher, Hans et al, 'Carbon Leakage Evidence Project: Factsheets for Selected Sectors' (ECORYS, Öko-Institut, Cambridge Econometrics and TNO, 2013).

Branger, Frederic and Philippe Quirion, 'Would Border Carbon Adjustments Prevent Carbon Leakage and Heavy Industry Competitiveness Losses? Insights from a Meta-Analysis of Recent Economic Studies' (CIRED, 2013).

Branger, Frederic, Philippe Quirion and Julien Chevallier, 'Carbon Leakage and Competitiveness of Cement and Steel Industries under the EU ETS: Much Ado About Nothing' (CIRED, 2013).

Bruce, Neil, 'Measuring Industrial Subsidies: Some Conceptual Issues' (OECD, 1990).

Burtraw, Dallas et al, 'Linking by Degrees: Incremental Alignment of Cap-and-Trade Markets' (2013) 1.

Bush, Marc L. and Krzysztof J. Pelc, 'The Politics of Judicial Economy at the World Trade Organization' (2010) 64 *International Organization* 257.

Calabresi, Guido, *The Costs of Accidents. A Legal and Economic Analysis* (Yale University Press, 1970).

Cambridge Econometrics, Climate Strategies and Entec, 'Assessment of the Degree of Carbon Leakage in Light of an International Agreement on Climate Change: A Report for the Department of Energy and Climate Change' (2010).

Chan, Hei Sing (Ron), Shanjun Li and Fan Zhang, 'Firm Competitiveness and the European Union Emissions Trading Scheme' (The World Bank: Europe and Central Asia Region, 2013).

Charnovitz, Steve, 'The Law of Environmental "PPMs" in the WTO: Debunking the Myth of Illegality' (2002) 27 *Yale Journal of International Law* 59.

Clean Energy Regulator, *LEPID for the 2013–14 Financial Year* (30 June 2015) Australian Government <http://www.cleanenergyregulator.gov.au/Infohub/CPM/Liable-Entities-Public-Information-Database/LEPID-for-the-2013-14-financial-year>.

Clò, Stefano, *European Emissions Trading in Practice: An Economic Analysis* New Horizons in Environmental and Energy Law series (Edward Elgar Publishing, 2011).

Collaborative Economics, 'Green Innovation Index: International Edition' (Next 10, 2015).

Commission, European, 'EU action against climate change. EU emissions trading – an open scheme promoting global innovation' (2004)

Commonwealth of Australia, 'Australia's Low Pollution Future: The Economics of Climate Change Mitigation' (2008).

Commonwealth of Australia, 'Strong Growth, Low Pollution: Modelling a Carbon Price' (2011).

Convery, Frank and Luke Redmond, 'The European Union Emissions Trading Scheme: Issues in Allowance Price Support and Linkage' (2013) *Annual Review of Resource Economics* 1.

Cosbey, Aaron and Petros C. Mavroidis, 'A Turquoise Mess: Green Subsidies, Blue Industrial Policy and Renewable Energy: The Case for Redrafting the Subsidies Agreement of the WTO' (2014) *Journal of International Economic Law* 1.

Cosbey, Aaron and Luca Rubini, 'Does it FIT? An Assessment of the Effectiveness of Renewable Energy Measures and of the Implications of the Canada – Renewable Energy/FIT Disputes' (TheE15Initiative, 2013).

Cosbey, Aaron and Richard Tarasofsky, 'Climate Change, Competitiveness and Trade' (Chatham House, 2007).

Council of the European Union, 'Presidency Conclusions of the Brussels European Council of 8–9 March 2007' (Presidency Conclusions 7224/1/07, 2 May 2007).

Dales, John H., 'Land, Water and Ownership' (1968) 1(4) *The Canadian Journal of Economics* 791.

Deane, Felicity, 'Subsidies of the Australian Clean Energy Package' (2013) 12(2) *The Journal of Law and Financial Management*.

Deane, Felicity, *Emissions Trading and WTO Law: A Global Analysis* (Edward Elgar Publishing, 2015).

De Cendra, Javier, 'Can Emissions Trading Schemes be Coupled with Border Tax Adjustments? An Analysis vis-à-vis WTO Law' (2006) 15(2) *RECIEL* 131.

De Perthuis, Christian and Raphaël Trotignon, 'The European CO2 Allowances Market: Issues in the Transition to Phase III' (2012).

Delimatsis, Panagiotis, *International Trade in Services and Domestic Regulations: Necessity, Transparency, and Regulatory Diversity* (Oxford University Press, 2007).

Delimatsis, Panagiotis, 'Financial Innovation and Climate Change: the Case of Renewable Energy Certificates and the Role of the GATS' (2009) 8(3) *World Trade Review* 439.

Demailly, Damien and Philippe Quirion, 'Leakage from Climate Policies and Border-tax Adjustment: Lessons from a Geographic Model of the Cement Industry' (2005).

Demailly, Damien and Philippe Quirion, 'European Emission Trading Scheme and Competitiveness: A Case Study on the Iron and Steel Industry' (2008) 30 *Energy Economics* 2009.

Denne, Tim, 'Impacts of the NZ ETS on Emissions Leakage: Final Report' (COVEC, 2011).

Department of Climate Change, 'Carbon Pollution Reduction Scheme: Green Paper' (2008).

Department of Climate Change, 'Climate Change Carbon Pollution Reduction Scheme: White Paper' (2008).

Department of Industry, Innovation, Climate Change, Science, Research and Tertiary Education, 'Australian National Greenhouse Accounts: Quarterly Update of Australia's National Greenhouse Gas Inventory, December Quarter' (2013) <http://www.climatechange.gov.au/climate-change/greenhouse-gas-measurement-and-reporting/tracking-australias-greenhouse-gas-emissio-0/quarterly-update-australias-national-green house-gas-inventory-march-13>.

Dimantchev, Emil et al, 'Carbon 2013: at a Tipping Point' (Point Carbon, 2013).

Dröge, Susanne et al, 'Tackling Leakage in a World of Unequal Carbon Prices' (Climate Strategies, 2009).

Dröge, Susanne and Simone Cooper, 'Tackling Leakage in a World of Unequal Carbon Prices: A Study for the Greens/EFA Group' (Climate Strategies, 2010).

Dworkin, Ronald, *Taking Rights Seriously* (Harvard University Press, 1977).

Egenhofer, Christian et al, 'The EU Emissions Trading System and Climate Policy towards 2050: Real incentives to reduce emissions and drive innovation?' (CEPS, 2011).

Ellerman, Denny, '*Ex-post* Evaluation of Tradable Permits: the U.S. SO2 Cap-and-Trade Program' (CEEPR, 2003).

Ellerman, Denny, 'The EU's Emissions Trading Scheme: A Prototype-Global System?' (MIT, 2009).

Ellerman, Denny, Barbara Buchner and Carlo Carraro (eds), *Allocation in the European Emissions Trading Scheme: Rights, Rents and Fairness* (Cambridge University Press, 2007).

Ellerman, Denny, Frank Convery and Christian De Perthuis, 'The European Carbon Market in Action: Lessons from the First Trading Period' (2008).

Ellerman, Denny, Frank Convery and Christian De Perthuis, *Pricing Carbon: the European Union Emissions Trading Scheme* (Frank J. Convery, Christian de Perthuis and Emilie Alberola trans, Cambridge University Press, 2010).

Environmental Protection Authority, 'The New Zealand Emissions Trading Scheme. ETS 2012 – Facts and Figures' (2012).

Environmental Protection Authority, '2014 Emissions Trading Scheme Report' (2014).

Environmental Protection Authority, 'The New Zealand Emissions Trading Scheme. ETS 2014 – Facts and Figures' (2014)

European Commission, *Climate Action* <http://ec.europa.eu/clima/policies/transport/aviation/index_en.htm>.

European Commission, *Consultation on structural options to strengthen the EU Emissions Trading System* European Commission <http://ec.europa.eu/clima/consultations/0017/index_en.htm>.

European Commission, *Reducing Emissions from Aviation* <https://ec.europa.eu/clima/policies/transport/aviation_en>.

European Commission, *Structural Reform of the EU ETS* <https://ec.europa.eu/clima/policies/ets/reform_en>.

European Commission, 'Green Paper on Greenhouse Gas Emissions Trading within the European Union' (2000).

European Commission (2011), Draft Commission decision on free allocation rules for the emissions trading scheme: Explanatory paper prepared by DG Climate Action for MEPs

European Commission, 'Guidance Document n°7 on the Harmonized Free Allocation Methodology for the EU-ETS Post 2012' (2011).

European Commission, 'Report from the Commission to the European Parliament and the Council: The State of the European Carbon Market in 2012' (European Commission, 2012).

European Commission, 'EU welcomes WTO ruling in support of clean energy' (2013) <http://trade.ec.europa.eu/doclib/press/index.cfm?id=895>.

European Council, 'Council conclusions 169/14 of 23 and 24 October 2014' (2014) <http://www.consilium.europa.eu/uedocs/cms_data/docs/pressdata/en/ec/145397.pdf>.

European Environment Agency, 'Market-based instruments for environmental policy in Europe' (European Environment Agency, 2005)

'EU ETS impacts on profitability and trade: a sector by sector analysis' (Carbon Trust, 2008).

Falcão, Tatiana, 'Providing Environmental Taxes with an Environmental Purpose' in Larry Kreiser et al (eds), *Market Based Instruments: National Experiences in Environmental Sustainability* (Edward Elgar, 2013) 41

Faure, Michael G. and David Grimeaud, 'Financial Assurance Issues of Environmental Liability' (Maastricht University and ECTIL, 2000).

Finland, 'Consultation on Structural Options to Strengthen the EU Emissions Trading System' (2013) <http://ec.europa.eu/clima/consultations/articles/0017_en.htm>.

Fischer, Carolyn and Alan K. Fox, 'The Role of Trade and Competitiveness Measures in US Climate Policy' (2011) 101(3) *The American Economic Review* 258.

Fischer, Carolyn, Richard Morgenstern and Nathan Richardson, 'Carbon Taxes and Energy-Intensive Trade-Exposed Sectors: Impacts and Options' in Ian Parry, Adele Morris and Roberton Williams III (eds), *Implementing a US Carbon Tax: Challenges and Debates* (Routledge, 2015).

Fisher, Brian, Anna Matysek and Paul Newton, 'The CPRS and the European Union Emissions Trading Scheme: The Trade Intensity of Australian Industry Sectors' (BAEconomics, 2009).

Ford, Robert and Wim Suyker, 'Industrial Subsidies in the OECD Economies' (OECD, 1990).

Garnaut, Ross, *The Garnaut Climate Change Review: Final Report* (Cambridge University Press, 2008).

Garnaut, Ross, 'Garnaut Climate Change Review Update: Global Emissions Trend' (Commonwealth of Australia, 2011).

Garnaut, Ross, 'Garnaut Climate Change Review Update: Progress Towards Effective Global Action on Climate Change' (Commonwealth of Australia, 2011).

Garnaut, Ross, 'Garnaut Climate Change Review Update: Carbon Pricing and Reducing Australia's Emmissions' (Commonwealth of Australia, 2011).

Garnaut, Ross, 'Garnaut Climate Change Review Update: The Science of Climate Change' (Commonwealth of Australia, 2011).

Gilbert, Alyssa et al, 'Comparative Analysis of National Allocation Plans for Phase I of the EU ETS' (ECOFYS, 2006).

Goldenberg, Suzanne, 'Obama Fails First Climate Test by Rejecting EU Aviation Carbon Regime' (2012) <http://www.theguardian.com/world/2012/nov/28/obama-fails-climate-test-aviation>.

Goulder, Lawrence H. and Ian W.H. Parry, 'Instrument Choice in Environmental Policy' (2008) 2(2) *Review of Environmental Economics and Policy* 152.

Government, New Zealand, 'The New Zealand Emissions Trading Scheme. ETS 2013 – Facts and figures' (2013)

Green, Fergus and Nicholas Stern, 'China's changing economy: implications for its carbon dioxide emissions' (2016) *Climate Policy* 1.

Green, Kenneth P., January, 2015, 'Polluter Pays Principle' in *Salem Press Encyclopedia of Science* (2015).

Grubb, Michael, 'Strengthening the EU ETS: Creating a Stable Platform for EU Energy Sector Investment' (University of Cambridge Centre for Mitigation Research, 2012).

Grubb, Michael and Karsten Neuhoff, 'Allocation and competitiveness in the EU emissions trading scheme: policy overview' (2006) 6(1) *Climate Policy* 7.

Habermacher, Florian, 'Is Carbon Leakage Really Low? A Critical Reconsideration of the Leakage Concept' in Larry Kreiser et al (eds) *Carbon Pricing, Growth and the Environment* (Edward Elgar Publishing, 2012).

Hahn, Robert and Robert Stavins, 'The Effect of Allowance Allocations on Cap-and-Trade System Performance' (2011) 54 *Journal of Law & Economics* S267.

Hardin, Garret, 'The Tragedy of the Commons' (1968) 162 *Science* 1243.

Hausotter, Tobias, Sibyl Steuwer and Dennis Tänzler, 'Competitiveness and Linking of Emission Trading Systems' (Federal Environmental Agency (Germany), 2011).

Henschke, Lauren, 'Going it Alone on Climate Change. A New Challenge to WTO Subsidies Disciplines: Are Subsidies in Support of Emissions Reductions Schemes Permissible Under the WTO' (2012) 11(1) *World Trade Review* 27.

Hepburn, Cameron et al, 'Auctioning of EU ETS Phase II Allowances: How and Why?' (2006) 1.

Hintermann, Beat, 'Allowance Price Drivers in the First Phase of the EU ETS' (2009) *CEPE Working Paper*.

Holzer, Kateryna, *Carbon-related Border Adjustment and WTO Law* (Edward Elgar Publishing, 2014).

Howse, Robert, 'Climate Mitigation Subsidies and the WTO Legal Framework: A Policy Analysis' (iisd, 2010).

Howse, Robert and Antonia L. Eliason, 'Domestic and International Strategies to Address Climate Change: An Overview of the WTO Legal Issues' in Thomas Cottier, Olga Nartova and Sadeq Z. Bigdeli (eds), *International Trade Regulation and the Mitigation of Climate Change* (Cambridge University Press, 2009) 48.

Hufbauer, Gary Clyde, Steve Charnovitz and Jisun Kim, *Global Warming and the World Trading System* (Peterson Institute for International Economics, 2009).

IEA and OECD, 'Coal medium term market report: market trends and projections to 2018' (IEA, 2013).

Intergovernmental Panel on Climate Change, 'Climate Change 2007: Mitigation of Climate Change' (2007).

'Intergovernmental Panel on Climate Change (IPCC)' (2013) <http://www.ipcc.ch/>.

Intergovernmental Panel on Climate Change, 'Climate Change 2013: The Physical Science Basis – Summary for Policymakers' (2013) <http://www.ipcc.ch/>.

Intergovernmental Panel on Climate Change, 'Climate Change 2013: The Physical Science Basis – Technical Summary' (2013) <www.ipcc.ch>.

Intergovernmental Panel on Climate Change, 'Work Group III Assessment Report 5: Mitigation of Climate Change' (2014).

Intergovernmental Panel on Climate Change, 'Climate Change 2014: Synthesis Report. Summary for Policymakers.' (2015).

International Accounting Standard (IAS) 20 – Accounting for Government Grants and Disclosure of Government Assistance.

International Accounting Standard (IAS) 37 – Provisions, Contingent Liabilities and Contingent Assets.

International Accounting Standard (IAS) 38 – Intangible Assets.

International Civil Aviation Organization, *Carbon Offsetting and Reduction Scheme for International Aviation (CORSIA)* ICAO Environment <http://www.icao.int/environmental-protection/Pages/market-based-measures.aspx>.

International Energy Agency, 'Redrawing the Energy-Climate Map: World Energy Outlook Special Report' (IEA, OECD, 2013)

International Energy Agency, 'Key Trends in CO2 Emissions' (2015)

International Energy Agency, *IEA Finds CO2 Emissions Flat for Third Straight Year Even as Global Economy Grew in 2016* (17 March 2017) <https://www.iea.org/newsroom/news/2017/march/iea-finds-co2-emissions-flat-for-third-straight-year-even-as-global-economy-grew.html>

Irwin, Douglas A., Petros C. Mavroidis and Alan O. Sykes, *The Genesis of the GATT* (Cambridge University Press, 2008).

Jegou, Ingrid and Luca Rubini, 'The Allocation of Emissions Allowances Free of Charge: Legal and Economic Considerations' (ICTSD, 2011).

Johnston, Angus, 'Free Allocation of Allowances Under the EU Emissions Trading Scheme: Legal Issues' (2006) 6 *Climate Policy* 115.

Juergens, Ingmar, Jesús Barreiro-Hurlé and Alexander Vasa, 'Identifying Carbon Leakage Sectors in the EU ETS and Implications of Results' (2013) 13(1) *Climate Policy* 89.

Kachi, Aki et al, 'Linking Emissions Trading Systems: A Summary of Current Research' (2015) 1.

Kettner, Claudia et al, 'Stringency and Distribution in the EU Emissions Trading Scheme: First Evidence' (2008) 8 *Climate Policy* 41.

Kettner, Claudia, Daniela Kletzan-Slamanig and Angela Köppl, 'The EU Emission Trading Scheme: is there a need for price stabilization?' in Larry Kreiser et al (eds), *Environmental Taxation and Green Fiscal Reform*, Critical Issues in Environmental Taxation (Edward Elgar, 2014) vol XIV, 113.

Kirk, Alexandra, *Woodside wants LNG Exempt from Carbon Tax* (11 April 2011) ABC News <http://www.abc.net.au/am/content/2011/s3187564.htm>.

Koch, Nicolas et al, 'Politics Matters: Regulatory Events as Catalysts for Price Formation Under Cap-and-Trade' (2015) *Journal of Environmental Economics and Management* 1.

Kolshus, Hans H. and Asbjorn Torvanger, 'Analysis of EU Member States' National Allocation Plans' (CICERO, 2005).

Kruger, Joseph, Wallace Oates and William Pizer, 'Decentralization in the EU Emissions Trading Scheme and Lessons for Global Policy' (2007) 1(1) *Review of Environmental Economics and Policy* 112.

Lewis, Barbara and Valerie Volcovici, 'Insight: U.S., China Turned EU Powers Against Airline Pollution Law' (2012) <//www.reuters.com/article/2012/12/10/us-eu-airlines-climate-idUSBRE8B801H20121210#Drb1Yz7Q8WepdLKB.99>.

Low, Patrick, 'The Treatment of Subsidies in the WTO Framework' in Claus Dieter Ehlermann and Michelle Everson (eds), European Competition Law Annual 1999: Selected Issues in the Field of State Aids (Hart Publishing, 2001).

Lyster, Rosemary, 'Australia's Clean Energy Future Package: Are We There Yet?' (2011) 28 *Environmental and Planning Law Journal* 446.

Lyster, Rosemary and Adrian Bradbrook, *Energy Law and the Environment* (Cambridge University Press, 2006).

Lyster, Rosemary et al, *Environmental and Planning Law in New South Wales* (The Federation Press, 3rd edn, 2012).

Mace, M.J. et al, 'Analysis of the Legal and Organisational Issues Arising in Linking the EU Emissions Trading Scheme to Other Existing and Emerging Emissions Trading Schemes' (FIELD, IEEP, WRI, 2008).

Malmgren, Harald B., *International Order for Public Subsidies* (Trade Policy Research Centre, 1977).

Manne, Alan S. and Richard G. Richels, 'The Kyoto Protocol: A Cost-Effective Strategy for Meeting Environmental Objectives?' (1998).

Matthes, Felix Christian and Franzjosef Schafhausen, 'Germany' in A. Denny Ellerman, Barbara K. Buchner and Carlo Carraro (eds), *Allocation in the European Emissions Trading Scheme* (Cambridge University Press, 2007).

Mavroidis, Petros, *Trade In Goods: The GATT and the Other WTO Agreements Regulating Trade in Goods* (Oxford University Press, 2012).

Miller, R. and R. Brapties, *Transboundary Harm in International Law: Lessons from the Trail Smelter Arbitration* (Cambridge University Press, 2006).

Milne, Janet E. and Mikael Skou Andersen, 'Introduction to Environmental Taxation Concepts and Research' in Janet E. Milne and Mikael Skou Andersen (eds), *Handbook of Research on Environmental Taxation* (Edward Elgar Publishing, 2012).

Ministry for the Environment, 'A Guide to Landfill Methane in the New Zealand Emissions Trading Scheme' (2011).

Ministry for the Environment, 'Report on The New Zealand Emissions Trading Scheme' (2011).

Monjon, Stephanie and Philippe Quirion, 'Addressing Leakage in the EU ETS: Results from the Case II Model' (2009).

Monjon, Stephanie and Philippe Quirionn, 'How to Design a Border Adjustment for the European Union Emissions Trading System?' (2010) *Energy Policy*.

Monjon, Stephanie and Philippe Quirion, 'A Border Adjustment for the EU ETS: Reconciling WTO Rules and Capacity to Tackle Carbon Leakage' (2012) *X Annual Conference of the Euro-Latin Study Network on Integration and Trade (ELSNIT): Trade and Climate Change*.

Nash, Jonathan Remy, 'Too Much Market? Conflict Between Tradable Pollution Allowances and the "Polluter Pays" Principle' (2000) 24 *Harvard Environmental Law Review* 445.

Neuhoff, Karsten, *Climate Policy after Copenhagen: the Role of Carbon Pricing* (Cambridge University Press, 2011).

Neuhoff, Karsten and et al, 'Emission Projections 2008–2012 Versus National Allocation Plans II' (2006) 6(4) *Climate Policy* 395.

Neuhoff, Karsten and et al, 'Implications of Announced Phase II National Allocation Plans For the EU ETS' (2006) 6(4) *Climate Policy* 411.

Numan-Parsons, Elisabeth, Kris Iyer and Matthew Bartleet, 'The Surprising Vulnerability of New Zealand Manufacturing to CO2 Emissions Pricing: The Lessons of an International Comparison' (2010) 40(3) *Economic Analysis and Policy* 313.

O'Gorman, Marianna and Frank Jotzo, 'Impact of the Carbon Price on Australia's Electricity Demand, Supply and Emissions' (Centre for Climate Economic & Policy, 2014).

OECD, *Council Recommendation on Guiding Principles Concerning International Economic Aspects of Environmental Policies* (1972).

OECD, 'Recommendation of the council on guiding principles concerning international economic aspects of environmental policies' (1972) <http://acts.oecd.org/Instruments/PrintInstrumentView.aspx?Instrument>.

OECD, 'Environmentally Harmful Subsidies: Challenges for Reform' (OECD, 2005).

OECD, 'The Sectoral Competitiveness Issue: Theoretical Studies' in *The Political Economy of Environmentally Related Taxes* (OECD, 2006) 67.

OECD, *Glossary of Statistical Terms* (OECD, 2007).

OECD, 'Subsidy Reform and Sustainable Development: Political Economy Aspects' (OECD, 2007).

OECD, *The Polluter Pays Principle: Definition, Analysis, Implementation*, OCDE/GD(92)81 (OECD Publishing, 2008).

OECD, 'Mitigating Climate Change in the Context of Incomplete Carbon Pricing Coverage' in *The Economics of Climate Change Mitigation: Policies and Options for Global Action Beyond 2012* (OECD, 2009).

OECD, *The Economics of Climate Change Mitigation: Policies and Options for Global Action Beyond 2012* (2009).

OECD, 'Linkages Between Environmental Policy and Competitiveness' (OECD, 2010) <http://www.oecd-ilibrary.org/environment/linkages-between-environmental-policy-and-competitiveness_218446820583>.

OECD and IEA, 'Act Locally, Trade Globally: Emissions Trading for Climate Policy' (2005).

Olivier, Jos, Greet Janssens-Maenhout and Jeroen Peters, 'Trends in global co2 emissions: 2012 Report' (The Hague: PBL Netherlands Environmental Assessment Agency; Ispra: Joint Research Centre, 2012) <edgar.jrc.ec.europa.eu.>.

Olivier, Jos et al, 'Trends in Global CO2 Emissions' (2013).

Palombino, Fulvio Maria, 'Judicial Economy and Limitation of the Scope of the Decision in International Adjudication' (2010) 23 *Leiden Journal of International Law* 909.

Paltsev, Sergey V., 'The Kyoto Protocol: Regional and Sectoral Contributions to the Carbon Leakage' (2001) 22(4) *The Energy Journal* 53.

Parliament of Australia, 'Hill Signs Historic Agreement to Fight Global Warming' (1998) <http://parlinfo.aph.gov.au/parlInfo/search/display/display.w3p;query=Id%3A%22media%2Fpressrel%2FP1205%22>.

Pigou, Arthur, *The Economics of Welfare* (Macmillan, 4th edn, 1962).

Polish Ministry of the Environment, 'Consultation on Structural Options to Strengthen the EU Emissions Trading System' (2013) <http://ec.europa.eu/clima/consultations/articles/0017_en.htm>.

Posner, Eric and David Weisbach, *Climate Change Justice* (Princeton University Press, 2010).

Reinaud, Julia, 'Issues Behind Competitiveness and Carbon Leakage: Focus on Heavy Industry' (IEA; OECD, 2008).

Reinaud, Julia, 'Trade, Competitiveness and Carbon Leakage: Challenges and Opportunities' (Chatham House, 2009).

Report of the United Nations Conference on Environment and Development, UN Doc A/CONF 151/26 (3–14 June 1992).

Resolution A39-3, Adopted at the 39th Session of the Assembly, Consolidated statement of continuing ICAO policies and practices related to environmental protection – Global Market-based Measure (MBM) Scheme, ICAO (Montréal, 27 September–6 October 2016).

Rio Tinto, 'Australian Carbon Tax will Hold Back Export Industries, Investment and Jobs Growth' (10 July 2011) Rio Tinto <http://www.riotinto.com/media/media-releases-237_1156.aspx>.

Rossnagel, Alexander, 'Evaluating Links Between Emissions Trading Schemes: An Analytical Framework' (2008) 2(4) *Carbon & Climate Law Review* 394.

Rubini, Luca, *The Definition of Subsidy and State Aid: WTO and EC Law in Comparative Perspective* (Oxford University Press, 2010).

Rubini, Luca, 'Ain't Wastin' Time no More: Subsidies for Renewable Energy, The SCM Agreement, Policy Space, and Law Reform' (2012) 15(2) *Journal of International Economic Law* 525.

Rubini, Luca, 'What Does the Recent WTO Litigation on Renewables Energy Subsidies tell us about Methodology in Legal Analysis? The Good, the Bad, and the Ugly' (2014) *EUI Working Papers* 1.

Sandbag, 'Forecasting the EU ETS to 2020' (Sandbag, 2014).

Sandbag, 'Slaying the Dragon: Vanquish the Surplus and Rescue the ETS' (Sandbag, 2014).

Sands, Philippe, *Principles of International Environmental Law* (Cambridge University Press, 2003).

Sands, Philippe et al, *Principles of International Environmental Law* (Cambridge University Press, 3rd edn, 2012).

Sartor, Oliver, 'Carbon Leakage in the Primary Aluminium Sector: What evidence after 6½ years of the EU ETS?' (2012) <http://ssrn.com/abstract=2205516>.

Schmalensee, Richard and Robert Stavins, 'The SO2 Allowance Trading System: The Ironic History of a Grand Policy Experiment' (MIT Center for Energy and Environmental Policy Research, 2012).

Sépibus, Joëlle de, 'The European Emission Trading Scheme Put to the Test of State Aid Rules' (WTI, 2007).

Shavell, Steve, *Economic Analysis of Accident Law* (Harvard University Press, 1987).

Sijm, Jos, Karsten Neuhoff and Yihsu Chen, 'CO2 Cost Pass-Through and Windfall Profits in the Power Sector' (2006) 6(1) *Climate Policy* 49.

Smith, Stephen, 'Environmentally Related Taxes and Tradable Permit Systems in Practice' (OECD, 2007).

Sopher, Peter, Anthony Mansell and Clayton Munnings, 'Australia' (EDF IETA, 2014).

Stavins, Robert, 'The Problem of the Commons: Still Unsettled after 100 Years' (2011) 101 *American Economic Review* 81.

Stern, Nicholas, *The Economics of Climate Change: The Stern Review* (Cambridge University Press, 2006).

Stone, Christopher D. 'Common but Differentiated Responsibilities in International Law' (2004) 98(2) *The American Journal of International Law* 276.

The Canberra Times, 'Tony Abbott's speech on the carbon tax' (2011) <http://www.canberratimes.com.au/environment/tony-abbotts-speech-on-the-carbon-tax-20110914-1wopf.html>.

The European Commission and the Hon Greg Combet, Minister for Climate Change and Energy Efficiency, Australian Government, 'Australia and European Commission agree on pathway towards fully linking emissions trading systems' (Media release, 28 August 2012).

The Netherlands, 'Consultation on Structural Options to Strengthen the EU Emissions Trading System' (2013) <http://ec.europa.eu/clima/consultations/articles/0017_en.htm>.

Tiche, Fitsum G., Stefan E. Weishaar and Oscar Couwenberg, 'Carbon Leakage, Free Allocation and Linking Emissions Trading Schemes' (2013) *University of Groningen Faculty of Law Research Paper Series*.

Trotignon, Raphael and Anais Delbosc, 'Allowance Trading Patterns During the Trial Period: What Does the CITL Reveal?' (Mission Climate, 2008).

Tuerk, Andreas et al, 'Linking Carbon Markets: Concepts, Case Studies and Pathways' (2009) 9(4) *Climate Policy* 341.

Twomey, Paul, *Obituary: The Carbon Price* UNSW Australia <http://newsroom.unsw.edu.au/news/business/obituary-carbon-price>.

Verschuuren, Jonathan and Floor Fleurke, 'Entracte: Report on the Legal Implementation of the EU ETS at Member State Level' (Tilburg Sustainability Center, 2012).

Weishaar, Stefan, *Emissions Trading Design* (Edward Elgar Publishing, 2014).

Wettestad, Jorgen, 'EU Energy-Intensive Industries and Emission Trading: Losers Becoming Winners?' (2009) 19(5) *Environmental Policy and Governance* 309.

Wilson, Lauren, 'Steel Giants Back Howes Over Carbon Tax', *The Australian* (Canberra), 16 April 2011 2011 <http://www.theaustralian. com.au/news/nation/steel-giants-back-howes-over-carbon-tax/story-e6fr g6nf-1226039943407>.

Windon, James, 'The Allocation of Free Emissions Units and The WTO Subsidies Agreement' (2009) 41 *Georgetown Journal of International Law* 189.

Woerdman, Edwin, Stefano Clò and Alessandra Arcuri, 'European Emissions Trading and the Polluter-Pays Principle: Assessing Grandfathering and Over-Allocation' in Michael Faure and Marjan Peeters (eds), *Climate Change and European Emissions Trading: Lessons for Theory and Practice* (Edward Elgar Publishing, 2008) 128.

Woerdman, Edwin, Oscar Couwenberg and Andries Nentjes, 'Energy Prices and Emissions Trading: Windfall Profits from Grandfathering?' (2009) 28 *European Journal of Law and Economics* 185.

Wood, Tony and Tristan Edis, 'New Protectionism under Carbon Pricing: Case Studies of LNG, Coal Mining and Steel Sectors' (Grattan Institute, 2011).

World Bank Group and ECOFYS, 'State and Trends of Carbon Pricing' (2014).

World Bank Group, ECOFYS and Vivid Economics, 'State and Trends of Carbon Pricing' (2016).

World Trade Organization, 'Basic Instruments and Selected Documents' (GATT Secretariat, 1962).

World Trade Organization, 'World Trade Report: Exploring the Links Between Subsidies, Trade and the WTO' (2006).

World Trade Organization, *WTO Analytical Index: Guide to WTO Law and Practice: Agreement on Subsidies and Countervailing Measures* (Cambridge University Press, 3rd edn, 2011).

Zahariadis, Nikolaos, *State Subsidies in the Global Economy* (Palgrave Macmillan, 2008).

Zarbiyev, Fuad, 'Judicial Activism in International Law – A Conceptual Framework for Analysis' (2012) *Journal of International Dispute Settlement* 1.

AUSTRALIAN LEGISLATIVE MATERIALS

Australian National Registry of Emissions Units Act 2011 (Cth).
Carbon Credits (Consequential Amendments) Act 2011 (Cth).
Carbon Farming Initiative Act 2011 (Cth).
Carbon Farming Initiative Amendment Act 2014 (Cth).
Carbon Pollution Reduction Scheme Bill 2009 (Cth).

Clean Energy Act 2011 (Cth).

Clean Energy Amendment (International Emissions Trading and Other Measures) Act 2012 (Cth).

Clean Energy (Charges–Customs) Act 2011 (Cth).

Clean Energy (Charges–Excise) Act 2011 (Cth).

Clean Energy (Consequential Amendments) Act 2011 (Cth).

Clean Energy (Household Assistance Amendments) Act 2011 (Cth).

Clean Energy (Tax Laws Amendments) Act 2011 (Cth).

Clean Energy (Unit Issue Charge – Auctions) Act 2011 (Cth).

Clean Energy (Unit Issue Charge – Fixed Charge) Act 2011 (Cth).

Clean Energy (Unit Shortfall Charge – General) Act 2011 (Cth).

Clean Energy Legislation Amendment Act 2012 (Cth).

Clean Energy Legislation Amendment (International Linking) Regulation 2013 (Cth).

Clean Energy Legislation (Carbon Tax Repeal) Act 2014 (Cth).

Clean Energy Regulator Act 2011 (Cth).

Clean Energy Regulations 2011 (Cth).

Clean Energy Regulations 2012 (Cth).

Climate Change Authority Act 2011 (Cth).

Climate Change Authority (Abolition) Bill 2013.

Climate Change (Eligible Industrial Activities) Regulations 2010 (Cth).

Explanatory Memorandum, Clean Energy Bill 2011 (Cth).

Explanatory Memorandum, Clean Energy Legislation Amendment (International Emissions Trading and Other Measures) Bill 2012 and related Bills (Cth).

National Greenhouse and Energy Reporting Act 2007 (Cth).

National Greenhouse and Energy Reporting (Safeguard Mechanism) Rule 2015 (Cth).

National Greenhouse and Energy Reporting Amendment (2015 Measures No. 2) Regulation 2015 (Cth).

National Greenhouse and Energy Reporting (Audit) Amendment Determination 2015 (No. 1).

Steel Transformation Plan Act 2011 (Cth).

FOREIGN DOMESTIC MATERIALS

Belgium

Vlaams decreet houdende de organisatie van de elektriciteitmarkt [Flemish decree on the organization of the electricity market] (Belgium) 17 July 2000, Belgisch Staatsblad [Belgian Official Gazette] 2000, 32166 [author's trans].

New Zealand

Climate Change Response Act 2002 (NZ).
Climate Change Response (Emissions Trading and Other Matters) Amendment Act 2012 (NZ).
Climate Change (Unit Register) Amendment Regulations 2014 (NZ) SR 2014/364.
Minister for Climate Change, New Zealand Government, 'The Climate Change Response (2050 Emissions Target) Notice 2011', *New Zealand Gazette*, No 2067, 31 March 2011, 987.
Ministry for the Environment, 'Doing New Zealand's Fair Share. Emissions Trading Scheme Review 2011: Final Report' (2011).
Ministry for the Environment, 'Updating the New Zealand Emissions Trading Scheme' (Consultation document, New Zealand Government, April 2012).
Ministry for the Environment, New Zealand Government, *Energy's Obligations: Reporting emissions and surrendering NZUs* (3 December 2012) Climate Change Information <http://www.climatechange.govt.nz/emissions-trading-scheme/participating/energy/obligations/index.html>.
Ministry for the Environment, *Regulations Banning the Use of Certain International Units in the ETS* (17 December 2012) Climate Change Information, New Zealand <http://www.climatechange.govt.nz/emissions-trading-scheme/building/regulatory-updates/restricting-cers.html>.
Ministry for the Environment, New Zealand Government, *Liquid Fossil Fuel Suppliers' Obligations: Reporting Emissions and Surrendering NZUs* (21 December 2012) Climate Change Information <http://www.climatechange.govt.nz/emissions-trading-scheme/participating/fossil-fuels/obligations/>.

United States

American Clean Energy and Security Bill 2009.
Clean Air Act Amendments of 1990, 42 USC (1990).
Climate Security Bill 2008.
Low Carbon Economy Bill 2007.
Trail Smelter Case (United States, Canada) 16 April 1938 and 11 March 1941.

European Supranational Materials

Directive 2003/87/EC of the European Parliament and of the Council of 13 October 2003 Establishing a Scheme for Greenhouse Gas Emission

Allowance Trading within the Community and Amending Council Directive 96/61/EC [2003] OJ L 275/32.

Directive 2004/101/EC of the European Parliament and of the Council of 27 October 2004 Amending Directive 2003/87/EC Establishing a Scheme for Greenhouse Gas Emission Allowance Trading Within the Community, in respect of the Kyoto Protocol's Project Mechanisms [2004] OJ L 338/18

Directive 2008/101/EC of the European Parliament and of the Council of 19 November 2008 amending Directive 2003/87/EC so as to include aviation activities in the scheme for greenhouse gas emission allowance trading within the Community [2009] OJ L 8/3.

Directive 2009/29/EC of the European Parliament and of the Council of 23 April 2009 Amending Directive 2003/87/EC so as to improve and extend the greenhouse gas emission allowance trading scheme of the Community [2009] OJ L 140/63.

Proposal for a Directive of the European Parliament and of the Council Amending Directive 2003/87/EC to Enhance Cost-Effective Emission Reductions and Low carbon Investments [2015] COM/2015/0337 final/2.

Proposal 2014/0011 (COD) Concerning the Establishment and Operation of a Market Stability Reserve for the Union Greenhouse Gas Emission Trading Scheme and Amending Directive 2003/87/EC [2014].

Proposal 2015/148 (COD) for a Directive of the European Parliament and of the Council Amending Directive 2003/87/EC to enhance cost-effective emission reductions and low-carbon investments [2015].

Regulation 176/2014 of 25 February 2014 amending Regulation (EU) No 1031/2010 in particular to determine the volumes of greenhouse gas emission allowances to be auctioned in 2013–20 [2014] OJ L 56/11.

Regulation 421/2014 of 16 April 2014 amending Directive 2003/87/EC Establishing a Scheme for Greenhouse Gas Emission Allowance Trading within the Community, in View of the Implementation by 2020 of an International Agreement Applying a Single Global Market-Based Measure to International Aviation Emissions [2014] OJ L 129/1.

European Commission

Commission Decision Concerning the National Allocation Plan for the Allocation of Greenhouse Gas Emission Allowances Notified by Germany in Accordance with Directive 2003/87/EC of the European Parliament and of the Council [2006].

Commission Decision 2010/2/EU of 24 December 2009 Determining, Pursuant to Directive 2003/87/EC of the European Parliament and of the Council, a List of Sectors and Subsectors Which are Deemed to Be

Exposed to a Significant Risk of Carbon Leakage (notified under document C(2009) 10251) [2010] OJ L 1/10.

Commission Decision 278/2011/EU of 27 April 2011 Determining Transitional Union-wide Rules for Harmonised Free Allocation of Emission Allowances Pursuant to Article 10a of Directive 2003/87/EC of the European Parliament and of the Council [2011] OJ L 130/1.

Commission Decision 377/2013/EU of 24 April 2013 Derogating Temporarily from Directive 2003/87/EC Establishing a Scheme for Greenhouse Gas Emission Allowance Trading Within the Community [2013] OJ L 113/1.

Commission Decision 746/2014/EU of 27 October 2014 Determining, Pursuant to Directive 2003/87/EC of the European Parliament and of the Council, a List of Sectors and Subsectors which are Deemed to be Exposed to a Significant Risk of Carbon Leakage, for the Period 2015 to 2019 [2014] OJ L 308/114.

Communication from the Commission COM/2005/703 Further guidance on allocation plans for the 2008 to 2012 trading period of the EU Emission Trading Scheme [2005].

Communication from the Commission to the Council and to the European Parliament COMM/2006/275, on the Assessment of National Allocation Plans for the Allocation of Greenhouse Gas Emission Allowances in the Second Period of the EU Emissions Trading Scheme Accompanying Commission Decisions of 29 November 2006 on the National Allocation plans of Germany, Greece, Ireland, Latvia, Lithuania, Luxembourg, Malta, Slovakia, Sweden and the United Kingdom in accordance with Directive 2003/87/EC [2006].

European Commission (2011), Draft Commission decision on free allocation rules for the emissions trading scheme: Explanatory paper prepared by DG Climate Action for MEPs.

European Commission, 'Green Paper on greenhouse gas emissions trading within the European Union' (COM/2000/0087 final, European Commission, 8 March 2000).

European Commission, *Phase 2 Auctions* (08 May 2015) Climate Action <http://ec.europa.eu/clima/policies/ets/pre2013/second/index_en.htm>.

European Commission, State Aid n 416/2001: United Kingdom Emission Trading Scheme. Brussels, 28.11.2001 C(2001)3739fin.

European Case Law

Air Transport Association of America and Others v Secretary of State for Energy and Climate Change (C-366/10) [2011] ECR I-1133.
Billerud Karlsborg AB and Billerud Skärblacka AB v. Naturvardverket (C-203/12) [2013] ECR I-664.

Bundesrepublik Deutschland v Nordzucker AG (C-148/14) [2015] ECR I-287.

Commission of the European Communities v Italian Republic (C-158/94) [1997] ECR I-5789.

EnBW Energie Baden-Württemberg AG v Commission of the European Communities (T-387/04) [2007] ECR II-1201, II-1209.

Essent Belgium NV v Vlaamse Reguleringsinstantie voor de Elektriciteits-en Gasmarkt (C-204/12) [2014] 2192.

Federal Republic of Germany v Commission of the European Communities (T-374/04) [2007] ECR II-4441.

Iberdrola SA and Gas Natural SDG SA (C-566/11, C-567/11, C-580/11, C-591/11, C-620/11 and C-640/11) [2013] ECR I-0000.

PreussenElektra AG v Schhleswag AG (C-379/98) [2001] ECR I-2099.

TREATIES

General Agreement on Tariffs and Trade, opened for signature 30 October 1947 [1947] 55 UNTS 194 (entered into force 1 January 1948).

International Convention on Oil Pollution Preparedness, Response and Cooperation, 1990 (with annex and procès-verbal of rectification). Concluded at London on 30 November 1990 Vol 1891, 1-32194.

Kyoto Protocol to the United Nations Framework Convention on Climate Change, opened for signature 11 December 1997, 2303 UNTS 148 (entered into force 16 February 2005).

Marrakesh Agreement Establishing the World Trade Organization, opened for signature 15 April 1994, 1867 UNTS 3 (entered into force 1 January 1995).

Marrakesh Agreement Establishing the World Trade Organization, opened for signature 15 April 1994, 1867 UNTS 3 (entered into force 1 January 1995) Annex 1A (Agreement on Agriculture).

Marrakesh Agreement Establishing the World Trade Organization, opened for signature 15 April 1994, 1867 UNTS 3 (entered into force 1 January 1995) Annex 1A (Agreement on Subsidies and Countervailing Measures).

Marrakesh Agreement Establishing the World Trade Organization, opened for signature 15 April 1994, 1867 UNTS 3 (entered into force 1 January 1995) Annex 1A (General Agreement on Tariffs and Trade 1994).

Paris Agreement to the United Nations Framework Convention on Climate Change, opened for signature 26 April 2016, UNTS I-54113 (entered into force 4 November 2016).

Treaty Establishing the European Community, opened for signature 7 February 1992, [1992] OJ C 224/6 (entered into force 1 November 1993) ('EC Treaty').

Treaty on European Union, opened for signature 7 February 1992, [2009] OJ C 115/13 (entered into force 1 November 1993).

Treaty on the Functioning of the European Union, opened for signature 7 February 1992, [2009] OJ C 115/199 (entered into force 1 November 1993).

United Nations Framework Convention on Climate Change, opened for signature 9 May 1992, 1771 UNTS 107 (entered into force 21 March 1994).

Vienna Convention on the Law of Treaties, ('Vienna Convention') 23 May 1969, 1155 U.N.T.S. 331; 8 International Legal Materials 679.

UNITED NATIONS MATERIALS

Conference of the Parties, United Nations Framework Convention on Climate Change, *Report of the Conference of the Parties on Its Fifteenth Session, Held in Copenhagen from 7 to 19 December 2009 – Addendum – Part Two: Action taken by the Conference of the Parties at Its Fifteenth Session*, UN Doc FCCC/CP/2009/11/Add.1 (30 March 2010).

Rio Declaration on Environment and Development, UN Doc A/CONF.151/5/Rev.1 (12 August 1992).

INTERNATIONAL ECONOMIC MATERIALS

WTO Panel Reports

Panel Report, *Brazil – Export Financing Programme For Aircraft*, WTO Doc WT/DS46/R (14 April 1999).

Panel Report, *Canada – Certain Measures Affecting the Automotive Industry*, WTO Doc WT/DS139/R, WT/DS142/R (11 February 2000).

Panel Report, *Canada – Measures Affecting the Export of Civilian Aircraft*, WTO Doc WT/DS70/R (14 April 1999).

Panel Report, *European Communities – Conditions for the Granting of Tariff Preferences to Developing Countries*, WTO Doc WT/DS246/R (1 December 2003).

Panel Report, *European Communities – Countervailing Measures On Dynamic Random Access Memory Chips From Korea*, WTO Doc WT/DS299/R (17 June 2005).

Panel Report, *European Communities and Certain Member States – Measures Affecting Trade in Large Civil Aircraft*, WTO Doc WT/DS316/R (30 June 2010).

Panel Report, *Korea – Measures Affecting Trade in Commercial Vessels*, WTO Doc WT/DS273/R (7 March 2005).

Panel Report, *United States – Measures Affecting Trade in Large Civil Aircraft (Second Complaint)*, WTO Doc WT/DS353/R (31 March 2011).

Panel Report, *United States – Measures Treating Exports Restraints as Subsidies*, WTO Doc WT/DS194/R (29 June 2001).

Panel Report, *United States – Subsidies on Upland Cotton*, WTO Doc WT/DS267/R (8 September 2004).

Panel Report, *United States – Tax Treatment for 'Foreign Sales Corporations'*, WTO Doc WT/DS108/R (8 October 1999).

WTO Appellate Body Reports

Appellate Body Report, *Brazil – Export Financing Programme For Aircraft*, WTO Doc WT/DS46/AB/R AB-1999-1 (2 August 1999).

Appellate Body Report, *Canada – Certain Measures Affecting the Automotive Industry*, WTO Doc WT/DS139/AB/R (31 May 2000).

Appellate Body Report, *Canada – Certain Measures Affecting The Renewable Energy Generation Sector, Canada – Measures Relating To The Feed-In Tariff Program*, WTO Doc WT/DS412/AB/R WT/DS426/AB/R, AB-2013-1 (6 May 2013).

Appellate Body Report, *Canada – Measures Affecting the Export of Civilian Aircraft*, WTO Doc WT/DS70/AB/RW, AB-1999-2 (2 August 1999).

Appellate Body Report, *Canada – Measures Affecting the Importation Of Milk And The Exportation Of Dairy Products*, WTO Doc WT/DS103/AB/R WT/DS113/AB/R, AB-1999-4 (13 October 1999).

Appellate Body Report, *European Communities and Certain Member States – Measures Affecting Trade In Large Civil Aircraft*, WTO Doc WT/DS316/AB/R, AB-2010-1 (18 May 2011).

Appellate Body Report, *European Communities – Measures Affecting Asbestos and Asbestos-Containing Products*, WTO Doc WT/DS135/AB/R, AB-2000-11 (12 March 2001).

Appellate Body Report, *Japan – Countervailing Duties on Dynamic Random Access Memories (DRAMS) from Korea*, WT/DS336/AB/R AB-2007-3 (28 November 2007).

Appellate Body Report, *United States – Countervailing Duty Investigation on Dynamic Random Access Memory Semiconductors (DRAMS) from Korea*, WTO Doc WT/DS296/AB/R, AB-2005-4 (27 June 2005).

Appellate Body Report, *United States – Definitive Anti-Dumping and Countervailing Duties on Certain Products from China*, WTO Doc WT/DS379/AB/R, AB-2010-3 (11 March 2011).

Appellate Body Report, *United States – Final Countervailing Duty Determination with Respect to Certain Softwood Lumber from Canada*, WTO Doc WT/DS257/AB/R, AB-2003-6 (19 January 2004).

Appellate Body Report, *United States – Import Prohibition of Certain Shrimp and Shrimp Products*, WTO Doc WT/DS58/AB/R, AB-1998-4 (12 October 1998).

Appellate Body Report, *United States – Measures Affecting Trade in Large Civil Aircraft (Second Complaint)*, WTO Doc WT/DS353/AB/R, AB-2011-3 (12 March 2012).

Appellate Body Report, *United States – Standards for Reformulated and Conventional Gasoline*, WTO Doc WT/DS58/AB/R, AB-1998-4 (12 October 1998).

Appellate Body Report, *United States – Tax Treatment for 'Foreign Sales Corporations'* WTO Doc WT/DS108/AB/R, AB-1999-9 (24 February 2000).

Other International Economic Materials

New and Full Notification Pursuant to Article XVI:1 Of The GATT 1994 and Article 25 Of The Agreement on Subsidies and Countervailing Measures: Australia, WTO Doc G/SCM/N/253/AUS (11 September 2013).

New and Full Notification Pursuant to Article XVI:1 Of The GATT 1994 and Article 25 Of The Agreement on Subsidies and Countervailing Measures: European Union, WTO Doc G/SCM/N/284/EU (7 August 2015).

New and Full Notification Pursuant to Article XVI:1 Of The GATT 1994 and Article 25 Of The Agreement on Subsidies and Countervailing Measures: New Zealand, WTO Doc G/SCM/N/284/NZL (6 July 2015).

Index